FIGHT ON!

THE COLORFUL STORY OF USC FOOTBALL

FIGHT ON!

THE COLORFUL STORY OF USC FOOTBALL

STEVE BISHEFF
AND
LOEL SCHRADER

CUMBERLAND HOUSE
NASHVILLE, TENNESSEE

FIGHT ON!
PUBLISHED BY
CUMBERLAND HOUSE PUBLISHING, INC.
431 Harding Industrial Drive
Nashville, TN 37211–3160

Cover design: Gore Studio, Inc.
Text design: John Mitchell

Library of Congress Cataloging-in-Publication Data

Bisheff, Steve.
Fight on! : the colorful story of USC football / Steve Bisheff and Loel Schrader.
   p. cm.
Includes index.
ISBN-13: 978-1-58182-541-1 (hardcover : alk. paper)
ISBN-10: 1-58182-541-2 (hardcover : alk. paper)
1. University of Southern California—Football—History. 2. Southern California Trojans (Football team)—History. I. Schrader, Loel, 1924—II. Title.
   GV958.U5857U65 2006
   796.332'630979494—dc22

                                                                                    2006009068

Printed in the United States of America

1 2 3 4 5 6 7—12 11 10 09 08 07 06

For our wives, who offered love,
encouragement, and never complained,
and
for our friendship that never wavered

CONTENTS

FOREWORD

As I watched the Orange Bowl in 2005 and the Rose Bowl in 2006, I saw the greatness of Reggie Bush and the great decision-making skills of Matt Leinart. I saw a team of one-ness. I saw a spirit that resides in all of us to want to be a part of something special. I saw through the television lens in Florida and in person in Pasadena what Trojans football is all about. It creates a power to pull you in, to captivate you, to engulf you, to mesmerize you.

As I started thinking about this, I wondered what the 1920 team thought about. Were those players as exciting and daring? The 1928 team, which was the first national championship team to go undefeated (one tie) with the great Howard Jones as their coach, what were they thinking? Jones was known for being a coach of discipline. Do you think that some of those same characteristics reside in Pete Carroll? I think so. Not only do they reside in Carroll, but so does the philosophy that winning the game is not enough. It's also about being the best you can be in winning, and winning at the highest level to get respect on each and every play.

The more you understand your past, the better you appreciate the future. When you know why, you never want to lose to Notre Dame. You never want to lose at all. The more you play for number one, the more you realize that is the only thing you play for. Being number one can be a way of life. Being number one—playing for USC, that's what we expect. Players like Frank Gifford and Mike Garrett would tell you the essence of winning is to be the best you can be. But by the way, being number one is the only way.

Coaches over the years would come to understand that being number one to USC was paramount. Coaches like Pop Warner, Knute Rockne, Bo Schembechler, and Woody Hayes would succumb to USC's desire and passion for playing the game of football. Those coaches would see the greatness of the McKeever brothers. They would come to understand the Student Body Right toss when the ball was given to the great Charles White. They would acknowledge tremendous defense played by people like Jimmy Gunn, Richard Wood, Mark Carrier, and Paul Cleary. They would marvel at offensive linemen such as Ron Yary, Brad Budde, and Anthony Munoz. What all these players had was an insatiable desire to be a part of something that was great. To be a part of something that would allow them to compete against some of the best football players to ever live.

I was standing in the tunnel at the L.A. Coliseum trying to see if I could hear all the voices of the players who had walked through there before me. I could hear defensive tackle Jesse Hibbs telling me, "We've got to play tough." I could hear Stan Williamson from the 1931 team say, "Make sure you wrap up." I could hear Tay Brown telling all of us, "We're going to dominate!" Harry Smith, from the 1939 team, was standing right next to him confirming what Tay just said. Coach McKay was saying, "We're not going to give an inch." O. J. Simpson was saying, "We're going to win the fourth quarter!" Pat Haden, calm and cool, was letting us all know: "Victory is ours." I could hear Sam Bam Cunningham leaning over to Lynn Swann, saying, "We're going to have a big game today," and Anthony Davis telling everybody, "I'm going to take the kickoff back!" There was John Robinson's voice predicting that we were going to wear the other guys down, and Marv Goux, in the middle of all the defensive linemen, screaming that we would "take no prisoners!"

As I hear these voices, I also hear the voices of the recent team, of Pete Carroll, Darnell Bing, Sam Baker, Dwayne Jarrett, and LenDale White. What is common is that they do understand and appreciate the voices of the past. What they understand is what I came to understand about USC football: there is a rich tradition that goes all the way back to the late 1880s and consists of teams that have been undefeated, teams that have won national championships, teams that have played the spoiler and beaten undefeated opponents, teams with great All-Americans like Charles Young, Ron Mix, Marvin Powell, Jon Arnett, John Ferraro, Junior Seau, and Troy Polamalu, to mention just a few. There were teams that had to come from behind to beat Notre Dame, teams with Heisman Trophy winners named Garrett and Simpson, White and Allen, Palmer and Leinart. As Marcus Allen once said to me: "We play to be great. Not just to play great, but to BE GREAT!"

This book is not just about USC football. This book is great because it *is* USC football. All the things that embody me today are all the things that I have learned from not only the 2003 and 2004 teams that won the national championship, or the 2005 team that came so close, but all the things that reside in this book.

I hope that when you read this, you will understand why I live the way I live. FIGHT ON!

Forever,
Ronnie Lott

ACKNOWLEDGMENTS

We want to thank the many people at the University of Southern California who helped us and cooperated with this project. We owe a great debt of gratitude to Athletic Director Mike Garrett, Director of Trademarks and Licensing Services Elizabeth Kennedy, Assistant Athletic Director for Marketing Jose Eskenazi , and Sports Information Director Tim Tessalone and his staff for all their assistance. We want to include Notre Dame Associate Athletic Director John Heisler, as well.

We owe much to Cumberland House Publishing for their usual great job. John Mitchell, our editor at Cumberland House, was reassuring and supportive throughout. For his exceptional copy editing assistance, we want to thank our friend and prominent USC alum, Joe Jares.

The countless former players, coaches , and officials who gave us hours of their time and insight deserve our gratitude, especially the seven Heisman Trophy winners, their teammates, coaches, and family members, all of whom were unfailingly cooperative.

We want to mention Scott Schrader and Josh Wertheimer, a couple of computer-savvy gentlemen who lent an occasional hand to a couple of aging sportswriters who admittedly have trouble merely finding their way on-line. We thank them for their time and especially for their patience.

Most of all we want to express our gratitude to our wives, Lois Schrader and Marsha Bisheff, and our children, Barbara, Wayne, Jack, Steven , and Scott Schrader, and Greg, Julie and Scott Bisheff. This project would have been impossible to complete without their love and support.

INTRODUCTION

"GLORY DAYS REDUX"

The football glory days are back at USC, back where they used to be, back where they're supposed to be. Not only that, the Trojans have become even more successful, exciting and colorful than ever, with the team consistently at the top of the national polls, Trojan players dominating the Heisman Trophy balloting, and home crowds averaging more than 92,000 per game in a city where popular pro teams like the Dodgers, Lakers, and Angels have been forced to take a back seat to college football.

If you had made that bold prediction during the slump of the mid-1990s, if you had told all the terribly disheartened USC alums and boosters that their favorite football team would eventually return to win two national championships in a row and come within inches of a third, produce three Heisman Trophy winners in four years, and roll off a school-record thirty-four consecutive victories, they would have sworn that somebody had slipped

15

something into that large, cardinal-and-gold souvenir cup from which you were drinking.

USC's golden eras are gone, they would have moaned. The great years of Howard Jones and John McKay never can be repeated. There are roster limits now, tighter academic standards, and much tougher competition, especially within the Pacific-10 Conference, where teams such as Arizona and Arizona State are luring many of the top prospects out of California. "The odds are too stacked against us," the Trojans boosters would say. "We just have to face reality."

Well, some ten years later, that reality has shifted quicker than Reggie Bush in the open field. Pete Carroll has arrived to return USC to the level of greatness achieved in those glorious seasons of yesteryear. In just five years on the job, Carroll has resurrected everything that had made Trojans football one of the storied programs in college football history. Once more, USC has the blue-chip athletes, the huge offensive numbers, and, yes, the recognizable swagger associated with previous eras. Carroll has given us Carson Palmer and Matt Leinart and Bush. He has rattled off two consecutive national titles and come within inches on a fourth-and-two attempt late in the fourth quarter against Texas of making it an unprecedented three straight national championships. He not only won thirty-four games in a row, he has put together an astonishing 45–2 record since mid-2002, with both of those losses coming by just three points.

Clearly, USC football is not just back, it's all the way back. In order to truly appreciate how far it has come, however, you need to understand where it has been. This book will help you grasp why USC was and is once again one of the two or three great programs in college football, with enough glittering history and rich tradition to fill several Rose Bowls. We will transport you to the beginning, from the earliest years of the 1880s when USC first kicked off a football season with victories over Alliance Athletic Club, a makeshift team consisting of youngsters from the downtown Los Angeles area. We will explain how the program was formed, how it gained the nickname "Trojans" and why its first truly renowned football coach, Gus Henderson, was given the colorful moniker "Gloomy Gus." There was really nothing to be gloomy about, not with a sparkling winning percentage of .865 in his first six seasons and the construction of such great football edifices as the Los Angeles Memorial Coliseum and the Rose Bowl in the greater L.A. area.

Henderson's success set the stage for Howard Jones and his "Thundering Herd." We'll take you through the magical era when Jones's teams were so dominant they won four national championships, registering 121 victories against only thirty-six losses and thirteen ties. More than that, Jones elevated USC to the highest tier, moving it from a parochial setting to a position of national eminence. It was under Jones that the Trojans first began traveling throughout the country and developed the rivalry with mighty Notre Dame that would become the greatest intersectional series in the sport.

Besides being a great coach, Jones was a fascinating personality, driven but absent-minded, stubborn, and aloof, intimidating and taciturn. You'll read what his players thought of him, what the sportswriters wrote about him, and why he would come to be called the "King of the Rose Bowl."

Long before the days of gossip columns and high-powered publicity agents and cheesy television shows like *Access Hollywood*, Jones became a major star in a city known for its glamour and luminaries. He played golf with Bob Hope and Bing Crosby and achieved the kind of fame many of the struggling actors of that day could only dream about. USC was the biggest sports team in a town that was still years away from embracing pro franchises like the Rams, Dodgers, and Lakers, and more than any of his players, Jones was the unquestioned star of the show. In 1926, Jones's USC team and Notre Dame drew a crowd of 76,378 to the Los Angeles Coliseum. A year later, the Trojans and Irish attracted a throng of 120,000 for a match at Chicago's Soldier Field, still the biggest crowd ever to watch a college football game.

Jones's great years, as well as most of his great games, will be recounted with profiles of many of his colorful players. The "Thundering Herd" set the standard for the future of USC football, and after you read this, you'll know why. In 1941, two months before he was set to begin another season, Jones suffered a heart attack and died at age fifty-five. His death was a terrible blow, not only to his family and friends, but also to a program that would take more than two decades to recover.

Because of Jones, the USC-Notre Dame game would become one of the most eagerly awaited sporting events in America each year. *Fight On!* will explain how the series began, how the famed Knute Rockne and the celebrated Jones would make it such a spectacular rivalry, and it will recount many of the most memorable games in this remarkable intersectional competition.

The first year the Trojans beat the Irish in South Bend, they came home to find a parade route packed with 300,000 people in Los Angeles celebrating their victory. Thanks to radio and television coverage, the series has grown even more popular over the years. We'll try to explain why football games between these two storied universities remain one of America's most priceless sporting treasures.

Part of the excitement and color of USC football stems from its close proximity to the entertainment capital of the world. Hollywood has played a major role in that history, and this book offers a rare glimpse into how that connection has continued, from the days when John Wayne played for the Trojans (under his real name, of course) to now, when such show-business notables as Will Ferrell, Henry Winkler, Snoop Dogg, and countless others are frequently seen on the sidelines.

In order to understand a school's football success, you sometimes have to explain its shortcomings, as well. We'll chronicle the problems that plagued USC in the post-Jones era, even if some of them were merely failures to live up to the ridiculously high level the "Herd" had achieved. We'll take you through the often-compelling Jeff Cravath years, the highs and the lows of the Jess Hill era, and the brief tenure of Don Clark.

All of that led up to the arrival of a silver-haired, wisecracking Irishman named John McKay, who would soon usher in the next great era of Trojans football. We'll not only cover the star-filled McKay years, we'll also offer a fascinating look into what made that coaching legend tick, from his days as a relatively unknown assistant at Oregon to the years when he racked up national championships at USC faster than noted Trojan alum George Lucas racked up *Star Wars* grosses.

McKay introduced the I-formation to the West Coast and made tailback at USC the most famous and glamorous position in the sport.

Almost as great a recruiter as he was a coach, McKay developed Heisman Trophy winners Mike Garrett and O. J. Simpson, as well as a slew of All-Americans on both offense and defense. We'll recount why he was so successful and what those who worked closest with him, especially his players and his assistant coaches, thought about him. We'll tell you why he was as complex as he was brilliant and how, despite all he achieved, he remained remarkably insecure. We'll also explain why McKay decided to leave for the National Football League and what he thought of that decision years later. You never will read or learn more about the real John McKay than you will in the following pages.

One John begat another at USC, as John Robinson followed McKay and continued to field national championship-caliber teams. We'll explain how the Trojans picked him when Robinson was a relative unknown and how, with his affable personality and media-friendly style, he became a popular coaching star in his own right in Los Angeles by carrying on the same Heisman Trophy-level tradition with such great players as Charles White, Marcus Allen, and Ricky Bell. You'll discover how Robinson thrived and, in his later years, what led to his decision to leave USC for what would eventually become his own shot at coaching in the pros.

Through it all, from the humble beginnings of the Jones and McKay glory years right up to the Carroll era, we'll give you all the accompanying sidelights, from what makes the USC-UCLA crosstown rivalry unique to the 1970 USC-Alabama game that in many ways cut across the racial divide and changed the culture and sporting habits of the South.

We will profile all seven of USC's Heisman Trophy winners, from Mike Garrett to Reggie Bush, offering rare insights into each of these special football players. And, of course, we will delve into the Pete Carroll explosion, explaining how the university was fortunate to hire him and analyzing the many facets that make this extraordinary new coaching legend so successful.

You know about the present, but what does the future hold for USC football? Will Carroll stay? And what is the secret that will keep the Trojans competing at the highest level of the sport for years to come? You'll learn all that and more, with additional profiles on everyone from Marv Goux, the program's most famous assistant, to Traveler, America's most recognizable mascot.

Then, just to spark the kind of debate USC fans and followers love, we will, based on a combined total of more than eighty years of covering and observing Trojans football, pick what we consider to be the ten greatest games and fifty greatest players in USC history. Not only that, we will select them in order. Who do you think are the five greatest players ever to wear USC colors? We'll give you our choices. You can make yours. And won't that be fun to argue about at the office water cooler?

It is our goal that, when you finish Fight On!, you will realize that this definitive history of USC football was as enjoyable for us to research and write as it was for you to read. So go ahead, please . . .

"Read On!"

FIGHT ON!

THE COLORFUL STORY OF USC FOOTBALL

USC FOOTBALL: THE BEGINNING

Thomas Carver, who had relocated with wife Flora from their farm near the village of Tustin to a two-room house at what is now the corner of Figueroa and Exposition, left home one afternoon in early September 1888 to explore his new surroundings.

Franciscan fathers riding mission trails over the years had sown fields with mustard seed, and the land was awash in a sea of yellow. Carver marveled at the beauty of the area adjacent to the fledgling campus of the University of Southern California, at which he would be enrolling during the approaching week.

Suddenly, Carver heard shouts in the distance, the sort of noise generally associated with a ruckus or recreation. Jogging to the area of commotion, Carver found both. Young men outfitted in strange-looking garb were tugging and heaving and shoving and wrestling in what appeared to be organized mayhem.

Which, in a way, is what the newly minted game of football was all about.

As he watched the fray with fascination, one of the players sustained an injury and was lifted to a non-combat area. "Would you care to join us as a substitute?" one of the players asked Carver. He pondered the invitation for a moment, then asked himself what red-blooded American boy could possibly resist an invitation to beat up on other people without being arrested.

On Carver's first football play, a boy lugging an egg-shaped ball ran into him, whereupon Carver picked up the egg-carrier and began hauling him in the opposite direction. No, no, other players advised Carver. In this game, he was told, one carries the ball, not the player.

By the time the shouting and shoving were over that afternoon, Carver was hooked on the sport and became a member of USC's first football team, a noteworthy activity for which he will be forever remembered. What Carver didn't realize was that football would become the unofficial glue that holds the parts together at the University of Southern California, the blood from which the school's family tradition flows.

It is a credit to USC that Carver went on to teach at Oberlin College in Ohio, serve thirty-four years on the faculty of Harvard University as professor of economics, and write eighteen books and author fifty-one major magazine articles. But, at the University of Southern California, he is singularly bejeweled as a football pioneer.

There may be those who dispute the importance of football in USC's rise to a position of eminence among the nation's institutions of higher learning, but perhaps they should be reminded that most college presidents have generally found it difficult to rally alumni 'round a math class.

Saturdays in autumn have been occasions of bonding for more than a century at the university, and in light of recent success, probably will continue to hold a position of prominence in welding university parts into one for at least another century.

USC and other West Coast institutions were latecomers to the sport of football. Rutgers and its New Jersey neighbor, Princeton, faced off in the first game of intercollegiate football on November 6, 1869, on a plot of ground where the present Rutgers gymnasium stands in New Brunswick. Rutgers triumphed, 6–4. The game bore little resemblance to the sport of football played today. Each team had twenty-five members, and the rules were more like rugby. The game spread quickly to Ivy League schools other than Princeton, and those elite eastern universities dominated the national football scene for nearly half a century.

The University of California at Berkeley was the first West Coast educational institution to field a football team, beginning competition in December 1882 against the Phoenix Club. However, initial intercollegiate activity commenced in 1886 when Cal faced Hastings College of Law in San Francisco. Two years later, USC, coached by Henry Goddard and Frank Suffel, launched football action with two victories over Alliance Athletic Club, consisting of youths from the downtown Los Angeles area, by scores of 16–0 and 4–0.

USC's first intercollegiate action ensued the following season when the coach-less Methodists, as the school's athletes were becoming known, defeated St. Vincent's, a forerunner of Loyola and Loyola Marymount, and followed with a triumph over a group of Pasadena players, some with eastern experience. Despite this success, there was no football in 1890, and after competition resumed in 1891, the team still had no coach and never played more than three games in a season until 1897, when Lewis Freeman coached the team to a 5–1 record.

Games were played at several sites, among them a vacant field bordered by Grand, Hope, Eighth, and Ninth in downtown Los Angeles; Sportsman's Park in Pasadena; Athletic Park at Seventh and Alameda; Fiesta Park at Grand and Pico; Washington Park at Washington and Grand; and Prager Park near Washington and Grand. As football became more popular among students, games were held at Bovard Field, located just east of where Heritage Hall now stands on campus.

During the period in which football was attempting to gain a foothold, the university suffered through several financial crises. At one point, the school was unable to guarantee teacher salaries, but classes continued when instructors agreed to a plan in which they would split tuition proceeds. Later, during another financial crisis, the Methodist Conference assessed members on a regular basis to raise necessary funds to keep USC in operation.

The university and a newly thriving community around the school lay about three miles from the center of downtown, and the area was known as West Los Angeles, or the West Side. Lots deeded to the school by founders of the university were popular purchases, and a fashionable tract of homes connected to downtown Los Angeles by a horse-drawn rail line soon sprung up around USC.

As the world moved into the twentieth century, college football grew immensely popular across America, and crowds viewing the sport were increasing markedly in the Los Angeles area, where USC competed against Cal Tech, Occidental, Pomona College, and occasionally lesser lights such as Los Angeles High, Chaffey College, Whittier Reform, Orange A. C., San Diego High, and Throop Academy. Interest in USC football ascended greatly under coach Harvey Holmes, who directed the team between 1904 and 1907, during which his teams went 19–5–3, won two championships in the Southern California Intercollegiate Conference, and began attracting crowds in the 4,000 range. University teams were well dressed and well equipped, a tradition that exists to this day.

Athletic activity was directed and funded by the Associated Students, but university officials, still pinched for funds of their own, certainly weren't unmindful of the revenue potential offered by football.

Al Wesson, who served as director of the university news service, described the rise in football interest:

> "The desire to win athletic championships along with scholastic honors was revealed early in the history of Southern California students. Within a few years after the founding of the university eleven, sturdy young men sporting handlebar mustaches and padded vests drew lines in a vacant lot, erected wobbly goal posts, and challenged all comers to contest in that 'new-fangled push-and-tug' business called football."

It should be noted that there was a minor glitch in the football program, one that also would plague the university in later years. At the conclusion of the 1903 season, it was revealed that Dan Caley, captain of a team that went 4–2, was receiving illegal payments for his services from the club's manager, J. F. Seymour Jr. The reported amount was $25, but there were rumors that total payments might have reached $1,000.

The *Los Angeles Times* of January 15, 1904, said the reported professionalism "created consternation among the students." Further, the *Times* said, "Faculty and students are all wrought up because Seymour took the reins in his own hands and cast the stigma of professionalism upon the school. . . . All afternoon the halls swarmed with students. The class rooms were practically deserted, and the whole student body seemed demoralized."

But the controversy passed, and USC won the Southern California Intercollegiate Conference championship in 1904, posting a 6–1 record, best in the university's history. Despite its success, USC was in and out of the SCIC. While it needed games with teams from that league during the building of its football program, there was no hiding the university's desire to compete in loftier company, particularly against such West Coast schools as California, Stanford, Oregon, Oregon State, Washington, and Washington State. USC's first game against Stanford occurred in 1905 and yielded a 16–0 defeat, and its first contest against Cal was held in 1915, a 23–21 loss.

College football across the nation was being vilified for the savage nature of the game, the criticism prompting Cal and Stanford to drop the sport in favor of rugby from 1911 to 1913, USC following suit in a move designed to gain favor with those schools for future conference alignment purposes.

During this period, USC acquired the nickname "Trojans," which has endured through the years. Until that time, teams had been known as the Methodists or Wesleyans, probably because of the financial support from the Methodist church. But Owen R. Bird of the *Los Angeles Times* found an occasion in which university teams were prevailing against great odds and felt an urge to give them a nickname.

"The term Trojan, as applied to USC, means to me that no matter what the situation, what the odds, or what the conditions, the completion must be carried on to the end, and those who strive must give all they have," Bird explained. While the university did not formally adopt the nickname after Bird's story appeared in the *Times*, other Los Angeles newspapers picked it up and began using it. Eventually, USC embraced it.

Unfortunately, the sport of rugby did not gain the popularity of the school's new nickname. In fact, it was a financial and athletic disaster for the university, and in 1914 the school returned to football in the Southern California Intercollegiate Conference. But there were also problems in that environment, Pomona, for one, demanding that USC not play freshmen. After one year, the university again withdrew from the SCIC and attempted to become a major power, scheduling games against Cal, Oregon, and St. Mary's.

Track and field coach Dean Cromwell, who handled varsity football in 1909 and 1910, returned to the head of the program in 1916. An acknowledged track and field expert and later coach of the 1948 U.S. Olympic team, Cromwell preferred not to be engaged in football, and after three seasons, the university was forced to search for a permanent coach of stature. USC found its man in Seattle, where Elmer C. "Gloomy Gus" Henderson had built a huge reputation as an imaginative coach at Broadway High School.

He taught a spread offense that rivaled those of late-twentieth century tacticians and was a recruiter of considerable repute.

In fact, when asked while interviewing for the USC job how many players he could bring to the university from his Broadway High team, Henderson replied confidently: "All of them."

And he delivered pretty much what he promised, particularly lineman Leo Calland, an outstanding performer from 1920 to 1922.

Henderson, who was given his nickname by Paul Lowry of the *Los Angeles Times* because of the coach's ability to find a dark cloud in every silver lining, recruited the university's first four All-America performers, lineman Brice Taylor, the school's first African-American player; running backs Mort Kaer and Morley Drury, and tackle Jesse Hibbs. Chet Dolley was another of the school's luminaries under Henderson.

Gloomy Gus could coach, too, compiling the highest winning percentage of any coach in USC history, including the record posted by the magician of recent seasons, Pete Carroll. In his six seasons with the university, Henderson's teams recorded a 45–7 mark, a winning percentage of .865. He never lost to Stanford in three meetings but was 0–5 against California.

Three events of prime importance during Henderson's years lifted football to a major-college level that attracted the focus of the eastern establishment:

1. The building of the Rose Bowl in Pasadena and the staging of the stadium's first game on January 1, 1923, a contest in which USC engaged Penn State, one of the elite teams from the East. "The new Rose Bowl made people sit up and take notice of the West Coast," says Julie Bescos, captain of the 1934 USC football team, one of the school's greatest athletes who lettered for three years in football, basketball, and baseball, and later served as an assistant football coach (1937–41, 1946) and head basketball coach (1941–42). "Attention was focused on Pasadena each New Year's Day."
2. Construction of Los Angeles Memorial Coliseum, a project that permitted USC to schedule the nation's better football teams and attract crowds upwards of 70,000. And when the 1932 Summer Olympics were awarded to the city, the Southern California area also became a world sports center. Jim Pursell, who witnessed his final USC game at the Coliseum at age 103 in 2003, recalled the Coliseum's inaugural. "Actually, we (varsity) didn't play the first game," said Pursell, a 160-pound guard. "Our freshman team played Santa Ana College in a preliminary game." The varsity followed with a 23–7 victory over Pomona College.
3. After a long quest, USC was admitted to the Pacific Coast Conference in December 1921, joining California, Stanford, Washington, Washington State, Oregon, and Oregon State.

Henderson acquitted himself superbly in this loftier environment. He went 4–1 his first season, 1919, then followed with seasons of 6–0, 10–1, 10–1, 6–2, and 9–2. Henderson was at the helm for the Rose Bowl inaugural on January 1, 1923, a contest that produced a bizarre incident between Henderson and Penn State coach Hugo Bezdek.

The game was scheduled to begin at 2:15 p.m., but the Nittany Lions hadn't even arrived at the Rose Bowl by that time. As 43,000 fans squirmed, Henderson paced the field, growing more agitated with each passing minute. When Penn State arrived, Gloomy Gus accosted Bezdek and demanded to know where he and his team had been.

"We got caught in a traffic jam," said the Penn State coach. Henderson said he didn't believe Bezdek, and with his veracity challenged, the Penn State coach suggested the two duke it out at midfield. "Bezdek told Henderson to take off his glasses and they'd settle it right there," Pursell recalled. "Henderson refused, saying he had just gotten over the flu." It was later learned Bezdek had worked his way through the University of Chicago by fighting professionally under an assumed name.

Henderson exacted his revenge on the field as the Trojans coasted to a 14–3 triumph over the Nittany Lions. Afterward, Henderson said, "The best team won. Good coaching, like the effect of cigarettes, always tells in the long run. It is my belief USC should have won by four touchdowns." Baloney, or something to that effect, said Bezdek. "The best team lost! A football team with the best coaching in the world could not win against the luck the Trojans had. When playing at its best, my team would beat USC by forty points. My only wish is that Elmer Henderson had left his glasses home."

Gloomy Gus survived this assault on his manhood, and his entertaining teams attracted sizable throngs to the Coliseum. A 1923 game against Cal drew 72,000 fans, and in 1924, the final three home games of the season, including a Christmas Festival contest against Missouri, were viewed by crowds of 45,000, 45,000, and 47,000. Suddenly, football was more than a sport, it was a cash cow for the university. Some of the new buildings on the USC campus, including the Student Union and the physical education plant, owed their existence to the success of the football program.

The USC administration began to view athletic teams as vital adjuncts to a university that had suffered from a small endowment almost from its inception. The university's common sense grew in inverse proportion to its success on the football field. Even though Henderson was knocking the stuffing out of nearly every school in sight, his inability to master the California Bears eventually created a problem. What those who began demanding his scalp failed to consider was the inability of any team, anywhere, to defeat what became known as Andy Smith's "Wonder Teams" at California.

From September 25, 1920, until October 10, 1925, the Bears never lost a game. During this stretch, they won forty-six games and tied four, the third-best showing in college football history. Also, despite a full investigation of USC before it was admitted to the Pacific Coast Conference, it was reported that Stanford and California retained "a spirit of distrust and intimated frequently that they did not believe Southern California was maintaining such high scholastic standards nor enforcing such eligibility rules as were they."

This may have been the first public display of institutional arrogance that later led a USC coach, John McKay, to refer to people from Stanford as "those snooty bastards."

Whether there was any truth to the allegations about USC's academic standards is immaterial—Stanford and Cal were determined to play hardball. Just prior to USC's game at Berkeley on November 1, 1924, Cal's student body president handed USC's student body president a letter stating that athletic relations were being terminated at the end of the football season.

Members of the press were notified simultaneously, and it didn't take long for word of what was happening to shoot through the crowd of 60,000. The Trojans were scheduled to face Stanford the following week at the Coliseum. Graduate manager Gwynn Wilson advised Stanford authorities, "If we are not good enough to play you in 1925, we are not going to play you in 1924." With that, the Stanford game was cancelled and St. Mary's substituted as an opponent. Unfortunately, St. Mary's registered a 14–10 upset.

Severance of relations with Stanford and Cal prompted changes in the USC football program. First, Henderson was fired, ostensibly for being unable to defeat Cal but almost certainly because his presence as coach was what triggered the hassle between north and south. He had to go, chiefly because USC could not afford to give up such huge-revenue football games as those with Cal and Stanford, once again evidence of how important football money was to the university during that period.

Soon, the situation was back to normal. Stanford returned to the USC schedule in 1925, and Cal was back the following season. But after six years of winning, exciting, and financially productive football, the university no longer had a head coach.

The search was on.

HOWARD JONES
AND THE
"THUNDERING HERD"

oward Harding Jones. The perfect man at the perfect time. At a moment in USC football when the school's academic credibility was being challenged by Stanford and the University of California, Jones brought the school what it badly needed.

He offered pedigree. Not just an ordinary pedigree, but a Yale pedigree, an Ivy League pedigree.

He was a son of Yale and a former coach at his old school, and he had distinguished himself as the head of such other well-established football programs as Syracuse, Duke, Ohio State, and Iowa.

From 1925 to 1940, Howard Jones delivered a bonus, building a nationally acclaimed football empire that yielded four national championships, posted a winning percentage of .750 on 121 victories, thirty-six losses and thirteen ties, and had a twenty-five-game winning streak from 1931 to 1933. But victories and championships were secondary to what Jones delivered to the university. Besides pedigree, he brought a reputation for dignity and sportsmanship, and his presence alone at the head of the football program swept

USC from its parochial setting to a position of eminence among national observers.

Within a year of his arrival, his Trojans faced mighty Notre Dame at the Los Angeles Coliseum, and a year later USC made its first trip beyond the Rockies, traveling to Chicago to face the Fighting Irish before 120,000 spectators at Soldier Field.

During his sixteen seasons as USC coach, the school developed a reputation for engaging the best opposition the country could furnish. Jones was a gentleman with simple tastes. Aside from football, his only diversions were bridge and golf, and he attacked each with the same passion he approached football.

No one ever had any question about who was leading the USC parade. Not long after he arrived at the university in 1925, he was christened with the nickname "Headman" by Al Wesson, director of the school's athletic news service.

And with good reason. While Jones was willing, and sometimes anxious to delegate authority and planning to assistant coaches, the Headman offered instruction in every phase of the game and was forever available in moments of deep crisis. Also, according to former assistants, he was a master innovator of defenses, usually mapping three for each game.

Yes, the Headman had his quirks, such as being:

Absent-minded. "One time he left his home in Toluca Lake and headed for school by way of Vermont Avenue," says Ambrose "Amblin' Amby" Schindler, a star running back who was Player of the Game in the 1940 Rose Bowl. "He drove right past the school and wound up in San Pedro. Jeff Cravath had to run practice." It was well documented that an almost daily task for assistant coaches and members of the school administration was locating Jones's parked car when it time came for him to return to Toluca Lake. It should also be noted that the Headman once went four months before remembering to pick up his paycheck.

Taciturn. "You didn't talk to him, you played for him," says Harry "Blackjack" Smith, an All-America and College Football Hall of Fame guard on Jones's 1939 national championship team.

Aloof. He had no office on campus, and according to Schindler, "Most years, you didn't see him from the end of the season until spring football, and after spring ball, you didn't see him until fall."

Stubborn. "He wanted to win running the ball," Schindler says. And, adds Julie Bescos, who played and served as an assistant coach under Jones, recalling the 1939 Rose Bowl game in which fourth-string quarterback Doyle Nave came off the bench in the final minutes and threw four passes to Al Krueger that yielded a 7–3 victory over previously unbeaten, untied, and unscored-upon Duke, "I think we could have scored

UNIVERSITY OF SOUTHERN CALIFORNIA

Tough, disciplined Howard Jones looks like he was in good enough shape to be a member of his famous "Thundering Herd."

two or three more touchdowns if Nave had been in there earlier."

Intimidating. "If he'd have said jump, I'd have asked how high," says Bobby Robertson, an all-star's all-star from 1939 to '41. Adds Bescos, "The kids respected Jones tremendously. I remember walking on campus one day with Jim Musick and Erny Pinckert, when we saw Jones coming across the street toward us. I said, 'Let's get the hell out of here,' and we did. He was very hard to talk to. He didn't volunteer anything unless you asked him a question."

Lovable? "No" says Bescos, "I tried as captain my senior season to get close to him, but I couldn't break the shell."

All right, so Howard Jones possessed imperfections—but few cared.

He was the "Headman," and he had taken a program that feasted principally on cupcake opposition during its first three decades and advanced it to a position of dominance. Jones's teams were known as the "Thundering Herd," a name reflecting the iron will of the coach and his stubborn attachment to running the football. During his sixteen seasons as coach of the Trojans, he produced nineteen All-America performers, nine of whom were inducted into the National Football Foundation's College Football Hall of Fame.

In later years, he was referred to as the "King of the Rose Bowl" for posting victories in all five of his Pasadena appearances, twice defeating teams that came into the New Year's Day Classic undefeated, untied, and unscored upon.

While Jones was in Los Angeles, the city doubled in population, climbing past the million mark, and he was the Big Man in Town, although he shied away from attention. In fact, he was reclusive, confining himself to a small circle of golf- and bridge-playing friends in the Toluca Lake area, among them actors Richard Arlen, Bing Crosby, and Bob Hope. His fame often eclipsed that enjoyed by the Hollywood stars who attached themselves to his program when he was riding the crest of his championship wave.

There was no other team in Los Angeles to challenge his position as king of the city. In those days, there were no Rams, Dodgers, Lakers, Angels, Kings, or Mighty Ducks competing with Jones's Trojans for headlines in Los Angeles, and until the Headman's last few seasons, the football team across town (UCLA), in its early years known as the Southern Branch, offered only token resistance. The city and the university were beholden to him for bringing acclaim to an outpost starved for attention and acceptance from folks beyond the mountains and desert, especially those among the New York newspaper crowd.

So, when his Thundering Herd captured the focus of the nation, in Los Angeles it was Hail to the Headman!

Perhaps it would be useful to explore Jones's path to Los Angeles and USC, because circumstances surrounding his hiring had a touch of drama and intrigue. Despite a 42–17–1 record over eight seasons at Iowa, a twenty-game victory streak during a 1920–23 span, and a 1921 triumph over Rockne and Notre Dame, Jones found himself out of a job after going 5–3 in 1923.

Strangely, Jones's problems at Iowa City did not stem from the three losses in 1923. In his well-researched book, *Shake Down the Thunder: The Creation of Notre Dame Football,* Professor Murray Sperber of Indiana University relates how Jones's devotion to sportsmanship led to the coach's departure from Iowa:

> "Iowa fans had become enraged at Coach Howard Jones's behavior during the 1923 season home loss to Michigan. Despite the fact that Jones's Hawkeyes had won the two previous Big Ten titles, when the referee allowed a Wolverine last-second winning touchdown and Jones, rather than join the crowd in howling protest, supported the ref's decision, the fanatics turned on him. A few months later he could smell the tar and feathers as he departed the state of Iowa."

Jones spent a year in relative exile, posting a 4–5 record during the 1924 season as head coach at unacclaimed Duke.

When Jones left Iowa, there was a spirited campaign in Iowa City to replace him with Rockne. But Rockne turned aside the courtship and helped place Jones at Duke, and he also reportedly trumpeted Jones later for the job at USC. First, however, USC made a run at Rockne, who was in town for the 1925 Rose Bowl with his famed Four Horsemen and Seven Mules. After Rockne vanquished Stanford in the Rose Bowl, 27–10, the hunt began in earnest.

Rockne, football's slickest operator, was engaged in one of his annual I've-got-a-great-offer-elsewhere gambits, attempting to squeeze additional concessions from the Notre Dame administration, a tactic that generally worked. So, when USC winked at him, Rockne, never one to turn away a suitor, winked back. He met with USC officials about the open football position.

Professor Sperber recounts what occurred:

> "On January 15, 1925, the USC comptroller wired Rockne: 'All conditions you suggested in recent conference met. Elmer is pleased with arrangement and sincerely hopes you can arrange affairs to come.' (Elmer 'Gloomy Gus' Henderson was incumbent USC coach,

and Rockne requested that Henderson be retained in another athletic department position.) The next day, however, when a Los Angeles reporter published details of the USC offer and the wire services jumped on the story, negotiations ended. The school telegraphed Rockne: 'We regret unfortunate publicity which has doubtless made your position embarrassing. Trustees unanimous in . . . extend[ing] invitation to you.'"

The Notre Dame coach was skillful and experienced at these trapeze acts, but this time he failed to put up a safety net to break his fall. When Rev. Matthew Walsh, Notre Dame's president, got word of what was transpiring behind his back, he handed Rockne a document and requested that the coach read it. The document was a ten-year contract Rockne had signed with Notre Dame, and Father Walsh alerted his coach to the legal ramifications of breaking that agreement and going to either Iowa or USC.

"They had me sweating blood," Rockne told a friend.

With Rockne no longer an alternative—there is considerable doubt that he ever was a serious candidate for the USC post—the way was cleared for the Trojans to hire Jones to lead their parade. He obtained a five-year contract at $12,500 a year, $2,500 more annually than Rockne was receiving under his contract at Notre Dame, although Rock, as he was popularly known, had several lucrative side arrangements.

And, oh, what a parade Jones put together at USC. In 1925, his first season with the Trojans, the team went 11–2, one of the victories an 18–0 decision over, ahem, Iowa, which had neither Jones nor Rockne nor, apparently, much of a football team.

Jones had chosen a propitious time to take over the Trojans.

Gus Henderson registered forty-five victories in fifty-two games, an .865 winning percentage, highest of any USC coach until Pete Carroll arrived on the scene, yet he accepted without rancor a $20,000 settlement for the last two years of his contract. Freshmen were not eligible to play in varsity competition at that time, and Henderson thought he had the makings of a future championship team among the younger players on the squad.

"I hate to turn that group over to someone else," he confided to friends.

Jones knew what to do with "material," as players were referred to in those days. Through his first nine seasons, he never lost more than two games in any, and achieved unbeaten records and national championships in 1928, 1931, and 1932. The Herd was thundering like no other football program in the country, with the possible exception of Notre Dame, which won two national titles during those years.

Revenge also was exacted from California for past transgressions. The Bears, who dropped USC from their schedule after the 1924 season over petty grievances and probably cost Henderson his job, found Jones more than they could handle. In his first eight games against the Bears, the Headman won six, tied one, and lost one, and one of the victories was a 74–0 payback in 1930 for California's conduct in the Henderson affair.

Arnold Eddy, former director of the General Alumni Association, tells in his book, *Traditionally Yours*, how the margin of victory happened to become so great in the 1930 game. Eddy writes that prior the 1930 game with Cal, assistant coach Gordon Campbell approached Jones with a request. Campbell and Cliff Herd scouted the Bears during the season and noted tendencies in the Cal defense they thought could be exploited. "Coach, I have helped you faithfully since 1925," Campbell said to Jones. "I have never asked for a favor, but today I want one. Let me do the substituting, OK?"

Jones acceded to the request, and the two shook hands. In the third quarter, with the Trojans leading, 54–0, Jones said, "Gordon, take the power out." Campbell replied, "Coach, I didn't hear you." Campbell kept the power in until the Trojans reached seventy-four points. The Henderson affair was avenged, thanks to Gordon Campbell and a compliant Headman.

Schindler and Bescos, both still buoyant and keen of mind as the years advance, love to talk about the idiosyncrasies of their old mentor.

Schindler tools Los Angeles freeways in a Jaguar that sports a license plate: EX SC QB. Yes, Amby played a single-wing tailback position that Jones designated as quarterback. "People pass me on the freeway, and when they see my license plate, they honk and give me the Trojan salute," he says, referring to the two-finger (middle and index) "V" that USC fans flash to each other.

Schindler laughs and adds: "If they give me one finger, I know they're from UCLA. Or maybe Notre Dame."

Amblin' Amby chuckles again as he tells of the Headman's chalk talks. "He never used an eraser," Schindler says. "He'd wet his index finger and erase with that. He'd have a lot of chalk all around his mouth most of the time at those chalk talks."

Bescos says Jones could be a "rascal" during practices. "The Headman would say, 'This is the way you're supposed to do it,' and you wouldn't be ready," Bescos recalls. "He'd knock you right on your tail. You never knew when he'd come at you. He was kind of cute that way." Bescos also found amusing the sparse instructions Jones gave him when he was hired as an assistant coach in charge of ends in 1937. "He told me to practice the players hard and I'd be notified when there was going to be a coaches meeting."

That's all? "Yes," Bescos responds with a smile. "That was it."

No pre-practice planning and instructions?

"No, that was it," says Bescos. "There was no weight room or anything, and we [assistant coaches] would arrange our own practices. The Headman would go from one group to another. We'd practice from three to five p.m."

Bescos says Jones was calm and cool during games. "He seldom got off the bench," says Bescos, who lettered for three years in football, basketball, and baseball, and was captain of Jones's 1934 team. "If he had a message he wanted delivered to one of the players, an assistant would do it."

Nor was Jones an active participant in recruiting athletes for his football team. In fact, Arnold Eddy said the Headman was so inept at recruiting that no one ever asked him to do it. That's markedly different from the modern era in which a head coach is expected to travel nationwide, often in a private jet, to whisper loving words into the ears of recruits.

Bescos says he never met Jones before arriving at school in the autumn of 1931. "The Headman was not a hands-on recruiter. In fact, Howard Jones never recruited anyone that I know of." Bescos says a football scholarship when he entered USC yielded tuition, training-table meals during the football season, and a $21-per-month job at "O and M," which stood for office and maintenance. "And don't believe those stories that we didn't have to work," says Bescos. "Every morning at five, Bob McNeish and I would sweep out the gymnasium, then we'd run to the Student Union to get a doughnut before classes started at eight."

Bobby Robertson, who eventually became a first-round selection in the National Football League draft, took a circuitous route to USC. Robertson was a high school football star in Omaha and appeared to be headed for the University of Nebraska until his father died. "This was during the time of the Great Depression," Robertson says. "I had to quit high school in order to help support the family. My mother went to Los Angeles to visit relatives, and I followed later. A friend of my mother's heard I was a football player, and he sent me over to USC with a letter."

While visiting USC, Robertson actually met the Headman. "He didn't talk much," Robertson says. "He was a very aloof man. I think he was a little self-conscious." USC sent Robertson to Black-Foxe Academy, a military school, to get his grades in order. "I got my high school diploma there and played football. Nine of the 11 starters on our freshman football team at USC in 1937 were from Black-Foxe Academy."

After enrolling at USC, Robertson says he learned it was common knowledge that Jones seldom involved himself in recruiting. "He left that up to Hobbs Adams, Julie Bescos, Gus Shaver, and Bob McNeish."

Following Jones's death in 1941, Al Wesson wrote a story for the school's *Alumni Review* that contained observations about the Headman. Among them:

- The Headman, being of retiring nature, hated to make speeches. But he was a pigeon for a service club and never refused an invitation to talk at a meeting no matter how small or unimportant.
- He never paid much attention to criticism of himself. But he burned and had plenty to say if anyone panned the game of football or any individual player.

- He demanded attention from his players when he talked. But when he was talked to, he never listened because he was always far away, mentally wrestling with some football problem.
- He was a perfect gentleman to strangers. But he never spoke a kind word to his closest friends.
- He liked people who stood straight up and looked athletic. But he himself was always in a slouch, and when standing in a group he always leaned on the guy nearest him.
- When Warner systems and Rockne systems and Model-T offense began trying to hide the ball in the backfield, the Headman became more determined to rely principally on one ball-carrying ace—his quarterback. But he proved by his record that the best way to deceive the opposition was not to hide the ball from it but to knock it down.
- He would hardly glance at a boy coming off the field after playing his heart out. But when the game was over, in the privacy of the training quarters, he would hunt out every boy who had played, thank him for what he had done, and be sure that any injuries, no matter how trivial, were immediately cared for.
- He never 'treated,' never carried enough money to buy anyone a lunch, and always figured on plucking his golf opponents of enough petty cash to pay his caddy. But his checkbook paid out generously to almost any charity that sought him out.
- He had a bad habit of staying up late over the clicking poker chips. But the white chips were marked with Trojan names and the colored chips represented the opposition as he worked out plays.
- He always told the athletic director that he couldn't prepare a decent schedule, his assistant coaches that they didn't know how to scout, the publicity boy that he couldn't write English, and the team doctors that they were quacks. But they liked to hear the Headman talk like that, for they knew it was his good-natured, rough kind of ribbing and that out of their presence he swore by them.

- He didn't belong to a church. But he lived every minute of his life according to the Golden Rule, the goal of a true Christian.

Whatever Jones's traits, they seemed perfectly suited for his new command.

Upon his arrival at USC, Jones demanded that the schedule be upgraded, and over the next ten years, such softies as Cal Tech, Pomona, Whittier, and Occidental were replaced by teams of substance, including Notre Dame. Bescos said he believes the construction of the Rose Bowl, which had its first New Year's Day game in 1923, also helped focus attention on USC football, and there's no question that after eastern powers began appearing in Pasadena, the West Coast was no longer considered a foreign outpost.

But perhaps nothing elevated the Trojans to national prominence as much as the annual game with Notre Dame, an intersectional series that began in 1926, and except for three World War II years, continues to this day. It is the only extended intersectional college football rivalry in the nation, and it mesmerized Jones, who could find no greater joy or challenge than matching wits with the storied Rockne and his successors.

The USC-Notre Dame series also captured the attention of the nation's press corps. Every meeting between the Trojans and the Fighting Irish during the Jones-Rockne era was heavily covered by the elite of the sporting press, usually including a sizable delegation from New York City.

Often, one school or the other, or perhaps both, would be contending for national honors, and each team was stocked with some of the greatest players in football. In those early years of the series, the Trojans had All-America performers such as backs Morley Drury, Mort "Devil May" Kaer, Don Williams, Orv Mohler, Erny Pinckert, Gus Shaver and Irvine "Cotton" Warburton, and such nationally acclaimed linemen as Jesse Hibbs, Nate Barragar, Francis Tappaan, Garrrett Arbelbide, Johnny Baker, Stan Williamson, Tay Brown, Aaron Rosenberg, and Larry Stevens.

The Irish countered with such luminaries as Frank Carideo, Marchy Schwartz, Art Boeringer, and Tommy Yarr.

Settings for the matches between Notre Dame and USC also were splendid, considering the state of stadiums in those days. The first game, in 1926, was played at the Los Angeles Memorial Coliseum, which had opened three years earlier and already was designated as the site for the 1932 Summer Olympics. It drew a capacity crowd of 74,378. The next meeting, at new Soldier Field in Chicago, attracted an overthrow throng of 120,000, still the largest crowd ever to watch a football game.

While games with Notre Dame were annual highlights, Jones's years also were marked by hotly contested games with Pacific Coast Conference teams and Rose Bowl confrontations with well-regarded programs from across the nation. Of particular note were games against California and Stanford. In his early years, Jones dominated both schools, especially Stanford, which was coached by Glenn "Pop" Warner, who achieved fame when he headed the Carlisle Indians and had one of the world's most acclaimed athletes of that era, Jim Thorpe.

Jones lost his first two meetings with Warner and tied a third before taking complete charge of the series. He won the next five, three of the victories occurring during national championship seasons, and Warner fled to more comfortable environs. Perhaps Jones would have been wise to ease up against Warner, because Warner's successor, Claude "Tiny" Thornhill, reversed the complexion of the series.

Humbled by USC's domination, Stanford's 1932 freshman team pledged not to lose to the Trojans during its three years of varsity competition. Among this group were halfback Bobby Grayson, tackle Bob "Horse" Reynolds, guard Bill Corbus, and end Monk Moscrip, all of whom were eventually elected to the College Football Hall of Fame. Given this level of talent, it probably was no surprise that they were able to fulfill their pledge. The "Vow Boys," as they became known, defeated the Trojans by scores of 13–7 in 1933, 16–0 in 1934, and 3–0 in 1935.

Jones also stuffed California in his early years at USC, winning six, losing one and tying one, before his fortunes sagged in the mid-thirties and the Bears dominated for four seasons.

While games with Notre Dame, which are chronicled elsewhere

in this book, were the centerpiece of the Howard Jones era, other contests also drew immense interest.

The Headman always had a quarterback of great repute, a player who called signals and also ran and passed the ball from a single-wing formation. Among the foremost was Morley Drury out of Long Beach Poly. Drury played both offense and defense most of the time but had to work himself up to quarterback, a position he claimed as a senior. Nicknamed "the Noblest Trojan of Them All"

UNIVERSITY OF SOUTHERN CALIFORNIA

One of the great running backs of USC's early glory years, Morley Drury was immortalized when he was given the nickname "the Noblest Trojan of Them All" by a sportswriter.

by sportswriter Mark Kelly, Drury rumbled and rambled for 1,163 yards and eleven touchdowns, was elected captain, and was a consensus All-American in 1927.

Perhaps one of the most touching moments in Trojan history occurred on December 3, 1927, when the Noblest Trojan left the Coliseum field for the last time after leading his team to a 33–13 victory over Washington. It was said the ovation hailing this conquering hero could be heard in downtown Los Angeles more than three miles away.

Interviewed at his Santa Monica home a few years before his death in 1989, Drury confirmed reports he had removed himself from the game in the closing minutes so he could walk toward the Coliseum tunnel in a final salute to USC fans. "I can still hear the roar," he said. "It sent chills up and down my spine."

In his excellent book, *Ten Top Trojan Football Thrillers*, published in 1949, *Los Angeles Times* writer Braven Dyer, later enshrined in the USC Athletic Hall of Fame, marveled at the heights to which USC ascended under Jones.

Among Jones's first major achievements was his 10–0 triumph over Stanford in 1928. Pop Warner had achieved two victories and a tie in his first three meetings with Jones, and USC was once-tied and Stanford undefeated in the Pacific Coast Conference going into the struggle before 80,000 at the Coliseum. An unimpressive 19–0 USC victory over Occidental the week prior to the Stanford game had left the Indians and their supporters highly confident of success. Wrote Dyer: "As shrewd a judge of athletic contests as 'Dink' Templeton, Stanford's track and field coach at the time, estimated Stanford's winning margin would be anywhere from one to four touchdowns."

There was further evidence of USC's impending demise, Dyer said: "News from the Trojan camp during the week preceding the game only served to emphasize SC's sad plight. Jess Hibbs, the team's captain and star tackle, was ill and missed two days of practice. Nate Barragar, a hard-hitting center who was a bearcat on defense, had been handicapped by injuries and spent half the week in the hospital.

"Then an epidemic of influenza broke out on the SC campus and forced Jones to move his squad to a Beverly Hills hotel. Looking back now, I wonder if any Trojan supporter even bothered to attend the game. It had all the advance promise of a wake."

But the Trojans had a surprise awaiting Stanford. Employing what was called a "quick mix" defense—what would be known as a blitz later in the century—USC completely stifled the Indians, as they were known as in those days, and rolled easily to a 10–0 triumph. Ever the gentlemen, Warner proclaimed that "USC was the perfect eleven."

The victory against this most difficult foe enabled Jones to complete successive seasons without a conference defeat, and the Trojans claimed their first national championship. But, to the surprise of many, USC declined a Rose Bowl invitation.

Another of Dyer's Top Ten victories was USC's smashing 47–14 win over Pittsburgh in the 1930 Rose Bowl. This game followed a season in which the Trojans scored 492 points while yielding only twenty-nine. Hopes for another national championship were dashed by losses of 15–7 to Cal and 13–12 to Notre Dame, the latter game played before 112,912 at Soldier Field in Chicago.

USC's total-season performance gave it the 1930 Rose Bowl bid, and Pitt came West because of its unbeaten record and a lust to avenge a 7–6 loss to Stanford in the 1929 Rose Bowl. The Panthers were led by Jock Sutherland, who had established a reputation as one of the foremost coaches in the game. Two of the nation's better-known authorities, Knute Rockne and John W. Heisman (for whom the trophy was later named), readily chose Pitt as the expected winner.

Jones outfoxed Sutherland, who gathered his forces to stop "Racehorse" Russ Saunders's runs. Instead, Saunders took to the air, and the Trojans raced to a 26–0 halftime lead before the Pitt coach altered his defense. The rest was easy in a 47–14 romp.

But Jones's greatest feat may have been a winning streak that began with a 30–0 victory over Oregon State on October 3, 1931, and went twenty-four more games before concluding with a scoreless tie involving the Beavers on October 21, 1933. The Trojans added a victory after the Oregon State contest to extend their unbeaten streak to twenty-seven games before losing to Stanford's Vow Boys.

While amassing these victories, the Thundering Herd won national championships in 1931 and '32, and dispatched Tulane and famed coach Bernie Bierman, 21–12, in the 1932 Rose Bowl, and Pittsburgh and Jock Sutherland again, 35–0, in the 1933 Pasadena game.

During the winning streak and the 10–1–1 season that followed in 1933, Jones was blessed with the running skills of 148-pound Cotton Warburton, the Reggie Bush of his day. Warburton, it was said, could stop on a dime and make change. On the last game of USC's twenty-seven-game unbeaten streak, a 6–3 victory over Cal at Berkeley, Warburton did the impossible—but couldn't remember what he had done after sustaining a second-quarter concussion.

As Dyer reported the action:

> "A little kid, half out of his head and hiding behind a grotesque goblin-like mask, turned what looked like a certain defeat into a Trojan Halloween party here late this afternoon by running 59 yards to give Southern California a 6-to-3 triumph over California's ferocious Golden Bears. Stunned and blinded from a terrific tackle of Harry Jones in the second quarter, this 148-pound midget, Irvine (Cotton) Warburton by name, re-entered the game soon after the start of the fourth quarter and in one lightning thrust knifed the big bad bear where it hurt most. Cotton was able to take a shower and dress himself after the game but had no recollection of what had taken place."

For the next three seasons, Jones learned how the other half lived. His teams went 4–6–1 in 1934, 5–7 in 1935, 4–2–3 in 1936, and 4–4–2 in 1937. Yes, wolves were howling for his hide.

"Things had been pretty rough for Howard Jones," says end Bill Fisk, who joined the varsity in 1937. "We picked him up in 1938."

Indeed, the Headman rebounded in 1938, thanks to an influx of top talent rounded up by assistant coaches Hobbs Adams, Julie Bescos, and Bob McNeish. After losing the first game of the '38 season to Alabama, the Trojans rumbled through eight of nine opponents, losing only to conference foe Washington, 7–6, at Seattle. At 6–1, they finished in a tie with Cal for the conference championship and received a Rose Bowl bid because they had defeated the Bears.

USC's Rose Bowl opponent was Duke, a fierce defensive team that came to Pasadena unbeaten, untied, and unscored upon. The Blue Devils were led by halfback Eric "the Red" Tipton, whose booming punts forced opponents to go long distances for touchdowns. On January 2, 1939, the teams played the game between the twenty-yard lines, rarely mustering any semblance of a scoring threat. But the Blue Devils finally mounted a drive late in the third quarter and moved into position for Tony Ruffa to kick a forty-yard field goal on the second play of the fourth period.

USC's Phil Gaspar missed a twenty-seven-yard field goal after the Trojans recovered a Duke fumble, and all seemed lost. But somehow, USC put together a closing surge.

Quarterback Grenny Lansdell led a charge that began at the USC thirty-four and reached the Duke thirty-four with just under two minutes remaining. Although the advance was steady, it wasn't fast enough to yield a touchdown before time would run out. Drastic action was necessary.

There are two versions of what occurred next, but in each, fourth-string quarterback Doyle Nave, the team's best passer, was inserted into the game, despite the fact he had played only thirty-five minutes all season. But Nave was ready for his moment in history, and he had been instructed to employ the "27" series. His first pass gained twelve yards and his second picked up a first down near the left sideline.

"We didn't have much room in which to work," Nave recalled later. "In those days, the ball was left where it was downed and wasn't moved to a hash mark. I attempted to get the ball closer to the center of the field on the next play on 'Twenty-seven End-Around' but it lost some yards."

With under a minute remaining, Nave went for "27 Down-and-Out." He described the final pass from the fourteen-yard line: "I faded over to the east side of the field, and I saw Al [Krueger] break away from Tipton," he said. "I threw the ball into the left corner, and Al made a great catch for a touchdown."

With the extra point it was 7–3 for USC, and Duke was unable to mount a threat in the forty seconds that remained.

Nave's name remains a legend in USC football. He hadn't played enough that season to earn a letter but was told after the game he could have "a whole alphabet." He was, in fact, given a lifetime pass to USC games.

There are, to this day, two versions of how Nave got into the game.

UNIVERSITY OF SOUTHERN CALIFORNIA

The legendary Jones was known for his creativity and his no-nonsense approach to coaching the game.

Years after the 1939 Rose Bowl, sportswriter Maxwell Stiles unveiled his version, told to him by Joe Wilensky, a former USC lineman who also is referred to as an ex-assistant coach [athletic department records do not list him as such]. According to the Wilensky version, he wanted Nave in the game and feigned receiving an instruction from coaches in the press box to do so. As the story goes, Wilensky nudged athletic director and assistant coach Bill Hunter and said, "The word is to send in Nave and have him throw to Krueger."

Beautiful story, and it has been picked up and spread by several writers over the years. But, says Julie Bescos, who was in the press box with Bob McNeish, another assistant, it ain't necessarily so.

"I'll tell you the true story of what happened," says Bescos. "It's this: Bob [McNeish] and I decided the defensive back [Tipton] guarding Krueger was a little loose. So, we decided to call Twenty-seven Down-and-Out. We called Sam Barry, who had gone down to the bench. He went to the Headman and told him what we were going to do. Nobody else was involved in it.

"Others have tried to take credit, but that stuff wasn't true. Sam put Nave in the game. Bob called Sam and said, 'We have a play called—an end-around pass. The Twenty-five play. Get Nave in there.' What was the response to the Nave-Krueger success? "Well, I'll tell you something," said Bescos. "That night, Sam Barry, Bob McNeish, Ray George, and I got together at the hotel and had a few belts."

With the Headman back in form, the Trojans sailed through the first eight games of 1939, their only blemish a season-opening 7–7 tie with Oregon. Among their achievements was a victory over Notre Dame at South Bend.

But looming in their path to another Rose Bowl was UCLA, also undefeated in nine games but with three ties. The Trojans had polished off UCLA the year before, 42–7, but this time the Bruins had two great black players, Kenny Washington and Jackie Robinson, the latter of whom would become a baseball pioneer and Hall of Famer.

Amby Schindler recalls the Trojans' first day of preparation for the Bruins. "He [Jones] is drawing up defenses," said Schindler. "He was respecting Jackie Robinson's ability at running the reverse play. Even though Kenny Washington was their best player, the Robinson reverse was the key to their offense. The play would come to the right side of our defense. Jones decided he was going to shift our defensive guys on the right side out wide, with one particularly large gap. He'd move our right end, Bob Winslow, and our right tackle out quite wide to stop the Robinson reverse. He paused and said, 'There's a big hole here, but, you know, they'll never find it.' And he laughed and laughed. And he was right. They never did."

Schindler says Winslow was given one assignment. "He was supposed to tackle Robinson on every play, whether he had the ball or not. We called Winslow 'Dirty Bob,' even though he wasn't dirty. He was just strong and mean. Jackie got so he'd show Winslow he didn't have the ball when they faked the reverse."

Schindler expresses great admiration for Washington. "The game was scoreless, and late in the game the Bruins had the ball at our four-yard line," he says. "They gave the ball to Kenny on the first play, but that's all. If they'd given it to him four times, we wouldn't have been able to stop him. But the fourth-down play was a pass in the flat to end Bob MacPherson that our great defensive back, Bobby Robertson, batted down."

The contest ended in a scoreless tie, and USC received the 1940 Rose Bowl bid, a game against Tennessee.

For the second successive year, the Trojans were facing a Rose Bowl team that was unbeaten, untied, and unscored upon, and the

Volunteers also possessed a twenty-three-game winning streak. Tennessee, coached by able Bob Neyland, possessed some of the most acclaimed players in college football, among them All-America guards Ed Molinsky and Bob Suffridge, quarterback George Cafego, and halfback Bobby Foxx.

But Jones owned the Rose Bowl.

"Howard Jones did something he never would have done before," says quarterback Schindler, who called all the plays. "I put on two drives, the first about seventy yards with only one forward pass. Funny thing about it, we scored at the north end of the Rose Bowl, where all the family tickets were. I scored the touchdown practically in my mother's lap. She saw everything.

"My second drive was about ninety yards and included two passes. The last one was to Al Krueger, who caught the winning touchdown from Doyle Nave in the '39 Rose Bowl against Duke.

"Anyway, we got to the two-yard line, where I remembered a play Jones had given us in my sophomore year for the Stanford game. It was designed to make two yards for a first down in the middle of the field or at the goal line. I remembered that play and threw a pass in the flat to Krueger for a touchdown. Tennessee figured we would run a power play."

When the contest was over and Schindler had been chosen Player of the Game, Jones approached him. "You didn't forget that play," he said, slapping Schindler on the back. "But, you know, we won this game the way I like to win 'em—with power."

Schindler laughs when he remembers something else. "While we're marching down the field, I thought I was mixing things up pretty well during that ninety-yard drive. I found out later that our two guards, Ben Sohn and Floyd Phillips, on every play were telling Tennessee's All-America guards that we were coming right at them. We were cocky enough to know what we could do."

The Trojans emerged with more than a Rose Bowl triumph. They also were chosen national champions by the prestigious Dickinson System, which was operated by a University of Illinois math professor and took into account strength of schedule and other measuring sticks.

This was Jones's fourth national title in fifteen seasons. His sixteenth season, in 1940, was a disaster by the Headman's standards—

three victories, four defeats, and two ties—but Jones was confident he had the personnel to rebound the following year.

But on July 27, 1941, precisely two months before the football season was to begin, Jones suffered a heart attack and died at age fifty-five.

His death was a devastating blow, and it would be more than two decades before the Trojans would return to the head of the football parade.

TALES OF TRAVELER

He is college football's most regal mascot, or, as many an opposing head coach has called him: "That #*%#%* horse."

He is Traveler, the noble white steed that appears at all USC football home games, ridden by a trusty Trojan warrior, galloping around the field of the Los Angeles Coliseum. He appears, racing in full stride, in front of the USC rooting section after each touchdown by the home-team Trojans as the refrains of "Conquest" blare loudly in the background.

Notre Dame's Ara Parseghian admitted he used to hate the sight of Traveler. USC head coach John McKay always would wink at the horse's rider, the late Richard Saukko, every time he saw Traveler waiting in the Coliseum tunnel. Trojan fans cheer wildly when the sport's most recognizable mascot appears on the field. USC players get pumped up by Traveler's romps behind their bench. Everybody associated with the university loves the animal who, by now, is actually Traveler VII.

The Traveler tradition began at the 1961 home opener against Georgia Tech. Bob Jani, then USC's director of special events, and Eddie Tannenbaum, a student at the university that year, spotted Saukko riding his white horse in the 1961 Rose Parade. They approached him and asked if he wanted to ride Traveler around the Coliseum, serving as the football team's new mascot. Saukko happily complied.

"He was always so proud to do it," says Patricia DeBernardi, who was Saukko's wife. "I don't think he ever realized how popular Traveler was. He was always so humble about it." Saukko, who happened to be an artist, first appeared wearing a costume actor Charlton Heston had worn in *Ben Hur*. Later, Saukko created his own costume. "He was a great artist," says DeBernardi. "He made the outfit by copying the one Tommy Trojan [the campus statue] had. He was a very handsome man with a great profile. I thought he fit the part perfectly."

DeBernardi, who was Traveler's owner and trainer until she retired in 2002, confirmed that opposing coaches disliked Traveler, but USC's coaches loved having him around. "Richard told me Ara Parseghian hated to see that horse," she says. "He also told me that the Trojan coaches always gave him a thumbs-up, and many of them wanted to touch the horse for good luck before every game." The only real, semi-serious accident occurred one year after Al Davis, owner of the National Football League Raiders, had removed the track surrounding the field at the Coliseum during the off-season. A hard rain had flooded part of the field, and when Traveler II reared up, as Richard always had him do, he slipped and fell down. Traveler rolled over on his side and stayed there. Richard got up and motioned to him, as if to say, 'Are you going to get up?' Finally, he did, but he was all green on one side from the grass stains."

Saukko, forty-one years old when he first started riding Traveler, remained aboard until after the 1988 season, when he was in his late sixties. Health problems forced him to retire as the rider. "The fans loved him so, it was sad to see him stop," says DeBernardi. Saukko's successors have been Cass Dabbs, Rick Oas, Tom Nolan, Ardeshir Radpour, and current riders Hector Aguilar and Chuck O'Donnell, who happens to be Saukko's stepson. When DeBernardi retired, she asked Joanne Asman to take over with her own Traveler in 2003. The current Trojan mascot is Traveler VII. Travelers I through VI ranged from an Arabian/Tennessee Walker to a purebred Tennessee Walker and Arabian to an Andalusian. But whatever the breed, the color was always pure white.

Asman, who owns and trains the horse now, says it remains "an absolute thrill" to see the current Traveler, a fourteen-year-old Andalusian gelding, gallop around the Coliseum. "He takes your breath away every time," she says. "It's such a great tradition. The fact we can make that tradition happen gives you a rush."

Traveler has gone on the road at times, appearing at the 1995 Cotton Bowl and the 2005 Orange Bowl. "He doesn't go anywhere when I'm not there," Asman says. "He does photo shoots and lots of TV stuff. He was on the June cover of *Vogue* magazine with Salma Hayek. Everyone at USC has just been great to us. We definitely feel like we've become a part of the USC family."

Asman thinks the current Traveler knows exactly what he is doing. "He loves it," she says. "He knows people. He knows it's his crowd. The biggest high was at the Orange Bowl. The USC fans didn't know he was coming. To hear the roar from the stands when he appeared, it was just an amazing feeling."

Traveler is even a part of the L.A. celebrity scene. He has appeared in some forty-one Rose Parades and has had parts in several movies, including *The Road to El Dorado*, *The Battle of the Gunfighter*, and *Snowfire*. He's been onstage, once appearing in the Long Beach Ballet's version of the *Nutcracker* ballet and he has joined such well-known personalities as Janet Jackson, Jamie Foxx, LeeAnne Rimes, and Fabio in various film and stage ventures.

In the fall of 2004, USC alumnus Bill Tiley, class of 1961, and his wife, Nadine, donated $2 million to provide a permanent endowment to support Traveler. Bill is the owner of the B. J.'s Restaurant and Brewery chain, and Nadine is an avid breeder of champion Andalusian horses. Nadine and Bill hope that a future Traveler will be bred at their ranch in Hemet, Tiley's Andalusians, also now known as "the Home of Traveler."

In the meantime, Traveler remains one of the most recognizable mascots in all of sport. When a future Heisman Trophy winner named O. J. Simpson was asked why he chose to attend USC, he always replied that "I fell in love with the school watching that horse run around the track." Asman now talks about how much Traveler has to run, considering USC's teams have been among the highest-scoring in the nation for the past couple of seasons.

"I think he gets tired sometimes," Asman says. "One game alone, I think he ran for about seven hundred yards. Someone once said than he probably has more rushing yards than anyone on the team."

3

THE GREATEST
RIVALRY

I t has been forty years since Notre Dame manhandled USC, 51–0, at the Los Angeles Coliseum, the worst defeat in Trojan history, and Nick Eddy is asked if he feels any remorse over beating up on those poor little Trojans.

Eddy, an All-America running back who was one of the leading marauders for the Fighting Irish that gray November 26 afternoon in 1966, pauses to gather his thoughts.

"Truthfully," he says, "the only remorse I feel is that it wasn't worse."

Eddy also gathers himself for a laugh. He lives in Modesto, California, not far from his native Tracy, and reveals that the Trojans have exacted revenge.

"Our daughter is a graduate of USC and went on to dental school, where she was president of her class," Eddy says. "She and her husband have USC season football tickets. They sit right by the tunnel. Yes, they root for USC when the Trojans play Notre Dame, but they root for USC *and* Notre Dame in all other games."

Eddy laughs again. "You know, they made me go over by that Tommy Trojan statue and took a picture of me with it."

Oh, the embarrassment of it all?

Not really. USC vs. Notre Dame is a love-hate relationship, mortal enemies on game days but secret admirers at other times.

This annual game is an arrangement pitting Catholic-conceived *L'Universite de Notre Dame du Lac* (The University of Our Lady of the Lake) against a formerly Methodist-supported university representing *El Pueblo de Nuestra Senora Reina de los Angeles de la Porciuncula* (The Town of Our Lady Queen of the Angels of the Small Portion).

Notre Dame and the University of Southern California—one with twelve national championships, the other with eleven, both with seven Heisman Trophy winners, each possessing a famed playing arena, Notre Dame Stadium in South Bend and the Coliseum in Los Angeles, which has been the site of two Summer Olympics, a baseball World Series, and the first Super Bowl, in addition to dozens of historic college and professional football games.

They have been combatants since 1926, joined in partnership, as were so many institutions of that era, by the lure of money football could produce for cash-starved private institutions. Big, big money.

A story has been promoted for three-quarters of a century that the wife of Gwynn Wilson, who was a minor USC functionary at the time, persuaded the wife of Notre Dame's famed coach Knute Rockne that there would be nothing but milk and honey and flowers awaiting the Fighting Irish if only they would venture to Los Angeles in 1926 and begin a series of games with the little-known Trojans.

And then, the story continues, Rockne succumbed to wife Bonnie's beseeching and supposedly fell into the arms of the loving Trojans, saying he'd settle for any kind of a measly payday just so he could be bring his mighty Notre Damers to Los Angeles for all that milk and honey and flowers.

This tale of feminine complicity is "spurious," at best, according to Indiana University Professor Murray Sperber, who has produced two superbly researched books focusing largely on Notre Dame football of that era. Sperber adds: "Keith Jackson [TV sportscaster] has been peddling this story for the past twenty years."

Validating Sperber's premise was his access to newly discovered private Rockne papers from a seven-year period covering that era.

Rockne's footballers were the nation's leading tourists, traveling hither and yon and over and out in search of opponents and money the school desperately needed for academic purposes and campus construction. But sportswriters and other critics began describing Notre Dame teams as the "Ramblers," hinting strongly that education wasn't a priority for members of the football team and that they were hired guns in the university's pursuit of money.

These charges were supported by ample evidence. It was widely known that George Gipp, perhaps the university's best-known football player, seldom attended classes or football practices, spending most of his time playing cards for money at the Oliver Hotel in South Bend and pocketing additional cash as a "house player" at Hullie & Mack's billiards parlor.

According to Professor Sperber in his book *Shake Down the Thunder*, there is no evidence Gipp attended a class in 1918–19, although he participated in Notre Dame football games.

Adds Sperber: "On March 8, 1920, Gipp was kicked out of school [his transcript for the 1918–19 academic school year is blank] for 'too many class cuts.' Rockne immediately lobbied President Burns to reinstate his star player, receiving help from downtown South Bend interests, and on April 29, 1920, Gipp was reinstated. [Where would we have been without the Gipper on his deathbed?]."

Former Notre Dame quarterback Eddie Scharer, who lived in Long Beach, California, for nearly half a century, told the *Long Beach Press-Telegram* that he, Scharer, "seldom attended classes" and was suspended from school until Rockne also came to his rescue.

Scharer eventually was dismissed from Notre Dame and entered professional football, for which he was paid $100 a game. Asked how this compared with financial situation at Notre Dame, Scharer told the Long Beach newspaper: "At Notre Dame, I had a sponsor, Bill Hayes of Detroit. I got all of my clothing, all of my living expenses, and a couple of hundred dollars a month for spending money. If I needed anything, all I had to do was call Bill Hayes and there would be a check in the mail for me.

"The Four Horsemen got all of the proceeds, including the advertising money, from a book called *The Dome*. It was theirs."

Thus, it was apparent the football situation had gotten completely out of hand by the time Bonnie Rockne supposedly was arranging a series with USC through Marion Wilson, wife of Trojan graduate manager Gwynn Wilson. In fact, the Notre Dame Faculty Board of Athletics told Rockne after the 1922–23 season that it had veto power over all proposed games and would use that power on "any West Coast contest."

What occurred to alter the stand taken by the Notre Dame administration? Well, what makes the world go 'round?

Money, lots and lots of money.

Sperber's book quotes a Rockne letter to a friend: "The Southern California officials came to South Bend and offered the authorities such a fluttering guarantee that they could not turn it down." [*Fluttering* was 1920s slang for a large financial risk.]

Adds Sperber:

> "[President] Walsh and the faculty board justified their acceptance of the offer by arguing that the game was part of a home-and-home series and the trip to California would occur only once every two years; moreover, because of the bowl game ban, Notre Dame would make no other West Coast journeys and could cut down on the travel during the USC away-game years. This justification did not totally please N. D. fans or opponents, but it reflected the real world in which President Walsh existed—demands from Rockne and alumni for more big-time football as well as the financial rewards from a winning team versus pressure from the educational establishment to deemphasize sports. Walsh could never truly satisfy either side and instead chose a middle course for his school."

So, the USC-Notre Dame series was on, and it evolved into a cash cow for the universities, both of which needed the revenue football produced. Notre Dame's percentage of the gate for the first game of the series on December 4, 1926, at the Los Angeles Coliseum was a school-record $75,619, many millions of dollars by today's standards, and an amount that sent the university's season football profits soaring to the princely sum of $251,000. For a little Catholic school that a decade or so earlier was fighting to maintain academic credibility and financial stability, this was a heavenly gift from the City of Angels.

And it was all done without the help of Bonnie Rockne and Gwynn Wilson's wife. Tsk-tsk, so much for bedtime stories.

Bonnie or no Bonnie, the Trojans and Fighting Irish have engaged each other continuously since 1926, with the exception of World War II years 1943, 1944, and 1945. It is the nation's greatest long-running intersectional rivalry, perhaps because there is no other like it, in which two schools, more than 2,000 miles apart, meet annually, often with a great deal at stake in the national rankings.

What sent the series sailing off to a fast beginning was the presence of two established coaches—Notre Dame's Rockne, an orator and coach of great skill, and USC's Howard Jones, a virtual mute compared to the fast-talking Rockne but a brilliant football tactician fully capable of vying against the best in the business. And because of Rockne and what he had achieved in building interest in college football, there was a mystique surrounding the Notre Dame team.

New York writer Grantland Rice and a Notre Dame publicist named George Strickler gave the program a virtual moon shot with their contributions after a 13–7 Notre Dame victory over Army at the Polo Grounds in New York in 1924. Wrote Rice:

"Outlined against a blue-gray October sky, the Four Horsemen rode again. In dramatic lore, they are Famine, Pestilence, Destruction, and Death. These are only aliases. Their real names are Stuhldreher, Miller, Crowley, and Layden. They formed the crest of the South Bend cyclone before which another fighting Army team was swept over the precipice at the Polo Grounds this afternoon as 55,000 spectators peered down upon the bewildering panorama spread out upon the green plain below."

When the Fighting Irish returned to South Bend, Strickler, just a kid publicist, possessed the wisdom to round up four plow horses from the Notre Dame stable and place his "Four Horsemen" upon them. The picture was carried in virtually every American newspaper and magazine, and more than eighty years later remains the signature Notre Dame football photo.

Rice's story and Stickler's picture endure, enhancing the legend of Rockne and Notre Dame. Strickler wisely obtained a copyright to the photo, and over the years it contributed significantly to his bankroll.

So, when USC and Notre Dame were to meet at the Los Angeles Coliseum for the first time, on December 4, 1926, the contest dwarfed any event previously held in Southern California, including Notre Dame's appearance in the 1925 Rose Bowl game and anything staged by nearby Hollywood. Adding color to the occasion was the "Thundering Herd" appellation hung on the 1924 USC team by an enterprising Los Angeles writer (author unknown).

The Thundering Herd vs. the Fighting Irish. It had a lyrical quality to it.

Tickets, priced at $3.50 and held at that level at the insistence of USC President Rufus B. von KleinSmid, were sold out long in advance of the game, but scalpers cleaned up. There were reports that scalpers sold tickets between the goal lines at a dollar a yard. Fifty-yard line: $50.

Some of the game's glamour was diminished when Rockne skipped Notre Dame's meeting with Carnegie Tech the previous week in favor of doing some work for his agent while attending the Army-Navy game in Chicago. With assistant coach Hunk Anderson in charge, the Irish sustained a 19–0 defeat, an embarrassment Rockne never lived down.

But a fortuitous decision by the Notre Dame coach proved decisive when the Fighting Irish and Trojans confronted each other for the first time.

Rockne selected the squad he would bring to Los Angeles, but, at the last moment, decided to add halfback Art Parisien, a little left-hander from Massachusetts. "I almost got left home," Parisien later told *Times* writer Braven Dyer. But with four minutes remaining and the Trojans in front, 12–7, Rockne had one of those strokes of genius for which he was famous.

Rock looked down the bench at a frail-looking kid wearing No. 11. Calling Art Parisien to his side, he placed a hand on the young-ster's left shoulder, whispered some last-minute instructions into his ear and, pushing him toward the field, said, "Get in there and do your stuff." The move stunned the crowd, Rockne removing his standout quarterback, Charles Riley, for an untested, 148-pound Parisien. Six weeks earlier, Parisien had been smothered under an avalanche of Northwestern players and was carried from the field with what was diagnosed as a bruised heart. But he had a healthy heart this day.

On the first play, Notre Dame employed a hidden-ball trick that netted Parisien four yards. Another run yielded two. Whether any-one from USC, including the coaching staff, knew Parisien was a southpaw isn't known, but the diminutive signal-caller ran left on the next play and shot a pass down field that Johnny Niemic caught at the USC twenty.

Rockne's team stalled temporarily, losing three yards in two plays. Third down at the USC twenty-three. On the next play, Parisien rolled far to the left and threw again to Niemec, who was wide open at the five-yard line. Niemec cruised into the end zone for the winning touchdown. Little Art Parisien, brought west as an act of kindness by Rockne, had taken Notre Dame sixty yards in six plays.

Hail Artie, full of grace? It mattered not that USC's Jeff Cravath blocked Niemec's placement attempt as the Notre Damers pre-vailed, 13–12. A capacity Coliseum crowd of 74,378—this was before the stadium was enlarged for the 1932 Olympic Games—sat in stunned silence.

Howard Jones and Rockne met in the Notre Dame locker room after the game, Jones saying: "We almost did it. Congratulations, Knute [pronounced Kuh-newt]." Rockne was magnanimous. "Thanks," he said. "It was the greatest game I ever saw."

While USC's quest for national respect and recognition was stalled, there was always next year, this game between the schools scheduled to be played at Chicago's Soldier Field because the Notre

Dame campus facility, Cartier Field, had a capacity of 20,000. As it developed, it would have taken six Cartier Fields to find space for the 120,000—some estimates were as high as 124,000—who were in or on seats, rafters, flag poles or whatever kind of space could be found to view the USC-Notre Dame battle.

Morley Drury, known as "the Noblest Trojan of Them All," quickly drove the Trojans down the field, and when Notre Dame crowded the line to stop him, Drury fired a fifteen-yard scoring pass to Racehorse Russ Saunders. The Trojans botched a conversion attempt, not unusual since Jones stubbornly refused to devote much practice time to the kicking game. Rockne's team came back to score on a twenty-five-yard pass, and made its conversion attempt for a 7–6 edge that stood up for the remainder of the game.

There are no known living eyewitnesses to a controversial call later in the game. According to *Times* writer Dyer:

> "Drury's pass, intended for Lowry McCaslin, was intercepted by Riley near his goal line. The Notre Dame quarterback ran three or four steps with the ball under his arm, and then was hit a crashing tackle by Saunders. The ball bounded into the end zone, was touched by a couple of Trojans and finally went through the end zone, out of bounds. Officials ruled it an incomplete pass, claiming that Riley never had possession or control. Believe me, he did. Bob Zuppke, famed Illinois coach, a spectator at the game, said at the time that the decision was a bad one. Other critics agreed, but, of course, the score stood. It all added color to the series."

While the subject is color, nothing ever occurred at Notre Dame that is more colorful or quoted more often than an event that took place on November 10, 1928, three weeks before USC and the Notre Damers were scheduled to meet at the Los Angeles Coliseum.

At halftime, the Irish were trailing Army, 6–0, at Yankee Stadium in New York when Rockne gathered his players around him and told of being at the bedside of George Gipp in the hours before his former star's death by pneumonia in 1920. Rockne said, "I'm going to tell you something I've kept to myself for years. None of you ever knew George Gipp. He was long before your time, but you all know what a tradition he is at Notre Dame. And the last thing he said to me, 'Rock,' he said, 'sometime when the team is up against it and the breaks are beating the boys, tell them to go out there and with all they got and win just one for the Gipper. I don't know where I'll be then, Rock,' he said, 'but I'll know about it, and I'll be happy.'"

Naturally, the Irish went out and won one for the Gipper. Since Rock had killed off half his family in previous halftime pleas, it's quite generally believed this was just another clever ploy. But the supposed bedside event gathered permanent momentum when it was depicted in a 1941 film, *Knute Rockne, All-American*, and the actor portraying the Gipper was Ronald Reagan, who later served two terms as president of the United States.

One of Rockne's Four Horsemen, Jim Crowley, said that when Rockne wanted something bad enough, he wasn't reluctant to exaggerate. On one occasion, the Notre Dame coach told of his six-year-old son being hospitalized and in perilous condition. Naturally, Rock surmised that little Jimmy would survive if the Fighting Irish managed a victory. Notre Dame rallied to win and, sure enough, little Jimmy, having made a miraculous recovery, was standing on the railroad platform in South Bend when the team returned home. Another time, Rock attempted to inspire his players by claiming Indiana's fierce tackling contributed to Gipp's death.

"They were all lies, blatant lies," said Crowley. "The Jesuits call it mental reservation, but he [Rockne] had it in abundance."

The ghost of the Gipper apparently took a day off when USC and Notre Dame met in their 1928 game at the Coliseum, the eventual national champion Trojans winning, 27–14, ending Rockne's season with his worst record, 5–4, since he went 3–1–2 in 1918.

It should also be noted that Rockne, after sustaining four losses for the first time in his coaching career, converted to Catholicism during the off-season. Clearly, this was a man who covered all the angles.

When Notre Dame and USC met in 1929, again at Soldier Field, they kept fans off flag poles and rafters, thus reducing attendance to

112,912, and again the Trojans were victims of their ineptitude with extra points. The Irish won, 13–12. The following year, which turned out to be Rockne's last, yielded a smasher for the Trojans, a 27–0 triumph over Notre Dame at the Coliseum.

Four months later, on March 31, 1931, Rockne boarded a plane in Kansas City on his way to the Los Angeles, apparently to help out in the production of a movie, *The Spirit of Notre Dame*. The plane crashed in a Kansas cornfield, with no survivors.

It was the Kennedy death of its time. The fast-talking Norwegian immigrant, whose blarney was richly suited for the "Irish" Notre Dame atmosphere created by poets in the nation's press boxes, had an abundance of enemies and admirers, but his death was mourned all across America, among enemies and admirers alike. He was bigger than football, bigger than the university itself, and it would take another two or three decades before the Notre Dame administration would be able to recapture the reins of the school and regard football as a sport instead of a money machine.

In fact, three years after Rockne's death, when Notre Dame was under attack from an investigatory body, the Carnegie Foundation, a Notre Dame official counter-attacked a critical essay issued by Henry Pritchett, president emeritus of the Carnegie group. Said the Notre Dame statement: "Dr. Pritchett stated with false assumption that highly publicized football is inimical to the intellectual interests of the university. That has not been our experience at Notre Dame. We wish to reiterate at this time that if we ever find it to be the case, we will drop football without a moment's hesitation."

And, in a letter to an oil company executive: "We have a beautiful front yard (campus quadrangle) that we would not trade for the front yard of any other school. Dr. Pritchett hates to think that we got it the way we did [through football profits], but I would much rather have it that way than to have obtained it out of some of Andy Carnegie's old squeeze plays [that is, by union-busting and bankrupting competitors]."

It should be pointed out that USC, which was flat broke at the turn of the twentieth century, also was heavily dependent upon football receipts. In his book, *Traditionally Yours*, Arnold Eddy, once executive director of the university's General Alumni Association, noted that increased seating capacity offered by the Los Angeles Coliseum permitted USC to engage in building projects:

"The June 1923 audit showed the Associated Students with a $29,000 profit, and by June 30, 1925, the total surplus, after having built a training quarters building on Bovard Field and a 2,000 capacity gym on 37th Street [later known as the "Barn"], was $76,000. In the year 1926, the surplus grew to $184,000, due primarily to high attendance at the Cal and Notre Dame games in the Coliseum. At this point, the Student Union Building could be financed, and in early 1927 ground was broken for the building. Two years later, a new gymnasium with swimming pool was under construction."

Leaders of USC and Notre Dame should be saluted for shunning criticism and permitting football to thrive and help finance the climb of their universities to the upper echelon of educational institutions.

On the football front, the death of Rockne dealt a heavy blow to Notre Dame's program. With Heartley "Hunk" Anderson at the helm, the university would fall back into the football pack, and USC would be a major player in the demise of the Fighting Irish.

That old irritant, St. Mary's, which had dealt a major puncture to Gus Henderson in his final year as head coach of the Trojans, in 1924, threw another haymaker at USC in the first game of the 1931 campaign. Howard Jones had national championship aspirations heading into the season opener against the Galloping Gaels, but the Headman's plans were dealt an unexpected blow when St. Mary's prevailed, 13–7, before 70,000 at the Coliseum.

But the Trojans quickly regrouped, dispatching Oregon State, Oregon, California, Stanford, and Montana by a combined score of 162 to 6 before heading to South Bend, where they would appear for the first time at Notre Dame's new stadium and attempt to terminate a twenty-six-game unbeaten streak possessed by the Fighting Irish.

For three quarters, it appeared as though the Trojans should have remained in Los Angeles, where they at least could have enjoyed warmer weather. Jones's Trojans trailed, 14–0, going into the fourth quarter, and there had been little indication USC had a chance of overtaking Notre Dame. In fact, the *Los Angeles Times'* Dyer wrote that "the score of 14 to 0 looked as big as the population of China."

However, after USC's running back Jim Musick left the game with a broken nose, Orv Mohler came on and lit up Notre Dame Stadium, with help from Gus Shaver. The two, with the aid of Ray Sparling, moved the Trojans forty-seven yards for a touchdown, but Johnny Baker's conversion was blocked. Notre Dame 14, USC 6.

Regaining the ball forty-three yards from the Notre Dame goal, the Trojans marched powerfully, Shaver scoring from nine yards out on a lateral from Mohler. Baker's kick made it 14–13, Notre Dame.

There were four minutes remaining when USC began its final drive, the goal line seventy-three yards away. The march was kept alive by a thirty-two-yard pass from Shaver to Sparling, and another pass later moved the ball into position for Baker to attempt his heroics. The USC kicker came through handsomely, booming a thirty-three-yard field goal that gave the Trojans a 16–14 triumph that ended Notre Dame's unbeaten streak.

There was no television in those days, but hundreds of thousands followed the game by radio back in Los Angeles, and when the Trojans arrived home by train four days later, a huge civic celebration erupted. A crowd of more than 300,000 danced through downtown streets and USC students took over leadership of the parade. USC yearbook *El Rodeo* described the win as the "biggest upset since Mrs. O'Leary's cow knocked over that lantern."

A film of the game was placed on the bill of Loew's State Theater, the top movie house in Los Angeles. After the first day, business was so good that the manager dumped the movie, running the football film over and over. It reportedly broke all house records at the State.

USC went on to capture a national championship, its second in four seasons.

No history of the USC-Notre Dame series would be complete without mention of the 1936 game at the Coliseum. Final score: Notre Dame 13, USC 13. First downs: Notre Dame 19, USC 1. Rushing yardage: Notre Dame 274, USC 31. Passing yardage: Notre Dame 137, USC 18. Total yards: Notre Dame 411, USC 49. Oh, USC's lone first down was achieved on a penalty. Honest.

One of the Trojans' touchdowns was scored on a ninety-six-yard interception return by USC defender Bob Langley in which official Tom Louttit unintentionally blocked off a pursuing Notre Dame defender, Larry Danbom. The other USC touchdown was scored when Amblin' Amby Schindler ran eighteen yards and attempted to lateral—a designed play. Says Schindler: "Dick Berryman yelled to me, 'Lateral, lateral.' When he said that, the Notre Dame safety took his hand off my outside hand, and I kind of slapped the ball to Berryman, who scooped up the ball and ran sixty-five yards for a touchdown." Schindler laughs. "Some people said it was a forward lateral. I'm not going to comment on that."

It was just one of a number of disputed plays that have marked the USC-Notre Dame series.

Who could forget 1938? Twice-beaten USC defeated top-ranked Notre Dame, 13–0, at the Coliseum, but the Fighting Irish were declared national champions. And in 1947, by which time both Rockne and Jones were dead, Norte Dame was 8–0 and USC 7–0–1, as 104,953 witnessed the affair at the Coliseum. It was a romp for the Irish, 38–7, and another national title for Notre Dame.

There was nothing greatly significant about Notre Dame's 19–12 triumph over the Trojans at the Coliseum in 1951, but it was a great weekend for sophomore Johnny Lattner of the Fighting Irish. "We went to RKO Studios on Friday afternoon and visited with Marilyn Monroe in her dressing room," says Lattner, who went on to win the 1953 Heisman Trophy. "She was just wonderful to us. There were five of us. We talked for an hour and a half. I asked her to autograph a picture, and she asked me what I wanted on it. I said, 'To John, thanks for that wonderful night we had together. Love and kisses, Marilyn Monroe.' Then I said, 'Put your phone number on it, too.' She did. And she also drove us to our hotel on Wilshire. We had tickets for her to attend the game the next day. I called that night, and she said she couldn't make it. Had to pick up an athlete at the airport the next day. Joe DiMaggio."

Lattner played under Frank Leahy, who was, in his own way, as colorful as Rockne and even more successful, winning four national titles to Rockne's three. He called all players by their given first names. Thus, Johnny Lujack was "Jonathan," Ziggy Czarobski was

"Zygmont," and so on. Once, his wife, Flossie, called to report she had broken an arm. "Better me than Johnny Lattner, huh?" she said. Leahy was noncommittal.

Lattner was one of Leahy's favorites. Going into Lattner's senior season, 1953, Notre Dame athletic publicist Charlie Callahan approached Leahy about waging a national Heisman campaign for the star halfback. Leahy demurred. "I'll handle it myself," the coach told Callahan. Years later, Callahan would laugh at how absurdly successful the campaign was. "Every time a writer would come around, Leahy would bring up Lattner's name and say, 'The lad is just wonderful to his mother.' I guess he figured no one could vote against motherhood. Anyway, Lattner won the Heisman, and deservedly so."

Leahy also treated the Trojans as though they were some scrub team from the hinterlands. He won eight, tied one and lost one in ten games against USC. And, three days after his 1950 loss to the Trojans, USC fired coach Jeff Cravath.

The USC-Notre Dame series heated up when Ara Parseghian took over the Fighting Irish and faced John McKay, who had won a national championship for the Trojans in 1962, two years before Parseghian came to South Bend.

In a memorable 1964 match at the Coliseum, McKay and the Trojans broke Parseghian's heart. USC was trailing, 17–0, at half-time, when McKay told his troops, "If we don't score seventeen points in the second half, we're going to lose." With this in mind, the thrice-beaten Trojans staged a remarkable comeback in the final thirty minutes, achieving a victory over the No. 1-ranked and unde-feated Fighting Irish on a fifteen-yard pass from Craig Fertig to Rod Sherman with 1:33 remaining.

"It wasn't the loss that hurt so much, it was the way we lost," says Tom Pagna, who was Parseghian's top assistant. "There were two calls that were just awful." Pagna was referring to a holding call that deprived Notre Dame of a second-half touchdown, and a ruling that Fertig's arm was moving forward when he was tackled, the play being judged a pass instead of a fumble recovery by the Fighting Irish.

"The thing that struck me was the great presence of Parseghian," says Pagna. "The kids were absolutely devastated. Ara told them if they wanted to kick a locker, punch a towel, or say a profanity, to go ahead and get it out of their systems. He said, "Then we're going to let the press in and act like gentlemen, with no excuses."

Two years later, Parseghian exacted revenge with a 51–0 victory over the Trojans at the Coliseum, the worst defeat in USC history. There were those who thought the Fighting Irish poured it on, but halfback Nick Eddy says Notre Dame was so crippled from a brutal and meaningful 10–10 struggle against Michigan State a week earlier that Parseghian had few able-bodied players to use as substitutes.

"I really respect John McKay," Eddy says. "He never complained, never accused us of running up the score, and I saw him do one of the darndest things of my career. We had an injured center, George Goeddeke, who wanted to get into the game in the worst way. Well, on the last play, Ara sent him in. McKay saw what was happening, so he sent in a player with strict orders to stand over Goeddeke and not touch him. That was about the classiest thing I've ever seen in football."

With his great tailback O. J. Simpson aboard for the 1967 season, McKay began to take charge of the Notre Dame series. In the nine games between the schools after the 51–0 defeat, McKay lost only once. There were six USC victories and two ties.

When the Trojans went to South Bend for the 1967 game, McKay remembered something. He recalled that the Trojans had taken the field first in 1965, then stood in the cold for what seemed like an eternity before the Fighting Irish emerged from their locker room. McKay refused to send the Trojans onto the field first and won a battle of bluffs. Parseghian sent the Fighting Irish out first. Whether this game of chess bothered Notre Dame isn't known, but USC intercepted seven passes, four by linebacker Adrian Young, and followed Simpson's running for a 24–7 victory that gave a national championship season its legs.

The only game McKay lost among his last nine against the Fighting Irish was the 1973 contest in which Joe Montana led Notre Dame to a 23–14 victory. Eric Penick, whose long touchdown run also sparked the Irish attack, recounts his state of mind that day: "I was psyched up when I went on the field and I'm still psyched. I'll probably be psyched till the day I die."

Perhaps the most memorable game of the series that began in 1926 and continues to this day was the 1974 meeting at the Coliseum. Notre Dame was fifth-ranked and USC sixth going into the contest, but the Irish shredded the Trojans, racing to a 24–0 lead before Anthony Davis scored on a swing pass from Pat Haden in the final minute of the first half, which ended with Notre Dame in front, 24–6. And then Thunder and Lightning, all in one man, struck the Coliseum, as Davis returned the second-half kickoff 102 yards for a touchdown that set off a forty-nine-point explosion that lasted sixteen minutes.

"We were like wild men," Davis says.

Adds Notre Dame assistant Pagna, "Southern Cal taught us speed was everything. I think Bear Bryant was the first to say it—luck goes to those with speed. He was right."

Final score: USC 55, Notre Dame 24. The Trojans won a national championship.

McKay finished off his amazing run against the Irish with a 24–17 victory in 1975, then headed for the National Football League. His successor, John Robinson, continued USC's domination of the Fighting Irish by winning six of seven games before turning over coaching duties to Ted Tollner. The series went into a tailspin for the Trojans under Tollner, Larry Smith, Robinson a second time, and Paul Hackett. From 1983 to 1995, the Trojans were winless but salvaged a tie in 1994. Tollner was 0–4, Smith 0–6, Robinson a second time 2–2–1, and Hackett 1–2. Pete Carroll lost his first Notre Dame game, then hammered the Irish by thirty-one points three successive times before winning a 34–31 thriller at South Bend in 2005.

No summary of USC–Notre Dame interaction would be complete without recounting lighter moments.

One incident should attract the attention of the Trojans, who were forced to face the Fighting Irish in 2005 on a Notre Dame Stadium field that apparently hadn't been mowed in weeks. Eighty years earlier, Rockne encountered similar conditions at Lincoln, Nebraska. "Are we going to play football on it, or make it into hay?" Rockne asked. Nebraska made hay of the Irish, 17–0. To make matters worse, a Lincoln newspaper referred to Notre Dame as the "Horrible Hibernians" and the "Papists."

A fight broke out during the 1971 USC-Notre Dame game at South Bend, and coaches from both teams raced onto the field in an attempt to quell the violence. "I was trying to pull two guys apart when I felt someone kick me right in the butt," says USC assistant Craig Fertig. "I turned around and saw it was the Notre Dame Leprechaun. He ran up into the stands, and I sure wasn't going to chase him into that crowd."

After resigning as coach of the Tampa Bay Buccaneers of the National Football League, John McKay went to South Bend for a Notre Dame-USC game in the 1980s. The Irish shot to something like a twenty-four-point lead in the first half. Asked at halftime how things looked for the Trojans, McKay, apparently recalling the 1974 USC comeback, leaned over and whispered: "I think we got 'em right where we want 'em."

After the 55–24 USC victory in 1974, Parseghian complained that his team had to practice indoors most of the week in South Bend because of the cold weather, and said the weather problem affected Notre Dame's performance in the second half. He said he was thinking of attempting to get the Los Angeles game changed to October in future years. Informed of Parseghian's observation, McKay said, "That's funny. The weather didn't seem to bother them when they beat us 51–0 in 1966. We'll play him in July if he wants."

It was November 30, 1951, and Notre Dame was scheduled to face USC the following day at the Coliseum in the first nationally televised football game. Father Theodore Hesburgh, who later, as university president, built Notre Dame into the highly respected institution it is today, was serving as team chaplain at the time. Johnny Lattner recalls the occasion. "Father Hesburgh called us together and reminded us that this game would be seen all over the country for the first time. He said, 'Wouldn't it be nice if the priests and nuns all over the country could see us win?'"

Was this Father Hesburgh's win-one-for-the-Gipper speech?

And then there was Rocky Bleier's talk to the last pregame rally held in the old Notre Dame fieldhouse in 1969. It was a raucous affair, a hefty student group called the "meat squad" guarding the band as it marched in, fruit and vegetables flying into the tubas. Students in the rafters were dropping firecrackers into a jammed crowd below. During the proceedings, a gaunt young man helping himself along with a cane stepped to the microphone to address the audience of 8,000 to 9,000.

The man was Bleier, just home from Vietnam where he had sustained serious wounds in combat. Somehow, four Californians, among them the authors of this book, sensed what was about to occur. Bleier, who had been a rock-solid player for the Irish and later starred for the Pittsburgh Steelers of the National Football League, described the difficulties that all the guys in Vietnam were forced to endure. Then, turning toward members of the Notre Dame team, he said, "I hope you'll go out there tomorrow and win one for the guys in the rice paddies."

To heck with the Gipper or Father Hesburgh's nuns and priests. This one was for those poor grunts in Southeast Asia.

Can any other rivalry approach this one? Jones vs. Rockne, McKay vs. Parseghian, and now Carroll vs. Weis. The beautiful USC song girls and lovely Notre Dame cheerleader Terri Buck of the early 1970s. Traveler and the Leprechaun. The best bands in the land. The Thundering Herd and the Subway Alumni.

No, there's nothing like it anywhere.

Hey, turn on the lights, the party's just beginning.

THE NOTRE DAME KILLER

UNIVERSITY OF SOUTHERN CALIFORNIA

The inimitable Anthony Davis flashes his his famous high-stepping style on his way to returning yet another kick for a USC touchdown.

Anthony Davis ran four kickoffs all the way back in his first two seasons with USC, two of ninety-seven and ninety-six yards during a six-touchdown spree against Notre Dame as a sophomore in a 1972 national championship season.

He also opened the 1974 campaign with a kickoff touchdown against Arkansas. "It got so no one was kicking to me after that," says Davis. "Oh, there would be some dribblers along the ground, things to throw me off my timing. But no real kicks right to me."

So, as you might expect, with Notre Dame leading, 24–6, as it opened the second half against the Trojans on November 30, 1974, Davis was anticipating another dribbler. But a couple of things had occurred during the halftime break that created a tiny germ of anticipation in his mind.

During the mid-game break, the All-America tailback, who scored USC's lone first-half touchdown, had a cut on the palm of one of his hands treated, so he didn't hear most of USC coach John McKay's talk to the team.

75

"When I got back with the team, Coach McKay was his usual self," says A. D., as he is known. "He was calm and discussing things we should do. He said, 'You guys were well-prepared for this game, you just haven't played well. You can come back. In 1964, we were down, 17–0, at halftime and yet we came back and won. If they could come back, you can, too.' Well, I'm sitting there looking at J. K. McKay, Pat Haden, and Richard Wood, and we're all thinking the same thing. This man is crazy. There's no way we can come back against the number-one defensive team in the country."

Davis pauses. "Then Coach McKay says, 'They're going to kick it to A.D., and he's going to bring it all the way back.' I'm thinking the man has lost his mind. First of all, I know they're not going to kick it to me. Or, if they do, it'll be a squib along the ground, something to put me off balance."

As the Trojans prepared to exit the locker room and return to the field, Davis sought additional aid for his cut palm from assistant trainer Paul Williams. "So, the team is already out of the locker room and quite a bit ahead of me," says Davis. "The Notre Dame players are coming out of their locker room and starting down the tunnel. I'm maybe fifteen to twenty yards ahead of them when one of them yells, 'We're going to kick off to Davis and kick his ass.' I turned around and shouted back, 'If you kick it to me, I'm going to bring it all the way back.'"

So, considering what McKay had said and the Notre Dame player shouted, a few bells were clanging in Anthony Davis's head as the Fighting Irish lined up to kick to USC at the start of the second half. But his sense of anticipation waned when the Notre Dame kicker booted the ball out of bounds. Five-yard penalty, kick again. Davis couldn't believe what he was seeing on the second kickoff attempt by the Irish. The ball was sailing directly toward him in the end zone.

As ABC television announcer Keith Jackson called the action:

"Here's the kick, high and deep. And Davis, two yards deep in the end zone, will bring it back. The wedge gets him to the twenty, he breaks it at the twenty-five. He blows horn at the forty. It's now a footrace, and here goes Anthony Davis for one hundred two yards and a touchdown!"

The next sixteen minutes exploded into what Jackson later described as "the damnedest football game I've ever seen." USC scored forty-nine points in sixteen minutes against the No. 1 defensive team in America, and the staid old Los Angeles Coliseum rocked and rolled as never before in its fifty-one-year history. "I was the match to the wood," Davis says. "I lit the inferno."

Indeed. On the ensuing kickoff, David Lewis of USC raced down the field and put a thunderous hit on the Notre Dame return man at the eight-yard line—and the old joint shook as though struck by an earthquake. Davis added two more touchdowns, and until Charles Phillips closed the scoring by returning an interception for a score in the first minute of the fourth quarter, barely anyone sat down. The thunderclap of noise reportedly was heard miles away.

Final score: USC 55, Notre Dame 24.

Echoing Jackson, McKay said, "Damnedest thing I ever saw. I don't know what happened. Maybe one of my assistants can explain it to me." His prophecy on the kickoff? "What did I have to lose?" he said with a wink.

There's an additional wrinkle to the kickoff return. "I ran right by the Notre Dame bench, and there was one guy between me and the clear," says Davis. "I gave him an inside move that he bit on, then went outside. Just as I did that, I caught [Notre Dame coach] Ara Parseghian's eye. Their guy tripped me a little bit, but I kept going. You look at the film and you'll see it."

Davis had eleven touchdowns against the Fighting Irish in three years and told of meeting Parseghian at a 2005 college Hall of Fame dinner in New York. "Ara looked at me and said, 'You're still an SOB.' And then he laughed."

Jackson, the brightest light in football broadcasting, told of having a little fun with Parseghian. "I sent him a picture of a white horse after that 1974 game," Jackson says. "He could have killed me. Oh, we're good friends. As you may recall, I worked with him for four or five years when he was an analyst on college games after quitting Notre Dame."

USC went on to the Rose Bowl after defeating Notre Dame and wrapped up a national championship with a victory over Ohio State, 18–17. Pat Haden threw a thirty-eight-yard touchdown pass to J. K. McKay with 2:08 remaining, and Shelton Diggs caught a two-point conversion pass from Haden for the game-winner.

In 1975, Davis, a unanimous 1974 All-American and second in the Heisman balloting to Archie Griffin of Ohio State, signed a sizable bonus contract to play with the Southern California Sun of the World Football League with Haden and J. K. McKay. When the WFL folded, he went to the Canadian Football League, then Tampa Bay of the NFL with his old coach, John McKay, and closed out his active career with the Los Angeles Rams. He is a real-estate developer in Irvine who's still celebrated more than thirty years later as the "Notre Dame Killer."

When the Trojans went to South Bend in 1973, a year after A. D.'s six-touchdown performance against the Fighting Irish, the Notre Dame campus was plastered with anti-Davis signs, the cleverest of which was: "Our Father, who art in heaven, don't let Anthony Davis, score 7."

"People call me the greatest player in that rivalry," Davis said. "That's the greatest compliment anyone can pay me. Regardless of whether you're a player, student, fan or what, there is this rivalry to behold—USC vs. Notre Dame. We're all fortunate to get a new lesson every year."

Davis doesn't take kindly to remarks such as the one 2005 Heisman Trophy winner Reggie Bush made about the annual USC-Notre Dame game. "It's not any more important [to beat Notre Dame] than to beat UCLA or Cal or Colorado State or anybody else," Bush said.

Watch it, Reggie, says Davis. "He needs to go back and read a history book," said Davis. "When we were playing Notre Dame, the national championship was on the line for one team or the other all three years. We won it in '72 and '74, and

Notre Dame won it in '73. Let Notre Dame knock them out of a national championship, and then we'll see if it's just another game."

One point Davis wants understood is the McKay legacy. "I believe the McKay years were the basis of what USC football is all about," he says. "Those years were the crossroads of the program." And, he also insists that he never wearies of talking about his three games against Notre Dame.

"Every day, everywhere, more than thirty years after that 55–24 game, people come up to me and want to talk about it, especially that kickoff return," he says. "I'm just happy to oblige. It's a benchmark, kind of like Maris hitting his sixty-first home run, Gibson hitting that World Series home run, Reggie Jackson hitting those three home runs on first pitches. People remember where they were when they listened to it or saw it in person or on TV. Maybe they were at the beach or on a mountaintop or on a highway. One woman told me she was pregnant and my kickoff return induced her labor. Only a few athletes are blessed with those moments, and I feel very fortunate to have been one of them."

It should be noted that not everyone was thrilled with Davis's eleven touchdowns in three years against Notre Dame or his explosion-triggering kickoff return in this game. Afterward, he was mobbed by friends and well-wishers and was starting to walk up the Coliseum tunnel when he encountered a woman waiting for him, an angry Fighting Irish fan. Waving a crucifix in Davis's face, she shouted, "Nobody does that against Notre Dame. You must be the devil."

A. D. looked at the woman and smiled. "They shouldn't have kicked it to me," he said.

Amen.

HOORAY FOR HOLLYWOOD

obby Robertson was one of USC's brightest football lights. He knocked down a pass in the end zone to preserve a scoreless tie with UCLA and an unbeaten record that sent the 1939 Trojans to the 1940 Rose Bowl, where they upended previously undefeated, untied, and unscored upon Tennessee, 14–0, and validated the school's fourth national championship. He performed in the East-West College Football Classic in San Francisco and the College All-Star Game against the National Football League champion Chicago Bears in 1942. Robertson also was the third player in USC history to be chosen in the first round of the NFL draft, in 1942.

But wait—Robertson has one more distinction he loves to share with those exploring his past. "I was in *Gone With the Wind*, with Vivien Leigh," he says, referring to the 1939 movie, one of the film industry's all-time classics.

Really? "Oh, yes. If you rent the film, I think you'll be able to see me."

The scene? Robertson laughs. "Well, it's at the Atlanta railroad station. There are a bunch of dead bodies on the platform. I'm one of those bodies."

Yes, Robertson was an extra in Gone With the Wind but never got close enough to the stars of the film to confirm an assertion in later years by one of the actresses, Evelyn Keyes, that Scarlett O'Hara, played by Vivien Leigh, was plagued throughout the film by Rhett Butler's [Clark Gable] halitosis.

The convergence of USC and Hollywood began more than two decades before Robertson's flirtation with the film world. Thomas Edison invented the first motion-picture device in 1892, naming it the Kinetoscope and securing a patent that placed a vise on its use. The Kinetoscope's early use was for Nickelodeons, named as such because a nickel was the price to see features in arcades around the nation. Pioneering motion pictures were short adventures or comedies that rarely lasted longer than ten minutes. These short subjects were made primarily in New York and New Jersey, with occasional locations in Philadelphia and Chicago.

Lured by the scent of fortune, poachers soon emerged, employing Edison's motion-picture device but declining to pay royalties to him. In the early 1900s, Edison sued everyone in sight, and usually won. Realizing the perils of operating at close quarters with Edison in the East, where the inventor could detect their poaching, filmmakers headed west, landing in Southern California, where the ever-present sun made production much easier than under the dim lighting of eastern studios. All the new movie moguls needed was a horse, a cowboy, a buxom heroine, and a camera—and the world was theirs. These were the days of silent films, so production costs were attractively low, especially in this California Garden of Eden offering mountains, an ocean, and a desert, all within close proximity of the home base.

The move from East Coast centers began in 1908, and by 1915 it was estimated that 60 percent of the nation's movies were made in the Los Angeles area. Cecil B. DeMille, William Fox (creator of what is now called Twenty-First Century Fox), and Adolph Zukor, founder of Paramount Pictures, were among the early moguls. Most of the studios gravitated to an area that came to be known as Hollywood, a real-estate subdivision north and west of downtown Los

Angeles. The name was derived from a real-estate development called "Hollywood Land," a 500-acre tract with a giant sign atop Mt. Lee that overlooked the area.

While the film industry was planting its roots in Hollywood, about seven miles to the south, on Vermont Avenue, the University of Southern California was beginning to burst from its modest beginnings. Founded in 1880 on the edge of a city containing slightly more than 11,000 residents, the university took only eight years to field its first intercollegiate football team, and by the early 1920s, the school began to shed such scheduling cupcakes as Whittier Reform, Sherman Institute, Santa Fe A. C., and the 21st Infantry. USC was looking upward and outward, eyeing the prospect of competing on an even level, with California, the best of the West, and Notre Dame, the beast of the East. Since there was little industry and no major-league professional sports teams in Southern California in those days, Hollywood and USC football were kingpins in a city that had grown from 1,610 in 1850 to 576,673 in 1920. It was only natural they should court each other.

Howard Jones, who arrived from Duke to coach the USC team in 1925, recognized immediately that this would be a marriage made in heaven. What better way to help feed and clothe his players, and entice recruits to the program, than find them work in the film industry, where an extra made anywhere from $8 to $25 a day, heavenly wages, even in a city of angels? As the film industry moved from silent movies to "talkies" in the late 1920s, Hollywood cranked out a flood of grade-B football productions, occasionally with Howard Jones performing a bit role and his players often serving as extras and performers.

Jones's center, Ward Bond, who later became famous as the wagonmaster in television's *Wagon Train*, is listed as a credited performer in *Salute*, which was shot during the summer before his senior season at USC.

But first to seize upon opportunities presented by Hollywood and take them to a higher level was Marion Morrison, a brawny kid out of Glendale who had barely missed on a bid to win appointment to the U.S. Naval Academy. He had the nickname "Duke," a sobriquet given to him by some Glendale firemen while he was attending

Glendale High School. The Morrison family had a huge Airedale terrier named Duke who regularly accompanied young Morrison as far as the fire station when Marion was walking to school.

Soon, firemen began referring to Marion as "Little Duke" and the dog as "Big Duke." The "Duke" nickname stuck for the remainder of Morrison's life, which was spent as John Wayne, one of the biggest movie box-office draws in the history of the industry.

After failing to obtain an appointment to the Naval Academy, Morrison accepted a scholarship offer in 1925 to play football for USC. Prior to Morrison's sophomore season, Jones was approached by cowboy movie star Tom Mix, who wanted several seats together for USC games, which by then were being played at the Los Angeles Coliseum. Jones told Mix he would make the ticket arrangements if Mix would agree to help USC players get summer jobs at Fox Studio, only a few miles from the USC campus. Morrison and teammate Don Williams put together a cluster of prime seats for Mix, and in return, Morrison, Williams, and a couple of other players were given summer employment at Fox in 1925.

Meanwhile, Morrison's football career was encountering bumps. He was not eligible for varsity competition in 1925, his freshman season, and was a reserve in 1926. By 1927, he would have moved into more reserve action, but an injury sustained in a surfing accident at Newport Beach rendered him unable to play. Jones dropped Morrison from scholarship, and unable to pay his tuition and Sigma Chi fraternity bills, he quit school.

"He was a tough guy," said Jesse Hibbs, Morrison's teammate and fraternity brother. "The one thing I remember is that just as he was to be paddled at the fraternity house, he would wince perceptibly. But that didn't mean he was a softie. No way."

Morrison's first film appearance was in the silent movie *Brown of Harvard*, in which he doubled on the playing field for Francis X. Bushman, a major star at the time. He appeared in several more silent films as an extra before attracting the attention of director John Ford, who played a major role in Morrison's climb to fame. In *Hangman's House*, Morrison portrayed a horse-race spectator, and there are three shots of him, one in which he destroys a picket fence in his excitement. John Ford liked what he saw.

Recounting his time as a prop man at Fox and his relationship with Ford, Morrison said, "Well, I've naturally studied John Ford professionally as well as loving the man ever since the first time I walked down his set as a goose-herder in 1927. They needed somebody from the prop department to keep the geese from getting under a fake hill they had for the film *Mother Machree*. I'd been hired with Don Williams and a couple of players because Mix wanted those box seats. They buried us over in the properties department, and Mr. Ford's need for a goose-herder just seemed to fit my pistol."

Indeed. Ford made him "Duke Morrison" in his next film, *Words and Music*, and changed the name again, this time to "John Wayne," in a sound picture, *The Big Trail*, in 1930. The movie's director, Raoul Walsh, was a Revolutionary War fan and greatly admired General "Mad Anthony" Wayne. But the film's producer thought "Anthony" sounded "too Italian," so someone in the room suggested "John Wayne."

The Big Trail was designed to set up Wayne for stardom, but the picture failed to generate favorable reviews. Wayne appeared in dozens of low-budget films over the next decade, biding his time until Ford finally found the right part for him. It was the role of Johnny Ringo in the 1939 movie *Stagecoach*, a film for which he was paid only $3,000.

But it was John Wayne's ticket to fame and fortune. Over the next forty years, he would play the male lead in 142 films. Despite an output that would have overtaxed an ordinary man, he received only one Oscar award for best actor, which was given for his role in *True Grit*, in 1969. But he had an airport, John Wayne in Orange County, named after him, and was held in high esteem by fellow actors. When he succumbed to cancer in 1979, a Japanese newspaper ran this headline: "Mr. America Passes On."

Wayne was a pioneer in the USC football-Hollywood relationship, although there was a flurry of activity involving USC players and the film bombshell Clara Bow in the mid-1920s. Bow had a reputation for high living, and the film industry wasn't averse to using anything it could to capture attention for its stars. Given Hollywood's penchant for invention and its lust for publicity, it wasn't surprising that rumors began circulating that Bow, known as the

"It" girl, had serviced the entire USC football team. When the situation was investigated, it turned out Miss Bow, closely supervised by her father, held a postgame party at her home for some of the Trojans. Nothing more. Morley Drury, "the Noblest Trojan of Them All," was reputed to be Miss Bow's companion. Late in life, he told a writer, "It was a bunch of silly rumors. We were too innocent to get involved in anything like that."

With Howard Jones firmly in place as head football coach, USC began using Hollywood, rather than the reverse. There was generous employment, particularly during summers, for USC players, primarily as extras but also occasionally in credited parts. The money was great, especially for those times, and the company the players kept on the lots was the dream of young people. Among young film stars Trojan players socialized with were Shirley Temple, Elizabeth Taylor, Marilyn Monroe, Ann Sheridan, Sonja Henie, and Jean Harlow.

All the while, they were receiving wages as extras, sometimes earning as much in a day as an ordinary workingman might earn in a week. "I worked at Warner Brothers, Twentieth Century Fox, Paramount—all the major studios," says Bobby Robertson. "There was a fellow from the Screen Actors Guild named Ralph Hacton who favored USC guys, especially football players. You got eight dollars a day as an extra, which was good money in those days. You got twenty-five dollars if you spoke a line or made a tackle in a football film. On the film *Navy Blue and God*, I was a double for Bob Cummings and got twenty-five dollars a day. Huge money."

Robertson also recalls how film stars loved to consort with USC football players, treating Trojans as celebrities, rather than the reverse. "I was on a film with Errol Flynn," Robertson says. "I talked to him a lot. You have to understand, those actors were just as interested in USC football as we were in their work. They would talk to you for hours about football, and many came to games. I was on a film with Gary Cooper, and we talked."

Foremost among the Hollywood recollections of Ambrose Schindler, Player of the Game in the 1940 Rose Bowl, was working on *The Wizard of Oz*, one of filmdom's classics that was made at MGM Studios in Culver City. "I was subbing on a scene for the Tin Man, and we were climbing a hill," Schindler says. "I had hold of the Cowardly Lion's tail, and I pulled it off." [Laughs.] "Naturally, they had to shoot the scene over."

Julie Bescos, captain of the 1934 USC football team and a three-sport star, probably had the most lucrative Hollywood experience, perhaps because of injuries he sustained during the shooting of the first *Mutiny on the Bounty* in 1935.

"That was the biggest thing I ever did," he says about the film starring Clark Gable as Fletcher Christian and Charles Laughton as Captain Bligh. "I was one of the mutineers. There were twenty-three of us. I worked twenty-three weeks at the Isthmus of Catalina filming the ocean scenes. They built a miniature *Bounty*, and they built Tahitian huts on the beach. They would film all storm sequences off Catalina. They built three runways, which were a hundred twenty feet high, and had three-thousand-gallon tanks from which they could release water for storm scenes. Well, I got hurt. I fell fourteen feet onto some concrete and landed on my head. I was in a Culver City hospital for twelve days and had headaches for four years." The pay? "I got seventy-five dollars a week, which wasn't bad money in those days. I could have sued them for what happened, but I didn't. But I'll tell you this: After that happened, anytime I needed a job, I'd call casting and they would put me right on."

Bescos is amused about an incident that occurred during the filming. "I was chewing gum and, on the loudspeaker, the director—I think it was Frank Wright—said, 'Mr. Bescos, would you please get rid of that gum? Gum wasn't invented at the time of the mutiny on the *Bounty*.' I was embarrassed." Bescos appeared in fourteen films. "UCLA wasn't that much of a team in those days. USC was the big dog."

All-America guard Harry "Blackjack" Smith recalls with fondness one of his Hollywood assignments. "Ann Sheridan was so close to me I could have leaned over and kissed her on the cheek. But I didn't."

Jim Hardy, Player of the Game in the 1944 Rose Bowl, worked often at the studios. "I had cards in both the Screen Actors Guild and Screen Extras Guilt," Hardy says. "You could work one day a week at a studio and make more than you could in a week somewhere else. I worked in the location department at Warner Brothers for Pop Guthrie, who was a big Trojan fan. He got jobs for a lot of players. A director named David Butler walked into the office. He recognized me and said, 'What are you doing here? You can make more money on the other side of the camera.' I asked Pop Guthrie if that was right, and he said it was.

"So, I went with David Butler, and on some pictures, he would carry me for three or four weeks on pay and give me a speaking line. He sent me to actors school. After a month or so, I was supposed to have a screen test. My wife drove me to the Warner Brothers studio and waited for me. I got out of the car and walked around and around for about half an hour, and then went back to the car.

"My wife asked me how I had done. I said, 'I never went in.' That was the end of my acting days. I just wasn't cut out for acting. But I'll say this—if Frank Gifford had gone into acting, he'd have been another John Wayne. He'd have been terrific. But Frank wanted to play football, and he made it big as an announcer in TV."

Hardy apparently didn't know Gifford gave Hollywood a try. Gifford was in countless films as an extra—at $18.75 a day—and was a technical consultant on *The All American* with Tony Curtis and Janet Leigh. He also landed a speaking part in the film. At that point, Gifford became serious about the acting business. He studied under actor Jeff Corey and eventually landed a $450-a-week contract with Warner Brothers. But after many fits and starts, and stunt work, Gifford could see his film career was going nowhere. When he turned to broadcasting, doors began to open everywhere.

While hundreds of USC players have been employed as extras or in limited parts in Hollywood, four Trojan All-America performers had long and lucrative careers in the film industry. One of the university's greatest running backs, Cotton Warburton, was a film editor and won an Oscar for his work on *Mary Poppins*. Nate Barragar, Jesse Hibbs, and Aaron Rosenberg were motion picture and television producers and directors. Marshall Duffield was a director married to actress Dorothy Lee, while Ron Miller, an end in the early 1950s, married Walt Disney's daughter, Diane, and became a top executive at Disney Studios. Racehorse Russ Saunders, a great fullback in the late 1920s, was a top-level executive at Warner Brothers.

As mentioned earlier, among the most successful in building an acting career in Hollywood was lineman Ward Bond, who was close friends with John Wayne and entered USC about the time Wayne (then Marion Morrison) left.

Mike Henry, a hard-hitting linebacker from the 1950s who joined the Rams of the National Football League, played Tarzan in three films, and was "Junior" to Jackie Gleason in all three *Smokey and the Bandit* movies that starred Burt Reynolds, a former Florida State football player. Henry had a productive film career.

O. J. Simpson, the 1968 USC Heisman Trophy winner, appeared in several movies and was a much-seen television football analyst and commercials star. Tim Rossovich, Simpson's teammate on the 1967 national championship USC team, had a long film career. Among others who have carved out work in film and television are Lynn Swann, a member of both the college and professional football halls of fame; Anthony Davis, the "Notre Dame Killer"; Rodney Peete, television; Tim Ryan, TV and radio football analyst; Mazio Royster, television commercials; Paul McDonald, radio and TV analyst; Keith Van Horne, radio football analyst; Mark Carrier, radio football analyst; and Erik Affholter, a producer of television business commercials.

Nick Pappas, who became director of alumni support groups after his USC football career ended, served as actor Pat O'Brien's double in *Knute Rockne, All-American*.

Among the new breed, Allan Graf, a starting offensive guard on the 1972 national championship USC team, is moving swiftly ahead in the movie business. Graf's friend Lester Josephson, a member of the Rams football team, invited him to stunt-double for Dick Butkus in the 1976 film *Gus*, and Graf exploited his opportunity. He obtained his Screen Actors Guild card and, over a run of fifty films, has gone from stunt man to stunt coordinator to second-unit director. And he's become the expert when it comes to football filming. Graf is aligned with a group studying the feasibility of filming a story of how USC fullback Sam Cunningham "integrated" Alabama football by his performance in a 1970 game in Birmingham, the first football contest in Dixie involving a heavily integrated (USC) team against an all-white (Alabama) aggregation.

In addition to football players of acclaim, USC has educated the sons and daughters of celebrities for nearly a century. Among

FIGHT ON!

those attending the university were Marlo Thomas, daughter of TV and movie star Danny Thomas, who was known as Margie Thomas during her days at Kappa Alpha Theta sorority; Ron Howard, little Opie on *The Andy Griffith Show*, Richie Cunningham on *Happy Days*, and now a movie director of considerable repute; George Lucas, who brought the world *Star Wars*; Neil Armstrong, first astronaut to set foot on the moon; television host Art Linkletter's son, Jack; and actor Andy Devine's son, Denny, a Trojan swimmer.

Among those connected with movies, television, or both, and who root avidly for Trojan football teams, are alumni Will Ferrell, who once was an assistant in the USC sports information office; Henry Winkler, "the Fonz," whose wife is a USC graduate; singer Nick Lachey, a friend of 2004 Heisman Trophy winner Matt Leinart; and rapper Snoop Dogg.

Back in the Howard Jones era, it was not surprising to see Boris Karloff, Frankenstein's monster in the movies, wandering the sidelines at USC football practice. Humphrey Bogart was an avid Trojan football fan, as were Bing Crosby and Bob Hope.

A caveat on Crosby, who attended a Catholic university, Gonzaga, in Spokane, Washington. "He was for us except when we played Notre Dame," says Bescos. "Then Bing and Pat O'Brien and some others in the film colony would root for Notre Dame." But Bescos recalls with relish how he and a friend persuaded Crosby to name a thoroughbred horse "Fight On," a USC battle cry. "Bing was out of town the first time it ran, and he didn't get to bet it," said Bescos. "Well, we got money down on it, and it won. It never won another race."

One of the highlights of Trojan football during the Jones era was the running of "Trojan Specials," trains that would take the team and fans to distant games. John Wayne and Ward Bond rode on some of the specials and reportedly had uproarious times, once staging a friendly wrestling match in a bar.

Years after he rode his last Trojan Special, Wayne showed up in Austin, Texas, the night before USC faced the University of Texas on September 17, 1966. Sportswriters regularly traveling with the USC football team returned to the Stephen F. Austin Hotel from dinner early in the evening and followed the suggestion of one writer that they join a Trojan party in an upper-floor ballroom.

As the writers entered the party area, a booming voice rose above the noise.

"Hey, Ace," John Wayne shouted to one of the writers, "it's eight o'clock and you're still standing. What's wrong?"

"Up yours, Duke," Ace fired in return.

There was general laughter, and the Duke was among those laughing loudest. But a little guy standing near Ace growled and advanced on him in a belligerent manner, asking, "What did you say to the Duke?"

"I told him where he could put it," Ace said.

"You can't talk to him like that," said the little guy, whereupon he unleashed a punch that missed. He also fell. When the little guy arose, Ace swung, missed and also fell. Within seconds, the huge movie actor had both combatants in his grip. "Take them to their rooms," said Wayne, identifying the little guy as his hairdresser.

Returning to the bar, Wayne explained to the writers why he was in Austin. "We've been invited by the Texas student body, but we're also on our way to Mexico to film *The War Wagon*," he said, motioning to his companion at the bar, actor Bruce Cabot. As Wayne stood sipping tequila, he turned to Nick Pappas, USC's director of alumni support groups. "Nick, you know what I'd like to do?" he said. "I'd like to talk to the team before tomorrow's game. Do you think John McKay would let me do that?"

"Well, why don't I find out?" Pappas replied. "I'll go call Coach now."

He returned shortly and said, "Coach would love to have you," he said. "Nine a.m., Duke. I'll meet you in the lobby at five to nine."

After a couple of hours, the party broke up. Shortly after eight o'clock the next morning, a writer entered the hotel lobby and noticed Wayne and Cabot standing somberly near a hotel doorway to the street. "Anything wrong?" the writer asked. Wayne said, "My little buddy [the hairdresser] died in his sleep last night. Heart attack, I guess. We found his body this morning. We're waiting for a hearse now." Within minutes, two men came in the door of the hotel, pushing a gurney. "We're here to pick up a body," one of the men explained. "What's the gurney for?" Wayne asked. "We have to pick up the body," he was again told.

"Not my buddy," said Wayne. "Wait here, I'll get him." With that, Wayne and Cabot went to the elevator. About ten minutes later, the elevator opened and there was Wayne, carrying his friend's body. "I'll take him to the hearse," he said. After making his delivery, Wayne waited with Cabot until Pappas arrived and escorted them to a dining room where the Trojans were eating their pregame meal.

McKay introduced Wayne to the team, which sat spellbound as the Duke launched his pep talk, mentioning first his USC coach, Howard Jones.

"The Headman always told us that each of us should get the best of the man opposite us," Wayne said. "He said if we did that, we would be sure to win. And, if you do that today, you will win, too." There wasn't a sound. It was doubtful any players were breathing, so taken were they with the message Wayne delivered.

During the game, a writer in the press box noted that Wayne and Cabot were standing in front of the Texas student section, waving their arms and carrying on. "Let's go down and see what's going on," said one writer. The other agreed, and armed with field passes, they took the press-box elevator to a lower level and walked to the field area.

Wayne had the students aroused. He had his index and little fingers shaped into the "Hook 'em Horns" salute Longhorn fans employ. But as he raised his right arm toward the sky, he wasn't saying "Hook 'em Horns." He was telling the Texans where they could deposit their team. Wayne was enjoying himself to the fullest and was even happier when the Trojans hung on for a 10–6 victory. He and Cabot headed for the USC locker room, followed by the two writers. As both parties entered the locker room, McKay, who had been given the game ball for his brilliant play-calling in the final minutes, spotted Wayne.

He tossed the ball to Wayne, twenty-five feet away. "To the greatest Trojan of them all," said the USC coach. Wayne was genuinely touched. And in keeping with the fun he had been having, he raised the ball over his head while he led the Trojans in a rousing rendition of "Bless 'em All."

Oh, the place was rocking. As Wayne headed for the door with Cabot, he turned around and said, "Gentlemen, I'm highly honored." With that, he was out the door and on his way to Mexico.

Wayne died of cancer in 1979, but it is difficult to forget his final appearance as a Trojan. Memories of that day in Austin in 1966 came cascading back on January 4, 2005, when the Trojans met Texas at the Rose Bowl with a national championship at stake.

Maybe if the Duke been there to give the Trojans the Headman speech . . . well, who knows?

THE TRANSITION
YEARS

oward Jones's death two months before the start of USC's
1941 football season left little time for the university administration to ponder options.

"I know they wanted Jeff Cravath for the job," says Julie Bescos,
one of the school's all-time athletic greats and an assistant under
Jones from 1936 to 1941. "But Jeff had just signed a contract as
head coach at the University of San Francisco and couldn't get out
of it."

That left only one option: Jones' longtime friend and assistant,
Sam Barry, who also was head coach in basketball and baseball.
Barry accepted, probably with reluctance, for football was not his
strength. He was basketball coach at Iowa when Jones was there, and
Jones had prevailed upon university officials to bring him to USC.

Out of loyalty to his departed friend and the university with
which he had established deep roots, Barry plunged into the task of
maintaining USC's hard-earned position among the upper echelon of
college football.

The challenge was daunting. Jones had gone through one of the worst campaigns of his coaching career in 1940, finishing seventh in the Pacific Coast Conference and compiling an overall record of 3–4–2. Barry fared worse, salvaging victories over Oregon State and Washington State and a tie with UCLA in nine games.

The 7–7 deadlock with the Bruins occurred on December 6, 1941, a day before the Japanese attacked Pearl Harbor, plunging the United States into World War II.

"I recall we were driving to Palm Springs the next day for a conference meeting when we heard over the car radio about the attack at Pearl Harbor," Bescos says. "We just turned around and came home. The conference meeting was canceled."

The war claimed Barry, who entered service in the spring of 1942 and didn't return to USC until after hostilities ceased on September 2, 1945. Fortunately for USC, Cravath was free after a year at San Francisco to take over head-coaching football duties in 1942.

Cravath played two seasons, 1925 and '26, under Jones and earned deep respect from the Headman for his fierce blocking and tackling as a 175-pound lineman and captain of the 1926 team. The new coach's demeanor is perhaps best described by Bobby Robertson.

"He was mean as hell," says Robertson. "If you got in his doghouse, you might as well leave school. If he didn't like you, you didn't play. Earl Parsons was a good example of someone who got on Cravath's list. Cravath was rough and tough. He might even tell the president of the school to get off the field."

But Cravath prospered during the war years, largely because of an influx of players from Navy and Marine training programs that had been set up at USC. He also was fortunate that Sam Barry, before his departure to the service, rescued multitalented Jim Hardy from the scrap heap.

"I fell in love with the Trojans when I was eight," says Hardy. "If the Trojans lost, it was a tearful weekend. My father was a Western Union operator who worked at SC games, so we [brother Don] would ride to the game with him and go through the kids gate. I went to Fairfax High in Los Angeles and played football. My senior year, I broke a leg and there was no chance I'd get a scholarship at USC. My dad couldn't pay for me to attend USC, but I enrolled there and walked on for football. I wound up being the starting tailback on the freshman team. I beat out a guy who was on scholarship. I ran out of money and didn't enroll for the second semester. Sam Barry called and asked why I wasn't in school. I told him I didn't have the money. He said, 'You get down here right away. You have a scholarship.'"

With Hardy available, Cravath switched to the T-formation, the sophomore from Fairfax as his quarterback.

"Our offense was so rudimentary," says Hardy. "He [Cravath] knew nothing about the T-formation, so we were running the single-swing offense out of a T. Our passing game was not that sophisticated, either. But he had some great players, particularly Don Doll [Burnside], and guys such as Bill Gray, Gordon Gray, Eddie Saenz, and Wally Crittenden who transferred in from other schools as part of the service programs. Cravath played favorites, too. He left me alone, mainly because there was no one else. If I made something up in the huddle and it worked, he didn't say anything. I did that many times."

The Trojans staggered through Cravath's first campaign, going 5–5–1, finishing fourth in the Pacific Coast Conference, and losing for the first time to UCLA, the school that had been dismissed for so long as the "Southern Branch." But when Hardy was given more freedom on offense, the Trojans prospered in 1943, compiling a 7–2 regular-season record and winning the Pacific Coast Conference championship. Their only defeats in the regular season were to powerful service teams from San Diego Navy and March Field.

Their success earned them a trip to the 1944 Rose Bowl, where Hardy threw three touchdown passes and earned Player of the Game honors as the Trojans romped, 29–0, over Washington.

A year later, after an unbeaten season that included ties with UCLA and Cal, the Trojans returned to the Rose Bowl, where Hardy, playing with a stomach disorder and a temperature, threw for two touchdowns and ran for another, thus accounting for six in two Pasadena appearances. USC easily outdistanced Tennessee, 25–0. "Hardy must be rated with the all-time Rose Bowl greats," wrote Al Wolf of the *Los Angeles Times*. Former Syracuse coach

Chick Meehan added, "Hardy's quarterbacking is on a par with the best of Sid Luckman of the Chicago Bears."

Hardy recalls with amusement an incident that occurred prior to the 1944 Rose Bowl game. "Each player was given an allotment of tickets for the game, and I bought up a batch from some of the freshmen on the team," he says. "There was no rule against selling tickets in those days, and I thought I could make a killing. Well, tickets weren't going very well, and I was desperate to get rid of them. So, I stood outside the Rose Bowl selling those tickets. Cravath came along and saw me. Made him mad as hell, and he didn't start me."

But Hardy achieved his purpose. "I got my money back," he says.

Cravath took the Trojans to another Rose Bowl on January 1, 1946, but he no longer had Hardy, and USC was hammered by Alabama, the second-ranked team in the nation, 34–14. This defeat terminated USC's eight-game Rose Bowl winning streak.

The USC coach's fortunes sagged after that, and he fielded only one more bowl team. His 1947 team finished the regular season with a 7–1–1 record and a No. 8 national ranking. But the Trojans had the misfortune of facing No. 2 Michigan in the Rose Bowl.

Cravath may have sealed his doom by the way he prepared his Trojans for this game. "Going into that Rose Bowl game, we were a very unhappy team," says Gordon Gray. "The first day of practice, we scrimmaged and three guys blew out knees. Then Cravath took us to Santa Barbara for eight or nine days and scrimmaged us hard. Well, you know what happened."

Yes, how the Trojans performed was there for everyone to see, including 93,000 at the Rose Bowl in Pasadena. Led by All-America halfback Bob Chappuis, the Wolverines embarrassed the Trojans, 49–0.

USC's failure to score deprived musician-placekicker Tommy Walker of an opportunity to display his Clark Kent act. Walker was a member of the USC band and wore his uniform to games, but whenever the Trojans needed a placekick conversion, he would shed band clothes that he wore over a football uniform and run onto the field. He made twenty successful conversions during the 1947 season. Cravath made him stay on the field for the 1948 Rose Bowl game. Walker was disappointed that he did not get a chance to kick a point-after, so, in the final moments of the game, Cravath wanted to insert him into the game as a defensive back, just so Walker could say he participated in the classic. But Walker was still donning shoulder pads when the final gun sounded. A music school graduate, Walker later provided halftime entertainment at three Super Bowls and fourteen Pro Bowls, and was director of the USC band from 1948 to 1955. USC adopted "Conquest" from *Captain from Castille* during his term as band director.

While Walker didn't get into the Rose Bowl game, the contest was the beginning of the end for Cravath. Powerful forces behind the USC program never forgot that embarrassment. Cravath hung on through 1948 and '49 with 6–3–1 and 5–3–1 records, but he had forged too many enemies to withstand a 2–5–2 season in 1950, although he finished the year with a 9–7 victory over unranked Notre Dame. It was Cravath's only losing season of the nine in which he directed the USC program, but he was fired in a bitter parting with his old university.

Los Angeles broadcaster Bob Kelley came to his defense. "They crucified Jeff Cravath," said Kelley. "The worst criminal in the world is entitled to certain considerations. A man as morally high as Cravath deserved a better lot. Jeff's only crime was, he didn't win every game. He had one losing season in nine years. The trustees of the University, meeting last night, under pressure from certain strong SC alumni, brutally fired Cravath—a loyal alumnus of the University with a marvelous coaching record wasn't even given the common courtesy of a chance to submit his resignation.. They crucified Jeff Cravath and his fine family just four days before Christmas."

Cravath didn't take his dismissal passively. "The players carried me off the field on their shoulders that glorious afternoon [Notre Dame game], and on the following Tuesday I was fired," he noted with undisguised sarcasm.

The rebuke he sustained from his alma mater apparently remained with Cravath through his remaining years. In the October 3, 1953, issue of *Collier's* magazine, Cravath co-authored with Melvin Durslag of the *Los Angeles Examiner* an article entitled, "The Hypocrisy of College Football—An ex-Bigtime Coach Tells

All." Cravath might not have told it all, but he didn't hold much back, and his revelations cast some doubt about the moral high ground broadcaster Kelley attributed to him.

Writing about the recruitment of Long Beach St. Anthony back Johnny Olszewski, Cravath told about taking the player to dinner and said that "the next day one of our wealthy alumni who lived in Johnny's hometown of Long Beach, California, got in touch with him. From what I understand—and a coach isn't supposed to know about such matters—the alumnus offered the athlete (a) a new car, (b) $150 a month during his four-year college career, (c) expenses through law school, and (d) a junior partnership in the alumnus's firm after graduation.

"I knew all along that an alumnus of the University of California, a traditional rival of USC, had also been keeping close track of Johnny all summer. I suspected by late August, too, that California was winning the decision. Still, I wanted to make one last bid for Johnny's services. It was arranged for us to have dinner again. But when he dropped up to my office in a new auto, I knew I was dead."

After citing other indiscretions practiced among major institutions, including USC, Cravath, living on a ranch in the El Centro area of California, added in his *Collier's* article: "Football is still my first love, but so far as coaching is concerned, I'm sort of reminded of what tourists are supposed to say about New York: 'It's a nice place for a visit, but I wouldn't want to live there.' Besides, I'm fond of my cows. They don't have alumni."

There was talk about USC seeking Notre Dame's Frank Leahy as Cravath's replacement—a rerun of the Knute Rockne ploy in 1925?—but the Trojans settled on Jess Hill, once one of the university's foremost athletes but a man with virtually no coaching experience.

In Hill's first year, he was blessed with the presence of Frank Gifford, who had been lured from Bakersfield College to USC with the promise of playing quarterback, only to languish for two seasons under Cravath as a safety, placekicker, and punter. In his book *The Whole Ten Yards*, Gifford describes how Hill turned his football life around:

"Shortly after being hired, he called me into his office and, in effect, asked me what he should do. Needless to say, I was dumbstruck. But what Jess finally decided upon made me ecstatic. Just like Homer Beatty at Bakersfield High, he switched us from the T-formation to a combination of the wing T and the single wing and built his attack around me at tailback. Besides continuing to play defensive back, I ran and passed and blocked—and we won our first seven games. Life was wonderful."

The Trojans lost their last three games, but Gifford won All-America honors and later was inducted into both the college and professional football Halls of Fame. His twelve seasons with the New York Giants forged a huge name for him in New York City, and he parlayed that fame into a bountiful television broadcasting career that included many years on *Monday Night Football*. Gifford is a member of the USC Hall of Fame and continues as a loyal and active alumnus of his old university.

Rarely raising his voice, Hill forged a 10–1 record in 1952, the only blemish a 9–0 loss to Notre Dame, and won an invitation to the 1953 Rose Bowl game. He capped this triumphal season with a 7–0 victory over Wisconsin, the Pacific Coast Conference's first Rose Bowl win over the Big Ten since the post-war contract calling for the leagues' champions to play each other on New Year's Day in Pasadena was put in place.

UNIVERSITY OF SOUTHERN CALIFORNIA

Jess Hill was a Rose Bowl-winning coach who went on to become a successful athletic director at the school.

Hill lost a 20–7 decision to Ohio State in the 1955 Rose Bowl. During his six seasons, he won forty-five games, lost seventeen and tied one. In his last year as head coach, Hill was involved in an event of high drama and sociological importance. The Trojans, who had three black players, were scheduled to go into segregated Texas to face the University of Texas in a contest at Austin on September 22, 1956. Upon his arrival with the team at their Austin hotel, Hill was informed that the black players would not be allowed to stay there. Hill quickly declared his position. "We all stay here or none us do," he told the hotel clerk.

It appears, in retrospect, that Hill had anticipated what he would encounter at the first hotel. He'd made a phone call, reportedly to a USC alumnus in Austin, who had arranged for all members of the team to stay at another hotel in the city, a place that also had been previously segregated. The three blacks were C. R. Roberts, Lou Byrd, and Hillard Hill.

Roberts still has vivid memories of what transpired that evening. "Most of the workers at the second hotel were blacks who had never seen a black allowed to stay at the place," he says. "I believe they began calling friends in the neighborhood to tell them about it, because it wasn't long before a crowd of African-Americans ringed the hotel, just staring at the building. One of the workers told me the people outside wanted to meet us, so I went out and talked to them. It probably was the first break in segregation they had seen. I urged them to go home, and they did."

Roberts, a fullback, also left his mark on Texas football. On the first play of the second quarter, he raced seventy-three yards for a touchdown. He had other touchdown runs of fifty and seventy-four yards, the latter on his first carry of the second half. He never carried the ball again and finished with 251 yards in twelve carries as USC defeated the Longhorns, 44–20.

"There were no racial incidents during the game," Roberts says. But the retired school teacher still bristles at racial bigotry he encountered in the National Football League. "It's one of the reasons I got out of football," he says.

In the year of the Austin assault on segregation, Hill and the university were caught in the middle of an explosion of charges and counter-charges among Pacific Coast Conference schools about illegal subsidies for athletes, particularly football players.

In his book, *Traditionally Yours*, former General Alumni Association Director Arnold Eddy reported what may have been the inception of problems concerning illegal subsidies for athletes with the formation of the Southern California Educational Foundation:

> "The object of the Foundation was to assist worthy high school graduates in securing a college education. The Foundation was supported by interested alumni and friends, and among them several of our University Trustees. Needy students (not all athletes) were assigned carefully selected elders who would provide a small sum of scholarship money each month, the money provided by the SCEF. Frankly, the plan was in a sense somewhat of a copy of what was then known as the Michigan Plan.
>
> "Our program was reported to the NCAA by a UCLA alumnus. An investigation was made. At its conclusion the NCAA field man told me that he had visited approximately 50 universities and this was the best plan and the best-run aid program he had investigated; he also said that he thought that all schools should have such a program—however, under NCAA rules it was illegal! As a result, the NCAA penalized us; our athletic recipients were denied a half season of play. If Michigan was ever penalized for their plan it was news to me."

In most sporting circles, the "carefully selected elders" to whom Eddy referred were more popularly known as "sugar daddies," and more than one USC football player from the 1930s to 1950s era has admitted to this book's authors that they were recipients of illegal aid. In fact, upon going from USC to the Los Angeles Rams of the National Football League, Leon Clarke stated publicly that he "had to take a pay cut."

Prior to the 1956 football season, USC, UCLA, Washington, and California were penalized by the conference because athletes from those schools were receiving under-the-table payments. Four years earlier, the Pacific Coast Conference, working with the American Council on Education, embarked upon a policy of further accenting enforcement of league rules. The endeavor was beginning to bear fruit.

C. R. Roberts was among those whose 1956 football season was reduced to five games, as was one of the school's greatest running backs, Jon Arnett. Both chose the first five games, and Arnett also opted for allegiance over money. "I met out in Malibu with a fellow from the British Columbia team in the Canadian Football League," Arnett says. "He offered me one hundred thousand dollars—a lot of money in those days—to go with them, with nothing binding about staying with them after one season. I chose to remain in school and play those five games, and I've never regretted my decision. You know, there are people from that era who have never forgotten what I did, and they show their appreciation."

Arnett's last game as a Trojan was against Stanford, a much-despised opponent at the time because it had taken a holier-than-thou attitude after escaping PCC and NCAA penalties. Arnett sparkled, but USC lost.

As USC sought to restore order to its house, Jess Hill was offered the athletic directorship of the university and accepted, handing off the head football coaching duties to an assistant, Don Clark, prior to the 1957 season.

The personable and capable Clark had a disastrous first season, going 1–9, and had a 4–5–1 record in 1958. Amid recriminations from all sides, the Pacific Coast Conference fell apart in 1958 after more than forty years of existence. It simply could not govern itself. In 1959, Clark hired a highly regarded assistant out of Oregon, John McKay, and the Trojans won their first eight games. They climbed to a No. 4 national ranking before losing to UCLA. They also dropped the season finale to Notre Dame and finished with a No. 14 ranking.

Clark resigned after the 1959 season. An incident during the USC-Cal game may have persuaded the personable and well-liked coach to get out of coaching. One of his players, Mike McKeever, was called for a late hit on Cal's Steve Bates as the Cal player landed out of bounds. Bates's face was torn up, and McKeever was pointedly vilified by *Life* magazine, which had assumed a self-appointed role as monitor of college football. Several sportswriters viewed a film of the game and saw one play in which a Cal player jumped on a pile with his fist raised and pounded it down on a Trojan player. The USC projector operator showed the fist going up and down several times. USC apologized to Cal over the incident, and there was a thought Clark might have been miffed over the school's handling of the case, including the apology to the Bears. Whatever his motive, he quit coaching to join a family business.

Administratively, a new conference, the Athletic Association of Western Colleges (later changed to Universities) was born, with USC, UCLA, Cal, Stanford, and Washington as members.

Ahead lay a dawn of prosperity for USC football.

"JAGUAR JON"

Jon Arnett not only had one of the more colorful nicknames in USC history, he had some of the most dazzling moves. For those not old enough to remember, maybe this is the best way to put him in perspective: He was the Reggie Bush of his time.

"Jaguar Jon" is the label sportscaster Gil Stratton gave him, and once you saw Arnett run, you never had to ask why. Give him the football in the open field, and he was a touchdown waiting to happen. He didn't have Reggie-like speed, but he was quick enough and amazingly intuitive, not to mention a master at cutting back against the grain. Yet what separated him from everyone else was the kind of remarkable balance even some of the truly great runners didn't possess.

"My older brother was always teaching me back flips and handsprings in the front yard as a kid," says Arnett, who was also a high school gymnast. "Looking back on it, I think he was probably doing it to hurt me." The only ones he wound up hurting with all those embarrassed opposing tacklers in the mid-1950s.

Arnett once explained how his gymnastic experience helped him on the football field: "Say you learn to do a back flip with a twist . . . after you master this maneuver, you become aware of the position of your feet and legs when you are upside down in the air. You have gained better control of your body, and you land in perfect balance. Now supposing you are upended by a tackler and your feet fly out form under you. There's no panic and the awareness of how to land in balance is there."

But Arnett wasn't just a great runner. He was a great football player. In his All-America junior year at USC in 1955, he scored 108 points on fifteen touchdowns and eighteen of twenty-two PATs. He rushed for 723 yards, threw for 150, and caught passes for 154 more. In his spare time, he returned sixteen punts for an eye-opening 27.9-yard average and also averaged

44.4 yards on eight punts. It is no wonder that then-coach Jess Hill, who also had Frank Gifford and Jim Sears in his time with the Trojans, called Arnett "the best back I ever coached." Red Sanders, the highly successful coach at UCLA said, "You watch Arnett some time. He even walks different than everyone else."

An all-city Player of the Year at Manual Arts High, a school located just a short punt return or so from the Los Angeles Coliseum, Arnett quickly established himself as a future star at USC in his sophomore season. Growing up in lower-middle-class surroundings as the son of a train mechanic, Arnett also realized that not everything was guaranteed to go his way.

"My first game as a sophomore, I scored three touchdowns and I was sharing the position with a guy who made All-Coast [Aramis Dandoy] the year before," Arnett says. "In fact, I scored seven touchdowns in my first three games, and believe me, I was walking on my tiptoes. I really thought I had it going. There were write-ups in the newspapers that I was going to be the first three-time All-American from the West Coast. Then, just about mid-season, I got leg whipped while playing defense and missed the next four games with a sprained knee. That brought me down to earth and proved to be a valuable lesson."

It wouldn't be the last lesson Arnett would learn at USC. Before a senior season in which he would have been one of the leading candidates for the Heisman Trophy, Arnett was among those cited by the commissioner of the then-Pacific Coast Conference, Victor O. Schmidt. The commissioner claimed Arnett and seniors on four conference teams had taken money from boosters for tuition, books, and rent. The ruling was that all those involved would be restricted to playing in just five games in their senior seasons. That killed any dream Arnett had of winning the Heisman. The trophy was won that year by Notre Dame quarterback Paul Hornung. A year earlier, Arnett and USC had defeated Hornung and the Irish, 42–20, with Arnett scoring twenty-eight of the Trojans' points. Arnett always called that his favorite game as a collegian.

In his abbreviated senior year, Arnett, at 5–11 and 195 pounds, was leading the nation in rushing with 150 yards per game after five games. He also led USC in tackles as a defensive back and averaged fifty-eight minutes per game. Even only playing half the schedule, he finished tenth in the Heisman balloting. A great long jumper for the Trojans who finished second in the NCAA in that event in 1954, Arnett teamed with C. R. Roberts to form one of America's great 1–2 punches in his senior season.

As a sophomore, he topped off his first big year with a brilliant performance in the Rose Bowl. "Someone figured I came within six yards of three Rose Bowl records," he says. The Trojans lost, 20–7, to Ohio State that New Year's Day in a heavy rain. "I had a seventy-yard run from scrimmage that was two yards short [of a record]," he says. "I had one hundred twenty-eight yards rushing, two more yards short, and a seventy-one-yard punt return. The record was seventy-three yards."

Even though his senior season was cut short, Arnett still talks about how enjoyable it was playing football at USC. "In college, every game day was exciting," he says. He proved how he felt when he turned down a chance to jump to the British Columbia Lions of the Canadian Football League before his senior season. The Lions offered him $100,000 to turn pro. "Do you realize how much a hundred thousand dollars was in 1956?" Arnett asks.

Looking back, he says he is only sorry about one thing. "My one regret is that I never got to run in a John McKay-type offense. I would have loved that. The game has changed. Runners are carrying twenty-eight to thirty times a game and lining up seven yards deep in the backfield. We used to line up only a couple yards deep, and our first move had to be laterally. That made it a lot more difficult."

After his senior season, Arnett was picked in the first round by the Los Angeles Rams in one of the more star-studded drafts in NFL history. Among the future greats to be selected that year were Hornung, Tommy McDonald, Jim Parker, John Brodie, Sonny Jurgensen, and Del Shofner. How impressed were the Rams with Arnett? They picked him ahead of another fair running back of that era—a fellow named Jim Brown.

"I think twenty guys out of that draft went on to be All-Pro," Arnett says. He was one of them. He was a six-time Pro Bowler who made first team All-Pro in 1959 when the other members of the All-Pro backfield that year were future Hall of Famers Johnny Unitas and Lenny Moore of the Baltimore Colts.

If Arnett had been drafted by the Green Bay Packers instead of Hornung, he, too, likely would be in the Pro Football Hall of Fame now. That's how good he was. Hornung was a remarkably versatile player, but as a pure runner, he was never in the same class as Arnett. "Arnett has more speed than most of them, he is bigger than some of them, and his ability as a gymnast enables him to keep his feet better than any of the backs of the Howard Jones era," said Cliff Herd, who was an assistant on Jones's staff back in the Thundering Herd days.

Arnett understands that USC tailbacks, or halfbacks, as they were known then, weren't the glamour players in his day that they would become years later. "At that time, there probably wasn't nearly as much history about the tailback as there has been written about in the past twenty years," he says. "I went to USC because it was the school I'd always followed as a kid. It had nothing to do with the tradition of tailbacks."

Most college football historians rank Arnett with Washington's Hugh McElhenny, another future Pro Football Hall of Famer, as the greatest broken-field runners of that era. Yet Arnett maintains that great running isn't something one works hard to achieve. It is a natural gift. "When you say someone is a great runner, it's not really a compliment," he says. "It's something you're born with. It's nothing I had to develop out of intelligence. You can be the greatest runner in the world and be dumb. So that doesn't make me better than anyone else. I have more respect for a great chess player because he had to learn to play the game."

Don't let Arnett fool you, though. He gained all those yards while playing full time on defense in the days of one-platoon football. "The tendency was to kind of catch your breath on defense," he says, with his usual candor. "Maybe you wouldn't support the run as well as you should. Maybe you wouldn't cover a receiver real tight. You'd guess a lot. You had to do it to survive."

Most of the time, those catching their breath were chasing Arnett. In his signature game as a Ram, against the Chicago Bears in 1958, Arnett had fifty-eight-yard and thirty-two-yard runs from scrimmage, punt returns of fifty-eight, thirty-six, and twenty-four yards, and a seventy-two-yard run with a screen pass to finish with 298 weaving yards in front of 100,470 people at the Coliseum that Sunday.

As great a pro as he was, he retired at age thirty, partly because he didn't want to incur a serious injury and partly because he'd lost a step or two. "I was thirty years old, and I'd had a good time," he says. "In my last year, I made close to fifty thousand dollars. I never had a career-ending injury, and I thought thirty was a good age to get out. So I did." Although he played a few years with the Chicago Bears at the end, most of his career was played within a few miles of his home in downtown L.A., both with USC and the Rams.

An original inductee in USC's Athletic Hall of Fame, in 2001, Arnett also was inducted into the College Football Hall of Fame. "I'm proud of it and grateful for it and pretty honored that I'm among the select group in the Hall," he says. Those who watched him play aren't surprised.

Jon Arnett belongs right there in the discussion of the great college running backs, not only of his era but of any era.

THE CROSSTOWN RIVALRY

Maybe people in Los Angeles are biased, but they think—no, they insist—that USC vs. UCLA is the best non-intersectional rivalry in college football. At the very least, they can present a strong case. The thing that makes the rivalry so extraordinary, besides the consistent quality of the teams, is the proximity. The two schools are twelve miles apart on the map of L.A. but closer than the guy in the next office cubicle, in reality. It's a prickly relationship so deeply rooted that it can affect you and your neighbor across the fence, or, in some cases, even you and the person you sleep with at night.

No one's ever checked, but the beginning of most Los Angeles-based divorces probably can be traced more to the third week of November than to any other time of year. This is serious stuff, folks. You're either a Trojan or you're a Bruin. There is no in between.

Ohio State-Michigan, Alabama-Auburn, Army-Navy, even Yale-Harvard are all great college football rivalries. But this is the only one with the two universities in the same town. In L.A., just about everyone has some kind of affiliation to one of the schools, if not both. You graduated from one, or your wife or husband did, or you son or daughter is currently attending one, or the person you share office space with was there fifteen years ago and still acts as if he's sitting in the middle of the rooting section on game days. Family gatherings, especially in the fall, are splashed with cardinal and gold and blue and gold colors. Many of us even laugh and talk about our "mixed marriages." You know, the husband went to UCLA and the wife went to USC, or vise versa.

What all this leads to is a passion that is unbelievably strong. USC-Notre Dame is steeped more in history, at least nationally. But USC-UCLA is *the* game in Southern California every year. It is the one that guarantees bragging rights at the water cooler for the next twelve months. The one that has etched more vivid memories than any other single match-up in the rich fabric of Southern California sports. The Trojans-Bruins game is always played for the crosstown championship, but more often than not, the conference title and the Rose Bowl bid have been at stake and, at times, even the national championship has been tethered to the result of this always tense, dramatic, and often traumatic late-season confrontation.

Ask the players. They'll tell you. Almost all of them, at least the ones who grew up in Southern California, will admit there is more emotion flowing the week of a USC-UCLA game than at any other time of the season. And as for game day, well, adrenaline levels in the region are never higher than they are moments before the kickoff of a Trojan-Bruin battle. Kids who grew up together, or met and became friends at various high school all-star games, suddenly act like bitter enemies.

"I remember just hating UCLA's players after our first loss to them," said Carson Palmer, one of USC's two Heisman Trophy-winning quarterbacks. "I didn't really know any of the guys that well, but I just hated them. Later on in my career, it was so much fun to beat them. It's funny, but I never met a player from UCLA that I didn't like when I was going to school at USC. But there was something about that rivalry. You grow to just hate them."

Ronnie Lott, the All-America safety of the late 1970s, says it felt more like "the Hatfields and the McCoys" than the Bruins and the

Trojans. "The thing is, you never forget those games," Lott adds. "Years later, you run into players who played in them with you or against you, and you describe the games as if they were yesterday. It was all about bragging rights on a lot of issues. You wanted to win so you could go to parties and impress those of the opposite sex. Everyone knew about the UCLA game. All your relatives from around the L.A. area knew about the game and watched it. You wanted to be able to look them in the face afterward and feel good about it."

There has been, for some time, a debate among members of the Trojan family whether the biggest game on the schedule every year is UCLA or Notre Dame. For Pat Haden, the star quarterback and Rhodes Scholar in the early seventies, it was no contest. "I always thought UCLA was the most important game," Haden says. "Notre Dame was big, but UCLA was bigger and more important, especially in my area. You have to remember, back then only one Pac-10 team was allowed to go to a bowl game. And almost every year, USC vs. UCLA had the Rose Bowl on the line.

"In 1972, we were unbeaten and eventual national champions, but if we had lost to UCLA, we wouldn't even have gone to a bowl game. In my era, both teams played in their home colors. I used to love that, the red against the blue. I wish they'd go back to that. The rooting sections also used to sit directly across from each other. That was great, too. Even today, I work in downtown L.A., and half my building is USC and the other half is UCLA. It's like split down the middle. You want your team to win so you can have the last word the next Monday. It doesn't matter what the teams' records are. There is still a special tingle associated with that game."

Make a big play in an average college football game, and people will compliment you and pat you on the back and say nice things about you. Make a defining play in a USC-UCLA game, and you become a hero for life.

The late Kurt Altenberg, who made one of the biggest plays in the history of the series, catching a Gary Beban touchdown pass to beat USC and clinch a Rose Bowl bid for UCLA in 1965, spent the rest of a life that ended too early constantly having that performance brought up to him. "It is just amazing," he said. "And the funny thing is, it's usually the USC people who remember first. They usually say, 'Aren't you the guy who made that catch?'"

David Bell is another who can attest to the celebrity that stems from doing something significant in the USC-UCLA game. Before the final seconds of the 2000 contest, nobody knew much about him, or cared much about him, for that matter—other than his family and friends, of course. Nobody paid much attention to the smallish, anonymous guy who was so adept at sailing kickoffs into the opposing team's end zone.

In that particular season, Bell, the back-up placekicker, had been 0-for-3 on field-goal attempts. He had tried one field goal early in the game against UCLA and missed a chip shot from twenty-four yards out. Then, with the game in its final seconds, Trojans coach Paul Hackett called on Bell to attempt a thirty-six-yard field goal. He managed one of the wobbliest, ugliest kicks ever, but it somehow fluttered through the uprights to give USC a 38–35 victory.

Later on, in an otherwise normal life, Bell was constantly stopped whenever someone noticed his name. "'Hey,' they'll say, 'aren't you the one who kicked that winning field goal against UCLA?' Some people will tell me how much they enjoyed the moment. Others just kid me and tell me I lost them money."

And so it has gone right from the beginning. UCLA didn't open as the University of California Southern Branch until 1919, some thirty-nine years after USC was founded. UCLA began as a two-year institution, developed into a four-year school in 1924, and grew swiftly enough so that by 1929, it was ready to take on its crosstown rival for the first time in football.

The first reaction, after a 76–0 loss in which USC piled up a staggering 712 rushing yards, was why bother? The mismatches continued until UCLA, deciding apparently that a little blue discretion was the better part of gold valor, put the rivalry on hold from 1931 until 1936, when an improved Bruins squad managed to squeeze out a 7–7 tie and a much sought-after sense of respect.

The rivalry began to flourish through the years, especially as UCLA's athletic fortunes grew in stature. The series began to run in cycles, with USC's Thundering Herd teams dominating one era and

Red Sanders's devastating UCLA single-wing teams consistently beating the Trojans in another.

There have been some great coaching match-ups through the years in this series, but none could compare to the one that began in the mid-1960s, pitting colorful John McKay and his brilliant tailback-oriented USC teams against introspective Tommy Prothro and his beautifully balanced UCLA squads. College football in Los Angeles was never more fun to watch or follow than when these two coaching giants were going at it.

This was a match-up made for Hollywood. It featured such a contrast in styles and personalities: Prothro was more withdrawn and introverted; McKay was more open and friendly. Tommy, a disciple of Tennessee's Robert Neyland and Red Sanders, was a slow-talking, slow-moving Southerner with a wry sense of humor; McKay was a wise-cracking cigar smoker from the hills of West Virginia. Prothro was Walter Cronkite; McKay was Johnny Carson.

If McKay was friendly, open, and a media delight who would often hold court after practice at Julie's, a popular hangout near the USC campus, Prothro was always careful with his words, as mysterious as that large leather briefcase he carried with him on the sidelines before each game. McKay produced the town's first Heisman Trophy winner in tailback Mike Garrett in 1965. Two years later, Prothro produced UCLA's only Heisman winner, quarterback Gary Beban.

These two coaching rivals were never great friends, but they had a deep, if unspoken, respect for each other. USC's coach captured four national titles. His UCLA counterpart never quite managed to win one, although he came close a couple of times. Yet it was Prothro, whose intelligence glowed like the tip of the cigarette he inevitably would be smoking, who was often described as more inscrutable and was more regaled for winning with seemingly smaller and inferior athletes, the latter a fact that never ceased to irk McKay.

Prothro established the tone of the rivalry in his first year, after coming to Los Angeles from Oregon State, returning to the campus where he once coached as an assistant under Sanders. Matched against a vastly superior USC team in his first taste of this crosstown adventure, his Bruins were roundly outplayed for most of that after-noon in 1965. Garrett, the stubby tailback who was the first of McKay's glorious running backs, dominated the game for more than three quarters. But then Beban, Prothro's precocious sophomore quarterback, stunned a sold-out L.A. Coliseum crowd and untold thousands of television viewers by unloading a couple of fourth-quarter touchdown bombs that not only beat USC, 20–16, but deprived Garrett and his teammates of a trip to the Rose Bowl.

If McKay and Prothro had a signature game, though, it came two years later. Rated No. 1 and 4 in the polls going into the contest, the Trojans and Bruins were playing for the conference title, the Rose Bowl bid, the national championship, and with Beban and USC's O. J. Simpson the two leading contenders, the Heisman Trophy. Other than that, the game didn't really mean much.

This was a time when the action lived up to the hype, too. For those of us who have watched college football through the years in

UNIVERSITY OF SOUTHERN CALIFORNIA

O. J. Simpson breaks away on his unforgettable sixty-four-yard run to help beat UCLA in a national title showdown game in 1967. Considering the stakes involved, it is probably the most famous play in USC history.

L.A., this game still ranks as the best one, the one played with more intensity from the opening kickoff until the final gun, not just in this series, but in the history of the sport in town. It was, quite simply, a classic.

Beban, the senior who was trying to put a cap on a magnificent career, was suffering from badly bruised ribs, often staggering off the field, bent over in pain, after a series of plays. Simpson, the junior tailback who had become the most exciting player in the sport, was brilliant all day long, scoring once from thirteen yards out while running through a gauntlet of UCLA tacklers in a demonstration of power and will that remains, to this day, difficult to forget.

But it was his later run, the one that will always be remembered by USC loyalists, the play called "23-Blast," that became the defining play of his career and maybe of this wildly competitive crosstown series. O. J. took a handoff from quarterback Toby Page, who had audibilized on the play, cruised to his left, cut back into the middle of the field, and with his buddy and track team sprint teammate Earl McCullouch providing the final protection, raced sixty-four yards for the fourth-quarter touchdown that proved the difference in a 21–20 game for the ages.

"It is the one game we still remember after all these years," said Beban, now a successful businessman in Chicago. "It was one none of us will ever forget," said Simpson, who became infamous for something other than football later in his life and now lives with his two children in Florida.

But that's the thing about this USC-UCLA series. There have been so many unforgettable moments, so many great games through the years. Space constraints preclude going into all of them, but here are just some of the other more memorable crosstown matches:

THE HISTORY-MAKER—For the first time in the history of the rivalry, the two teams were undefeated and untied when they met to determine the Pacific Coast Conference championship and the Rose Bowl representative in 1952.

A crowd of 96,869 witnessed a tense, taut duel that was decided when USC defensive lineman Elmer Willhoite intercepted a Paul Cameron pass and returned it seventy-two yards to the Bruins' eight-yard line. Four plays later, tailback Jim Sears lofted a pass to Al Carmichael for the touchdown that won the game and clinched the conference title and a trip to Pasadena, 14–12.

BEBAN'S BOMB—No ending was ever more shocking. USC and Heisman Trophy winner Mike Garrett dominated the 1965 game for almost four quarters, but then a couple of late fumbles, one of them by Garrett, let the Bruins back in.

Gary Beban, a marvelous sophomore quarterback who would win the Heisman two years later, did the rest, firing two long touchdown bombs in the final four minutes, the last one to Kurt Altenberg for forty-eight yards, to stun the Trojans, 20–16, and capture the conference championship and go on to the Rose Bowl, where Beban and the Bruins would pull off another shocker against No. 1 rated Michigan State.

THE GREAT COMEBACK—Never leave a USC-UCLA game early. That lesson was driven home in 1996, when UCLA somehow came back after being seventeen points down with six minutes to play to tie, then eventually beat USC, 48–41, in overtime. USC's R. J. Soward had dominated the game for most of the sun-splashed afternoon, catching six passes for a staggering 260 yards and three touchdowns to help pile up that huge lead.

But by the time the shadows had begun to creep into the historic old saucer in Pasadena that day, tailback Skip Hicks could be seen scoring the winning touchdown on a twenty-five-yard scoot. And just think how all those folks who left the Rose Bowl early that afternoon to beat the traffic felt when they heard the final score.

SUDDEN SAM—This 1969 contest was the game of all games for those with divided opinions. It provided water-cooler debates for months afterwards. If you were a UCLA fan, you fervently believed the Bruins' Danny Graham was whistled for a phantom pass-interference penalty on Trojan wide receiver Sam Dickerson. If you were a USC supporter, you argued just as strongly that the call was richly deserved.

In the end, this duel between two unbeaten and once-tied teams was decided by the same Mr. Dickerson, who escaped into the early-evening darkness of the Coliseum's corner end zone to spear a thirty-two-yard, last-second touchdown pass from Jimmy Jones for a heart-stopping 14–12 victory.

THE SHOOTOUT AT THE CROSSTOWN CORRAL—Fans of defensive football might not have appreciated it, but the 1990 shootout at the Rose Bowl between USC's Todd Marinovich and UCLA's Tommy Maddox was a game the fans loved. This one was almost like a tennis match, the way both teams marched up and down the field.

In a breathtaking finish, Marinovich found Johnnie Morton, who flew into the air to make a highlight-reel, fingertip catch of a twenty-three-yard pass with sixteen seconds left to win it, 45–42. "I've never been in a game quite like that one," said Maddox, who threw for 409 yards in a losing cause. Those in the stands could never remember watching one like that, either.

THE PRIMO PASS—The best team in UCLA history capped a perfect season with one perfectly executed forty-eight-yard pass from single-wing tailback Pimo Villanueva to Bob Heydenfeldt in 1954. It was the only touchdown of a pressure-filled first three quarters, but it helped Red Sanders's beautifully coached team blow the game open and eventually win, 34–0, to grab a share of the Bruins' only national title, with Ohio State.

JOHN WHO?—Then there are those storybook scripts everyone always cherishes. In 1992, it involved a fifth-string UCLA walk-on and former Saddleback College backup quarterback named John Barnes. This was a kid who never had made it off the bench. A kid who barely had made it into the game-day program. No one knew his name or anything about him before the day started. But no one could stop talking about him afterward.

Barnes emerged from obscurity that afternoon to throw for 385 yards and three touchdowns, including a ninety-yard bomb to J. J. Stokes with three minutes to play to upset USC, 38–37. "You dream about days like this," Barnes said afterwards. But this was a stretch even for the dreamers out there.

SAY HEY, WILLIE—It wasn't just that USC was losing the game, 3–0, late in the fourth quarter of this afternoon in November 1962. It was also losing its grip on the first precious national championship of the McKay era.

Then, just when all hope seemed to be evaporating, halfback Willie Brown, looking more like Willie Mays, soared into the air, contorted his body, and made a spectacular catch of a twenty-four-yard Bill Nelsen pass at UCLA's two-yard line. It led to the Trojans' first touchdown and an eventual 14–3 victory that helped secure McKay's first national title.

RODNEY TO THE RESCUE—Rodney Peete made many great plays on offense in a USC career culminated by a Heisman Trophy runner-up senior season at quarterback. But his best play in the crosstown series came on defense.

On the final play of the first half in 1987, with UCLA already leading, 10–0, cornerback Eric Turner intercepted Peete's pass on the goal line and appeared a cinch to return it 100 yards for a touchdown that basically would have put the game away. But Peete chased him down in what seemed like one long, extraordinary, freeze-frame moment, finally tackling Turner on the USC eleven. The play turned the momentum of the game around, and the Trojans and Peete came back to win, 17–13.

THE GREAT DEFLECTION—Jay Schroeder's pass sailed high into the air in 1980, and USC's Jeff Fisher, the current head coach of the NFL Tennessee Titans, settled under it, about to make what appeared to be a sure interception.

But the ball somehow bounced off Fisher into the waiting hands of Bruin tailback Freeman McNeil, who raccd fifty-eight yards for the touchdown that won the game for UCLA, 17–14. "An act of God," is how Bruins coach Terry Donahue later described the play.

God, a shrewd neutral observer in this USC-UCLA rivalry, declined all interview requests afterward.

THE BRUIN BLUDGEONING—If USC fans had their way, every game in the rivalry would be like the 2005 contest. This was the final game in the Coliseum for both Matt Leinart, who'd already won a Heisman Trophy, and Reggie Bush, who was on the verge of winning one of his own. This was the afternoon when Bush put on the kind of show that stamped him as one of the Trojans' all-time greats.

"On a scale of one to ten, it was a ten," Bush said, after streaking, swiveling, and leaping his way to 260 yards, most of them in the first half. The Trojans overpowered their crosstown friends upfront, pounding away for 430 rushing yards en route to a 66–19 mugging on a smog-free, problem-free afternoon for USC. When Bush wasn't manhandling the Bruins, LenDale White took his turn. The "other" tailback in perhaps the most effective offense in Trojans history ran for 154 yards and two touchdowns, giving him a school-record fifty-four for his career.

But when the game was over, it was still remembered as Bush's day, with the crowd of 92,000 chanting "Reg-GIE . . . Reg-GIE . . . Reg-GIE!" as the final minutes ticked off. Afterward, after he'd paused to direct the USC band and accept the cheers and gratitude of so many Trojans fans, the junior who would win the Heisman a few weeks later in New York smiled and said the day had been "every-thing anyone could dream of."

If it was a dream for USC, it was a nightmare for UCLA. Trojans fans would like to think it could always be that way, but based on the long, contentious history of this series, they'll never admit it.

But deep down, they know better.

STRIKE UP THE BAND

It is the Trojan Marching Band, known as "the Spirit of Troy," and it is widely regarded now as one of the best and most innovative collegiate bands in the country, playing at such prestigious events as the 1984 Olympics and the Academy Awards. But it wasn't always so. To truly grasp and appreciate the impact USC's band has these days, one must go back a few years to when things weren't so wonderful for the musicians trying to represent the university.

"The band was a joke," said Dr. Arthur C. Bartner, describing the years before he took over the baton in 1969. If that sounds like an exaggeration, it isn't. At one point, in fact, the band was actually using shills to fill out the available uniforms. Steve Harvey, now a columnist for the *Los Angeles Times*, was attending USC and writing for the school newspaper, the *Daily Trojan*, in 1966 when he and Editor Steve Harris uncovered the scandal.

"The shills had been signed up because the turnout for the band had been so small," Harvey says. "Band members were told to recruit kids who would come out, put on uniforms, and carry the instruments but only pretend to play them. It was kind of the Hollywood touch, a form of lip-synching, all for appearance's sake." Two former band members admitted that they and several others had faked it in the past. "Don't say faking," one told Harvey. "We like to call it improvising."

The story in the *Daily Trojan* was picked up by the *Los Angeles Herald-Examiner* and its always creative sports editor, Bud Furillo, and appeared along with a huge photo of the band on page one of the sports section. A day later, Harvey was walking on campus and saw a big crowd watching a dummy hanged in effigy. Harvey got closer and saw his name scrawled on the torso of the dummy. "No one knew what *Daily Trojan* writers looked like, so I went undercover and casually asked a member of the mob what was going on," Harvey says. "'Oh, we're hanging that bleep-bleep Steve Harvey,'" he said. 'Yeah I know him,' I responded. 'He's a real jerk.'"

All that silliness ended when Dr. Bartner, a graduate of Michigan, came in and began to revamp the image of the band. "One of my main mentors was Marv Goux [the popular assistant coach on John McKay's football staff]," Bartner says. "I actually started in the fall of 1970. We had eighty guys, half of whom didn't go to school. Marv stepped up and told me, 'This is what a band has to be. It has to be the spirit organizer on campus. The band and the football team have to bond together.'

"He started what we've come to call the Jock Rallies the Friday before every game. In the old days, when they were held downstairs in the old P.E. Building, it was all fire- and-brimstone speeches and people breaking lockers and X-rated language. It was wild stuff. I was barely thirty years old, and Marv took me under his wing.

"That's how we started to build the band. The main thing I emphasized is, we want to support our football team. I tried to run band rehearsals like football practice, with the same kind of energy level and people yelling and cheering. All that came from Marv." But a lot of it since has come from Bartner. "We're much more broad-based now. We have two hundred eighty band members, and we have a band camp that's kind of like a preseason football camp. We correspond with incoming freshmen and build a list of one hundred freshman candidates to join the band."

The results speak for themselves. The Trojan Marching Band was named one of the eight best marching bands in the nation by *USA Today* and is one of USC's most visible public relations tools. Herb Alpert, the leader of the Tijuana Brass, played in the trumpet section as a student. Some of the great artists who have appeared with the band include Henry Mancini, Quincy Jones, Chuck Mangione, Leonard Bernstein, Diana Ross, and Neil Diamond. "I'm very proud of what we've done," Bartner says. "I've been here thirty-five years, and we've enjoyed some great times with the football team through the John McKay and

John Robinson eras. And now, with Pete Carroll, the last four years have been just wonderful."

A typical halftime show by the band, complete with precision drills, special musical arrangements, and dance routes, takes more than 100 hours to prepare. The band marches some ninety miles a year while traveling across the country in support of USC athletics.

"People ask me what's the best part," says Bartner. "I tell them, 'When the football team comes over to the band.' They come before the game, and then they come again after the game. We have a tradition when a star player comes up and leads the band after a victory. Lynn Swann started it. Once when the team came out for pregame practice, he just ran over to the band and started directing it. Now, at our Jock Rallies at five o'clock on Fridays, a different player leads the band in 'Conquest' every week. After big games, especially, like UCLA and Notre Dame and bowl games, the star comes over. We've had Matt Leinart and Reggie Bush, and even Pete Carroll has taken a turn leading the band. Everyone who is a Trojan celebrates that moment. That's what we live for."

Over the years, the USC band has performed for seven presidents and appeared in numerous movies, including *Forrest Gump* and *The Naked Gun*. It has played at four Super Bowls, the 1988 World Series, the 1994 World Cup, and the 2002 NHL All-Star Weekend. In 1988, Bartner brought the band to Australia to perform during that country's bicentennial celebration. The band makes more than 300 appearances a year. It hasn't missed a Trojans football game, home or away, since 1987, and its trips to Notre Dame and the Bay Area, in particular, are much anticipated. Approximately 20 percent of band members are music majors, with almost every school and department represented. Bartner, along with longtime arranger Tony Fox, has brought a unique, contemporary "drive-it" style of marching.

"When I came out here, everyone wanted another Michigan-type band," Bartner says. "But we had to come out with our own image." Part of that was created, thanks to a band member's suggestion, when a new piece of apparel was added to the distinctive Trojan uniforms. "Everybody wears sunglasses," Bartner says. "I think it adds a certain mystique. We wear them at day games and night games. We never take them off. The kids think of them as part of their uniforms now."

Can you imagine what members of the Ohio State or Michigan bands would say about that? At USC, they don't seem to care what others think. They've come a long way from the days when they required non-playing shills to fill out the group. "This is a very unique program," Bartner says. "It's not like the Big Ten bands. They're very disciplined and structured. Out here, you have to be more laid back."

Bartner's philosophy is very simple. He says: "We try to play well, march hard, and have fun."

THE JOHN MCKAY ERA

I t was almost as if he just appeared one day, sauntering through the billowing smoke from one of his ever-present cigars, looking up with that Irish twinkle in his eye, and snapping off glib one-liners so fast you couldn't write them down in your notebook.

John McKay wasn't just a football coach. He was a state of mind. He was equal parts strategist and comedian. He was the foot-ball equivalent of Johnny Carson, as quick with a quip as he was drawing up a new play. He could be brilliant and moody, funny and quick-tempered, cocky and yet, somehow, surprisingly insecure. His players feared him, his assistants worshipped him, and the fans and media loved him. McKay was the top name on the marquee, the dominant personality in a city that couldn't wait to anoint successful people as stars and cared more about sports than it did about solving its smog problems. From the time he won his first of four national championships at USC, in 1962, until he left thirteen years later to take his shot in the NFL, McKay established himself as the greatest football coach, college or pro, in more than fifty years in Los Angeles.

Considering all that he accomplished, it's difficult to believe, in retrospect, that McKay was more of an afterthought than he was the unanimous selection of those in charge at the university. He wasn't the big-name coach boosters had fantasized about, not a Woody Hayes, or a Bud Wilkinson, or an Ara Parseghian. He was just a young, wisecracking assistant coach few people outside the program knew.

It was widely believed, following Don Clark's resignation after the 1969 season, that USC President Norman Topping had the foresight to pick a coach who would rewrite Trojan football history. Some years later, however, Topping set the record straight. "Well, I'd like to take credit for possessing such brilliance, but I can't," he said. "The truth is, I first called in [assistant] Ray George, who had previous head-coaching experience [at Texas A&M]. I offered Ray the job, but he turned it down. He said he thought John McKay [another assistant] was the right man for the job. So I called John McKay to my office and offered him the job. Happily for us, he accepted."

It proved to be fortuitous for everyone connected with USC football. Give George some belated credit and throw some more in the direction of Nick Pappas, the former USC player and assistant coach who became director of the university's athletic support groups. Pappas was a colorful guy who once doubled for Pat O'Brien in a Knute Rockne movie. But don't be confused, he always has been a loyal Trojan.

It was Pappas, when he was scouting as a coach for the Trojans, who first encouraged McKay, then an assistant at Oregon, to apply when a position on Clark's staff opened. Pappas remained a strong friend of the coach from then on. "Nick led the Trojans in rushing back in 1935," McKay used to say, "when he had more hair."

McKay, who loved to refer to himself in later years as "the old Irishman," was born of Scotch-Irish parents in Everettsville, West Virginia, a tiny coal-mining town that doesn't exist anymore. He grew up one of five children in a strong Catholic family in the town of Shinnston, where everyone worked hard, played hard, and spent every Saturday in the fall listening to Notre Dame football. McKay's father, John, was a tough, disciplined mine superintendent. His mother, Gertrude, stayed home and took care of the kids.

Called "Jack" by his parents, McKay was extremely close to his father, who was described as a fearless, sound decision-maker who was not comfortable glad-handing, as it was called then. McKay would grow up to be the same way. His father died at the age of forty-five in 1936. Death came without warning. Doctors later discovered the cause was pneumonia. Young John, only thirteen at the time, was devastated. Years later, he would describe it as "a terrible shock."

UNIVERSITY OF SOUTHERN CALIFORNIA

If you had to pick one classic pose of John McKay, this would be it: the cigar-smoking, wisecracking coach entertaining writers at a postgame press conference in Los Angeles.

The loss of the family's main provider changed the McKays' lifestyle and, in many people's minds, laid the foundation for the insecurity that would surface from the coach in so many future situations. Suddenly, the McKays were poor, and John found himself taking odd jobs, sweeping out restaurants, washing bathrooms, and delivering wet concrete in a wheelbarrow. It was not an easy life, and John was determined to find some other way than to spend the rest of his days working in the coal mines.

His athletic ability helped him discover the road out. He was an all-state running back in football and a star guard in basketball at Shinnston High School, where his football coach, Mickey McClung, impressed him so much that McKay's goal was to go to college, get a degree, and come back to Shinnston and replace McClung someday. World War II interrupted his plans, as it did those of so many others. But after spending years in the service, some of it as a B–29 tailgunner, he came out as a twenty-three-year-old college freshman and promptly enrolled at Purdue, where he played varsity football right away. He eventually became a starting running back and defensive back for the Boilermakers, until McClung convinced him to transfer to Oregon. It was that move, perhaps more than any other, that changed McKay's life.

He played two years as a big-play runner for the Ducks on a team that also featured future Hall of Fame quarterback Norm Van Brocklin and Woodley Lewis, who would go on to be a terrific player for the Los Angeles Rams. More important, McKay earned his degree at Oregon, met his future wife, Corky, got married, accepted a job as a Ducks assistant, and had four children while he was in Eugene. He also gleaned much of the football knowledge that would serve him so well from coaches Jim Aiken and Len Casanova before moving to USC to join Clark's staff.

While McKay was surprised to be offered the Trojans' head coaching job that day in 1959, he said it took him "about a half-second to say yes." It took considerably longer than that for him to enjoy any real success. He had to put in his own system, organize his recruiting procedures, and adjust to the sudden pressures from the media and alumni. It didn't help when he went 4–6 and 4–5–1 in his first two years, losing to Notre Dame both seasons. There were murmurs of discontent throughout Southern California, with columnists in the L.A. papers speculating on candidates to take over if the program didn't turn around.

The breakthrough came in 1962 when McKay split signal-calling duties between two future NFL quarterbacks, Pete Beathard and Bill Nelsen; utilized three units he identified as Red, Green and Gold; and fielded a tremendous defense led by a little fireball of a linebacker named Damon Bame, to take USC to an undefeated season and the national championship. The 10–0 Trojans beat Navy and Heisman Trophy winner Roger Staubach, among others, outscored opponents, 219–55, then held off Wisconsin, 42–37, in a wild, pass-crazy Rose Bowl game that ended in virtual darkness, prompting the Pasadena venue to put in new lights for the future.

Willie Brown, the first of McKay's tailbacks to line up deep in the new I-formation, is convinced it was the coach's innovation that propelled the 1962 team to such great heights. "By instilling the I-formation, we were doing things other schools and other defenses couldn't handle," Brown says. "We had a good team with some really talented people at the skill positions, but it was the changes that won it for us." Brown admits the coach treated him differently than some of his teammates. "A lot of players were scared of him, but not the tailbacks," Brown said. "You didn't touch the tailbacks. He was a real disciplinarian, and he really believed in running the football. I couldn't have any more respect for what he did in returning the program to prominence."

"McKay employed Red, Gold, and Green units and inserted them in groups in 1962," says Bill Fisk Jr., a guard from that era. "Everybody played, and there were no prima donnas, no big stars. It was a happy environment."

Dave Levy, one of his closest assistants, said McKay switched out of the wing-T he had used in 1960 and the sprint-out offense he'd run in '61. "In '62, McKay decided to pretty much go with the I-formation," Levy says. "He didn't invent it, but he certainly popularized it. I remember talking to Sid Gillman of the Chargers and asking him if it would work in the NFL. He assured me it wouldn't, but, lo and behold, a couple of years later he was using it. In addition, we began running what later became known as Student Body Left or Right. You know, when you win a national championship and are the only team in the country using something, you become the inventor. In truth, Moses probably invented the I-formation."

But he probably didn't have as much fun as McKay, who would win three more national championships, nine conference titles, and nine bowl games, including five Rose Bowl victories in eight appearances. He turned USC into Tailback U. and made Student Body Right famous in college football vernacular. He also coached two Heisman Trophy winners—Mike Garrett and O. J. Simpson—and forty All-Americans. He was named national Coach of the Year in 1962 and 1972.

"That 1972 bunch was my greatest team," McKay said. "We had three NFL first-round draft choices, and counting guys who were sophomores and juniors that year, the total was something like thirty-three NFL players. Gentlemen, you have to have players to win football games."

McKay always had players—but he also had so much more. His teams developed an aura about them; some called it arrogance, others confidence. "No, it was a swagger," says Lynn Swann, the great All-America receiver who went on to become a Hall of Famer with the Pittsburgh Steelers. "We swaggered because we believed we were better than you. We swaggered because we knew that when the third and fourth quarters come around, you were going to be ours. I don't call that arrogance. We just believed in ourselves."

They made believers of others, too. Mike Rae, quarterback of the 1972 national champions, said, "You could see other teams sneaking a peek at us in pregame warm-ups." They were probably sneaking a peek at McKay, too.

John McKay poses with four All-Americans from his 1967 national championship team, Ron Yary (77), Adrian Young (50), O. J. Simpson (32), and Tim Rossovich (88). All four went on to be stars in professional football.

The "old Irishman" was as colorful as he was creative. Covering him was like being part football beat man and part comedy writer. Often, you found yourself laughing too hard to scribble down his last quote. "What did you think of your team's execution?" someone asked when he was coaching in Tampa Bay. "I'm all for it," McKay answered. When one of his USC players, Mike Hunter, slipped and fell while fielding the opening kickoff at hostile Notre Dame in 1965, McKay turned to an assistant and said, "My God, they've shot him." When questioned why one of his tailbacks carried the ball so much, he cracked, "Why not? He doesn't belong to a union."

Still, seeing his jokes in print never did McKay justice. He was much funnier in person. His timing was as good as Bob Hope's, and he had a mischievous twinkle in his eye that matched Johnny Carson's on his famous late-night television show. But McKay didn't become famous because he was everybody's favorite after-dinner speaker. He became famous because he could coach the shoulder pads off any good football player he could find. And he found plenty of them.

Although it is often forgotten in the rush to froth over his offensive prowess and his many glamorous running backs, McKay was a masterful recruiter who also molded some of the finest defensive units of his time. Many of the great coaches in college football history were specialists on one side of the ball. McKay was different. His offense was fresh and innovative, but his overpowering defensive units were always the foundation of his best teams. His defense was magnificent in 1962. Then he had the famous "Wild Bunch" in the late sixties and developed what might have been his finest defense of them all in 1972 when he won his fourth national title.

There was a reason USC was as good at attracting blue-chip players as it was at generating big-game victories. Fred Hill, a wide receiver who played for McKay from 1962 through '64, recalls his recruiting experience with the coach:

"My father was a construction worker who didn't have much education. He was very nervous about going onto a college campus and talking to a coach. But Coach McKay put him at ease. He said to my father, 'Would you like a cigar?' My Dad said yes, so they lit up their cigars and my dad was completely relaxed. Coach McKay said to him, 'Mr. Hill, we're going to give your son a four-year scholarship that will be good even if he doesn't make the team. If he doesn't make the team, that will be our mistake. He'll still have his scholarship.' That did it. My dad wanted me to be a Trojan."

Ron Humenuik, who played for the Trojans in the mid-fifties and coached under McKay from 1966 through '70, said, "Coach McKay had a knack for keeping players focused, for putting emphasis on the right things at the right time. He'd give an overall view, break it into pieces, and each day start putting the pieces together."

Much like his close friend, Paul "Bear" Bryant at Alabama, McKay was bigger than life. He had a presence about him that made those who knew him and worked with him fiercely loyal. He also had a style that was as familiar as that little saunter of his that was evident every time he strolled into a room.

At Julie's, the off-campus hangout that used to be a USC favorite, McKay had his own corner booth, a rich, red leather one that was deemed his exclusively. After football practice, McKay would adjourn to that booth with his reverential assistants and, usually, a bunch of scruffy sportswriters, and hold court, the smoke from his cigars making small, wispy circles in the air while the laughter from his one-liners reverberated throughout the room.

McKay's ability to drink—and more specifically, to hold his liquor—was as legendary as his ability to coach. He'd walk into Julie's at six o'clock with his entourage, start drinking stingers non-stop, usually without eating anything, and while most of the others at the table slowly staggered away trying to keep up, he'd continue drinking. Then, at closing, or when no one else was there, or no other napkins on which to draw plays were left, he'd casually get up from the booth and stroll out into the nearby parking lot looking as sober as when he'd walked in.

On the practice field, he was a different kind of man, often overseeing practice on a portable tower. "I thought that was God up there watching me," said Manfred Moore, who played for him from 1971 through '73. "That's why I went full speed all the time."

Mike Rae called McKay "very intimidating, very standoff-ish." Rae said he had a closer relationship to the coach because he was the quarterback. "But most guys on the team rarely spoke to him. They feared him."

Bill Fisk Jr., who was on McKay's first national championship team, said, "If you saw him coming down the street, you tried not to meet him. I was just eighteen when I went to USC, so I was scared of him. We all were."

Pat Haden not only was McKay's quarterback in 1973 and '74, he was also like another son to the coach. He was J. K. McKay's longtime friend and teammate who lived in the McKay household during his senior year in high school after his parents had moved.

UNIVERSITY OF SOUTHERN CALIFORNIA

John McKay poses with son J. K., left, and Pat Haden, the quarterback who was like a surrogate son to him. J. K. and Haden remain close friends today.

"At home, he was a twenty-four-hour-a-day football guy," Haden said. "He was very smart, very bright. He did like Westerns, either movies or novels. That's all he watched on TV or read. As a coach, he was very tough, especially on game day. The sportswriters thought he was funny, but he wasn't funny to us. He was very, very tough. At home, he could be pretty funny—but not during football season. He loved steak sandwiches and vodka and liked to play golf. Most of all, he loved the university. He loved everything about it. He was pretty remarkable that way."

More than anything, though, McKay loved football. He lived it and breathed it and was obsessed with it. "I was always drawing plays on tablets," McKay said. "I'd draw them on cocktail napkins and I'd draw them on tablecloths. I'd draw them anywhere. If I was watching a movie on television, I'd be scribbling plays at the same time. I like to think of myself as an innovator, rather than an imitator."

Haden says McKay's greatest ability was his knack for spotting talent. "I think he was the best evaluator of talent that I've ever seen," Haden said. "He would have some high school kid who was an All-America linebacker, and the first day he'd watch him practice and say, 'You're a tight end.' Two years later, that kid was an All-America tight end. I think he had a great knack for piecing an entire team together."

One of the best examples was Bobby Chandler, a scrawny kid who came out of Whittier in the early 1960s as a prep quarterback. McKay realized immediately he couldn't play that position at USC, but every time he looked up in practice, Chandler was scrambling into the clear, showing great moves and agility. "We have to find some way to get that Chandler kid into games," he said one day. The next day, Chandler was a flanker who went on to become one of the more effective receivers of the McKay era and a Pro Bowler in the NFL.

Hal Bedsole was another. An all-city quarterback coming out of the San Fernando Valley area of Los Angeles, Bedsole arrived at USC and was immediately switched to wide receiver by McKay. By his junior season, the 6–5 Bedsole had become an All-American and the go-to guy on offense for the 1962 national champions.

Perhaps McKay's most famous move was transforming the I-tailback into college football's most glamorous position. A Florida State coach named Tom Nugent is credited with being the first to implement a T-formation with the running backs lined up directly behind the quarterback in an "I." But McKay was the one who refined it and developed it into what became a devastating weapon. Originally, he used it as a means to disguise other plays. Then he tinkered with it, deciding to use it exclusively, with one clever addition. He split out one end on the side opposite the flanker. That gave him the opportunity to shift and put men in motion.

But all that was just an appetizer to McKay's main course of action. His plan was to make the tailback a T-formation version of the old single-wing tailback who carried the ball on the majority of plays. The difference, of course, is that the tailback wouldn't take the center snap. He would, however, become as much, if not more, a focus of the offense as the quarterback. To McKay, the logic was obvious. "It's simple," he said. "The tailback is your best back. It's like having a choice of batting your best hitter every time, instead of every three or four innings. If I have a choice, I want to bat him every inning."

In 1962, his first national title year, the "I" wasn't as effective as it would be later on. Pete Beathard, the No. 1 quarterback, was a gifted runner as well as a passer, and he rolled out much of the time. The carries given to the alternating tailbacks, Willie Brown and Ken Del Conte, were limited. But in 1963, a sophomore named Mike Garrett appeared, and he became the prototype USC tailback who would go on to lead the Trojans in rushing for three years, roll up huge yardage on eye-popping carries-per-game totals, and eventually win the Heisman Trophy in 1965.

"Garrett allowed us to expand the role," McKay said. "The power-I really began with him." The more McKay used him, the more Garrett loved his new job. As an I-formation tailback, he could read his blocks better, make smarter cuts, and get into the kind of rhythm only those who carry thirty, thirty-five, or even forty times a game can understand.

Garrett, of course, begat O. J. Simpson, who would prove to be a bigger, faster version and become McKay's second Heisman winner. There are many people who still believe Simpson, with his ability to run over people between the tackles and outsprint them in the secondary, is the greatest running back in college football history. Anthony Davis, the next great tailback in the succession, was the star of what McKay later described as his best team, in 1972. Davis was somewhere in between Garrett and Simpson in size and actually made a bigger name for himself as perhaps the most famous kick-return runner in the annals of the sport, a label Notre Dame would sadly endorse.

Later, after McKay left and was replaced by John Robinson, there were two more Heisman Trophy tailbacks, Charles White and Marcus Allen, and another who probably should have been in Ricky Bell, all in the old, power-running, I-formation mold first introduced by McKay.

In its prime, the I-formation was sometimes criticized as too boring and conservative. But McKay didn't care. He was pounding other teams at will with his bruising tailbacks. Along the way, he was also using a series of shrewd variations of the same basic plays. "We run off tackle three straight times, and the average fan thinks we're getting into a rut," McKay said. "But that's not true. We run off tackle once, and then we run it again. But the second time, we will change our blocking assignments, and that makes it different. On the same play, we have three different ways we can block."

Noted adversary Woody Hayes of Ohio State said McKay had done more with blocking tactics than any coach in America. Ara Parseghian, another famous McKay rival, said, "The plays all look the same, but they're not."

McKay wasn't too stubborn to make changes when necessary, either. After his worst loss at USC, a 51–0 drubbing by Notre Dame, of all schools, in 1966, McKay was determined to alter some things. "Did you see the size of those Notre Dame linemen?" he asked after the game, referring to such stalwarts as Kevin Hardy and Alan Page. "Their arms are bigger than the legs of our linemen. That's what we have to do—recruit some big, fast linemen." And they did.

McKay's players got bigger and stronger, and a few years later, after failing to stop the flashy, new option attacks thrown at him by the likes of Barry Switzer's Oklahoma teams, the coach made another decision. He would have to get faster players. Eventually, the result was a perfect blend of size and speed and a roster that could compete with any team in the country.

In 1972, McKay said he had the quickest defense he'd ever seen, college or pro. To this day, even in light of the great teams Pete Carroll has produced during his remarkable run, the '72 squad is regarded by many as the greatest USC team and maybe the best of all college football teams. "It was a great team to coach," McKay said. "They absolutely refused to make a mistake. We never had a down game. Our closest margin of victory was nine points against Stanford. Only two college teams in the previous twenty-five years did better than that."

The '72 team went 12–0, scoring 467 points and limiting opponents to an average of 132 yards per game and a meager 2.5 yards per rush. "Mike Rae was a great quarterback for us that year, and Pat Haden came off the bench to throw some big touchdown passes," McKay said. "Anthony Davis was a fantastic sophomore tailback, and Sam Cunningham was the best blocking back I've ever seen and became famous for his dives for touchdowns. No defensive line was too high for Sam to dive over."

Through it all, McKay always had his soul mate, Corky, nearby. She was the perfect football coach's wife, maintaining a smiling demeanor, even after the most difficult losses. McKay often joked a lot about her, but it was clear that this was one of football's strongest marriages.

UNIVERSITY OF SOUTHERN CALIFORNIA

Dave Levy was one of John McKay's most trusted assistants and one of the legendary's coach's closest friends.

"If they gave out a Heisman Trophy for coaches' wives, she would have won it," says Haden, who had a close-up view of the family his senior year. "She was always on an even keel, win or lose. She was an upbeat, vibrant person."

McKay's other family was the collection of assistants who always seemed to be close by his side, whether he was coaching on the sideline or having a post-practice cocktail at Julie's. You almost never saw McKay when Dave Levy, Craig Fertig, Dick Beam, and Marv Goux, among others, weren't nearby. "He was basically a shy person," Levy says of McKay. "He wouldn't go anywhere by himself. One of us always had to go with him."

This relationship became something much more than just a head coach and the men who took orders from him. This was the college football equivalent of Hollywood's "Rat Pack," a bunch of the most proficient coaches in the business who all truly enjoyed spending time together. "We worked damn hard," said Goux, probably the most loyal of all McKay's men. "But we loved every minute of it."

Well, maybe not every minute. "He [McKay] would get ticked off if someone asked something that was totally unknowledgeable, and he would be in a bad mood," Levy says. "He was a person who held nothing inside. He was going to vent. We used to have this thing at the office. If he came in happy in the morning, we were all in trouble by noon. If he comes in and slams the door, we'll all be going to Julie's for lunch. On a bad day, you made sure your door was closed. But at five o'clock, he'd stop by and say, 'We're going to Julie's.' You didn't ever say, 'No, Coach, I have something else to do.' So, off we'd go to Julie's, and he was ready to let you forgive him for being a jerk all day. Believe me, you couldn't stay mad at him. I don't think we ever doubted his motives.

"One of his great strengths in controlling people or managing them was to always keep them on edge. This could be a little unnerving, but it was not a bad thing. He had to have someone, and I was that guy for most of the time who relayed things to other people on the staff. To be honest, he really didn't like managing people. For a guy who was really good at confrontation, he had to get mad. He couldn't sit down and say, 'Hey, we have a problem and let's discuss it.' I never really heard that once. So, if he was mad at Marvie [Goux], he called everybody in and kicked butt. I think he knew we knew he was mad at Marvie or someone, and this was his way of getting at them. But that's the way he operated. I look at this as an unusual strength.

"I'll never forget, we either won or lost a close game, and he called all of us in and said, 'All right, nobody talks football around here unless I'm in the room.' We all looked at each other. You know, like, hey, we're football coaches. How do we coach football if we can't talk about it? I said, 'Guys, he said not to talk football, so don't talk football.' But we had young guys, and they'd get up to the blackboard drawing plays, and invariably Coach would stick his head in the door and ask, 'Anyone talking football in here?' We'd say, 'No, Coach,' and he'd leave. You know, we won our next three games, one against Notre Dame, and he acted as if nothing had happened."

A measure of how caught up in football McKay could be came one night when none of his assistants was expecting it. "I think we were going to Julie's when he stopped us in the middle of the street," Levy says. "It was dark outside, but not that late. We had talked about a Tennessee defense that was Cover 2, or cover half the field with two safeties playing a zone. Well, he said, 'You go here and you go there,' and we worked it out right there in the street.

"I'm pretty sure it was a Notre Dame game, and one of our defensive backs wound up intercepting a couple of passes."

Beam was another former assistant who loved the time he spent working under McKay. "I've never been around a guy who had a wit like him," Beam says. "I've also never been around a guy who knew as much football. I would scout the team we were playing the next week, and when I got back, I'd go in a film room with McKay. I learned more football in one year than I had in my entire life. He knew how to diagnose teams and how to take them apart. He had no problem figuring out the weaknesses. You should remember, we shut down the wishbone offenses at a time in which no one else could do it."

Beam got to know McKay better than most. "He was a very shy person," Beam says. "He didn't like crowds, especially when he didn't know anybody. He didn't trust a lot of people. But if you got to know him and he trusted you, he would be completely free with you."

In 1972, McKay was named USC's athletic director to go along with his role as head football coach, and to many, things were never again quite the same for him or the Trojans. This was a football man who saw things changing in the university athletic department and wanted to shape them his way. But the other duties slowly overwhelmed him, and although he'd been tempted before by offers from NFL teams, including the hometown Los Angeles Rams, suddenly the idea of leaving for the pros began to sound better to him.

His 1973 team went 9–2–1, losing to Ohio State and his old friend Woody Hayes, 42–21, in the Rose Bowl. The next year, the Trojans went 10–1–1, highlighted by the most famous comeback in school, and maybe college football history, 55–24, against Notre Dame after being down, 24–0, late in the first half. In the Rose Bowl, McKay's son J. K. caught the winning touchdown pass from another of the coach's favorites, Pat Haden. Then the coach opted to go for two points, and Haden found Shelton Diggs for an emotional 18–17 victory over Ohio State.

Perhaps that season, with the unforgettable game against the Irish, and his son and surrogate son teaming up to win the Rose Bowl, made him feel he'd accomplished all he could at the collegiate level. Or maybe, as he seemed to indicate in September 1975, a month before he'd make his decision to leave for Tampa Bay, he was just fed up with all the politics and demands of the job.

"I don't know what I want to do," McKay said, his sixteenth season at USC already under way. "But I damn well know what I *don't* want to do. I don't want to go to conference meetings and listen to endless conversations about whether we're going to have the hammer throw in our conference track meet. I don't want to have to go to a postgame party every time we have a home football game. I don't want to keep on taking a midnight plane to Kalamazoo or someplace to speak at a clinic in order to make enough money to live the way I want to. I don't want to have to worry about every athletic program we have at the University of Southern California. But every time I assign an assistant to attend a meeting or handle a situation in my place, I get a lot of flak about it.

"I'm tired. Don't they realize that I come back from conference meetings and then spend two and a half weeks touring Trojan clubs we have around the state? My god, I'm only human. I can only do so much." Is it any wonder the multimillion-dollar offer from the NFL expansion team had piqued his interest?

"I've spent thousands of hours thinking about it," McKay said that day. "But for the moment, that's as far as it goes. The important thing is that I don't want to do or say anything that would harm my present USC team. Actually, I don't know if I should stay in coaching at all. I've got a business offer that's pretty good, and I've talked to some people who have left coaching—Bob Davaney, Jim Owens, Ara Parseghian. They tell me they don't miss it that much. I don't think I could stay around USC as just the athletic director. People would come up to me and ask me questions about what the new coach would be doing. It would be an awkward situation, and I'd rather not face it."

Some suspected McKay had leaked the news about Tampa's interest to give him some leverage over USC. "That's not true," he said. "I never said a word about Tampa to anyone until the owner down there said something to the press first. It was the same thing on the offers I had from the Rams—I didn't let it out first." Always a coach fraught with insecurity, McKay also had tired of the second-guessing by fans and alumni. "You would think that, after four national championships and nine conference titles, I might have built up some brownie points," he said, sarcastically. "But hell, no. You wait. If I lose one, I'll be a bum."

Dave Levy says everyone was shocked by the Tampa Bay news. "One day, he said he was talking with Tampa Bay of the National Football League and said '. . . the deal is pretty good, Davie.'" [McKay always put an "ie" after a name in conversations; thus John, Dick, and Dave became Johnnie, Dickie, and Davie.] "He said the contract was for about a hundred and twenty-five thousand dollars, and he'd get a couple of cars and the rent would be paid on his house and things like that. There were only two or three jobs in the NFL paying like that. He said President Hubbard had asked him about it and he denied talking to Tampa. A couple of weeks later, he said, 'I'm going to take the job,' and he asked me if I wanted to go with him."

Levy said no; he had two children at USC getting free tuition and didn't want to go. What he wanted was a chance to replace McKay at the helm of the Trojans. A lot of people associated with the program wanted the same thing. But it was not to be.

John Robinson, a former assistant who had been with the NFL Raiders, got the job. Later, McKay would confide to friends, "If Dr. Topping had stayed as president, I'd never have left." And years later, McKay told Levy, "I knew three days after I took the Tampa job that I'd made a mistake."

He didn't tell the media in Florida that, of course. "The big reason I took the job was to get the cigars," he quipped. The first couple of years with the expansion Buccaneers must have been a challenge to his sense of humor. McKay had to endure what must have seemed, especially to him, an interminable losing streak, dropping a record twenty-six games in a row at one point. "I'll tell you how bad we were," he would say years later. "We beat New Orleans, and their coach, Henry Stram, was fired the next day. Then we beat the St. Louis Cardinals, and they promptly fired their coach, Don Coryell.

"It was different coaching back then. It was more of an ordeal. You couldn't go out and sign free agents the way you can today. It was tougher to build a team. But we knew if we kept plugging, we'd get better. And we did."

Eventually, McKay turned the franchise around, winning two division titles and taking the Bucs to the NFC Championship Game in their fourth year, the earliest ever for a new NFL team. The coach was just one tick away from the Super Bowl that season, before losing to the Los Angeles Rams, 9–0, in the NFC title game.

"Coach had a lot of confidence in his ability and the system he believed in," Lee Roy Selmon, McKay's first draft pick in Tampa, told writers at the time. "He endured some criticism, especially in the early years. I really respected him and admired him during those times, because he stuck to what he believed in. Over the course of time, not only did it work for the Tampa Bay Buccaneers, but I also saw several other teams adopting some of the philosophies." McKay coached nine years with the Bucs and although he certainly proved his ability to direct an NFL team, he would always be remembered more for his remarkable success at USC. That's where his heart would always be, too.

In the fall of 2000, he made one of his last visits to Los Angeles to attend a roast for one of his favorite ex-quarterbacks and assistants, Craig Fertig, who had been like a son to him. Suffering from kidney disease, McKay looked tired and weak, but he sat in a hotel bar before the dinner that night with Fertig and a couple of other friends and the two authors of this book, pausing to reminisce and tell stories. "I don't look that bad, do I?" he said. "I probably could go ten rounds with Mickey Rooney."

Asked if he felt nostalgic about Los Angeles, he said, "I missed it at first, but it's been twenty-five years now. I'll tell you what I don't miss. I don't miss the traffic. I don't think I could take driving around here anymore. My biggest drive where I live now in Tampa is to my country club. It takes me five minutes."

Later that night, McKay didn't have to drive. He was driven to an Anaheim entertainment complex where he sat in on the roast for Fertig. The most dramatic moment of the night came when the audience of more than 700, almost all of them avid USC alums and rooters, rose en masse when the old coach was introduced. The ensuing ovation was almost as long as it was loud. McKay hobbled up to the microphone, cracked a few jokes, and the crowd laughed uproariously. But some tears were shed, too, as McKay made his way back to his seat, because many in the audience knew he had diabetes and kidney problems and realized this would probably be the final public appearance the coaching legend would make.

A few months later, with his health failing, McKay eventually was moved to Rancho Mirage, where he was admitted to the Eisenhower Medical Center. It was there that Levy, Fertig, and Beam went to see him for what would prove to be the final time. "We wanted to be sure we got to see him because we knew some decisions would have to be made regarding his health and Corky might have to take him home to Tampa," Beam says. "Because of his diabetes, there was a possibility of a leg amputation. We were reminiscing, and he was in good humor. He was sharp as a tack, still very coherent. That was my last time to see him. He was in pretty good spirits.

"When they got him home to Tampa, they told him they would have to amputate a leg. He said, 'No, I'm not going to do that.' He didn't want Corky or anyone to see him around in a wheelchair. So he opted to go off dialysis. Corky told me when you go off dialysis, you usually die within seven to ten days. Well, the ol' coach went twenty days before he died. He was one tough cookie."

McKay succumbed to kidney failure on June 10, 2001, at age seventy-seven. He was survived by his two daughters, Michelle and Teri, and two sons, J. K., a lawyer in Los Angeles, and Rich, currently the president-general manager of the Atlanta Falcons and, in the eyes of many, perhaps the future commissioner of the NFL. McKay also had ten grandchildren.

His overall record at USC was 127–40–8. His winning percentage was .749. Howard Jones's percentage was .750. McKay won four national titles, nine conference championships, and had nine finishes among the Top Ten.

"With the passing of John McKay," said Garrett, his first Heisman Trophy tailback and current USC athletic director, "part of my life flashes in front of me, probably one of the most important parts of my life, when I learned to have an identity and I learned to be a man. I think there are all sorts of experiences in which young men may have a rite of passage. Mine was on the football field of USC, being coached by John McKay."

A few months after McKay's death, a standing-room only memorial was held for him in Bovard Auditorium on the USC campus. Fittingly, the service was alive with the indomitable spirit and crackling humor of a man who was as charming and witty as he was single-minded and successful. "We were married for fifty years," said his wife, Corky, who passed away four years later. "It wasn't always easy, but thank God, it was never boring. John called his family 'the Irish Mafia,' and they loved it. "But the University of Southern California was home for John. He was the happiest here."

Son J. K. McKay recalled a time he had taken a frightful hit during a game that knocked out several of his teeth. He was taken to the trainer's room when his father approached. "What are you looking so sad about?" the coach had asked. "Well, I just lost some of my teeth," the son answered. "Yeah, but how do you think I feel?" his dad pressed. "I paid three thousand dollars for you to have braces."

Haden, Levy, and Goux, among others, spoke and tried to fight back tears. The series of speakers was followed by a video that brilliantly captured the essence of McKay. From guesting with Carson on NBC's *Tonight* show to standing alongside his players on the sideline. From addressing a room full of alumni to schmoozing with Bob Hope. From his classic pose in front of a blackboard to a shot of him joking with sports writers. Then, before the applause for the video had faded, the strains of the USC Marching Band could be heard, and band members, in full game regalia, surged down both aisles playing "Conquest."

The crowd roared its approval, the guest speakers stood on stage waving the traditional USC two-finger victory sign, and a lasting photo of a smiling McKay, his arms folded and one hand on his chin in a classic pose, beamed down on everybody.

On the way out of the auditorium that day, one elderly gentleman turned to a friend and asked what he thought McKay's opinion of the memorial service would have been. His friend's comment was lost in the ensuing noise, but it really wasn't necessary. Anyone familiar with McKay knew the answer.

The old Irishman would have loved every minute of it.

THE WIT AND WISDOM
OF JOHN McKAY

- *After a close victory over UCLA:* "I just checked my heart, and I don't have one."

- *What do you think of your team's execution?* "I'm all for it."

- *On O. J. Simpson carrying the ball so much:* "It's not heavy, and he's not in a union. He can carry the ball as many times as we want him to."

- *After a 51–0 defeat by Notre Dame:* "There are 700 million Chinese who don't care whether we won or lost."

- *In the USC locker room after that same 51–0 loss to the Irish:* "Gentlemen, those of you who need showers, take them."

- *On Mike Hunter slipping and falling to the ground after fielding the opening kickoff during a game at always-hostile Notre Dame:* "My God, I think they've shot him."

- *On playing with more emotion:* "My wife, Corky, is emotional as hell, and she can't play football worth a damn."

- *When asked if his team prayed after a victory:* "God's busy. They'll have to make do with me."

- "I keep a picture of O. J. Simpson at my side at all times to remind me of the day when I knew how to coach."

- *On why he always played to win at the end of games:* "Ties are for Father's Day."

- "Intensity is a lot of guys that run fast."

- "You want to know what confidence is? I went duck hunting with Bear Bryant, he shot at one but it kept flying. 'John,' he said, 'there flies a dead duck.' Gentlemen, that's confidence."

- "Kickers are like horse manure. They're all over the place."

- "I'll never be hung in effigy. Before every season, I send my men out to buy up all the rope in Los Angeles."

- *About a placekicker named Pete Rajecki in Tampa Bay:* "Rajecki says I make him nervous when I watch him kick. Tell Mr. Rajecki that could be a problem. I plan to attend all games."

- *On Tampa Bay's orange uniforms:* "I didn't give it too much thought until I saw our buses, and I said, 'My God, we're dressed just like that bus.'"

- After USC's legendary 55–24 comeback victory against Notre Dame and Ara Parseghian in 1975, Father Theodore Hesburgh, the president of Notre Dame, walked over to McKay on the field and said, "Johnny, what's a nice Catholic boy like you doing beating us like that?" Never lost for an answer, McKay responded: "Sorry, father. Serves you right for hiring a Presbyterian."

- During a USC game at the Coliseum, a crowd of Craig Fertig's friends began chanting for the then-third-string quarterback to get into the game. McKay called Fertig over. "Are those your friends up there chanting your name?" he asked. "Yes, Coach," Fertig replied. "Well," said McKay, "why don't you just go sit with them?"

- One year at Notre Dame, USC hadn't come out of the locker room yet, and Notre Dame didn't want to be the first team on the field. A referee came to the door to tell the Trojans to come out. McKay asked if the Irish had taken the field. When he was told they hadn't, McKay said his team wouldn't come out until the Irish did. Told by the ref that USC would have to forfeit the game, McKay asked what the score would be if that happened. The referee explained it would be 2–0, to which McKay replied: "That would be the best damn deal we've ever gotten here."

- *On recruiting his son, J. K. McKay:* "I have a distinct advantage. I sleep with his mother."

- At a breakfast following a loss to UCLA, a waitress dropped a load of coffee cups. Quipped the coach, "Gentlemen, you saw her before only a couple of days ago. She was our top pass catcher against the Bruins."

- Before the 1970 Rose Bowl with Michigan, he was asked what effect Michigan's 48–0 victory in the 1948 Rose Bowl would have. "Not too much," McKay said. "In fact, if Michigan puts its '48 club on the field, I think we'll knock the hell out of them."

Heisman I

MIKE GARRETT

*Mike is not only the greatest player I have coached,
but the greatest college player I have ever seen.*
JOHN MCKAY
after Mike Garrett's senior season

Fate often can swerve like a great running back in the open field. If they didn't know that at USC before, they do now that Mike Garrett, maybe the most influential figure in Trojan athletics for the past fifty years, explains for the first time how he happened to land at the university that should forever be grateful.

"I've never told this story before publicly," says Garrett, the school's first Heisman Trophy winner and the current athletic director,

UNIVERSITY OF SOUTHERN CALIFORNIA

who hired Pete Carroll. "Cal was the first school to recruit me, then schools like Minnesota and Pittsburgh called. While I was being recruited, I made several visits, to Utah, to New Mexico State, to Arizona State. I didn't much care for any of them. I really had wanted to go to UCLA, since I was a big Bruins fan since I was a little kid. I loved all their single-wing tailbacks at the time. But UCLA wanted me to attend a junior college first, and I didn't want to do that.

"So now I was making my official visit to USC with my mom.

I'd come one other time and sat in John McKay's office, with him smoking a cigar and sitting behind that big old desk of his. But this time McKay wasn't there. Charlie Hall, one of his assistants, was sitting at the desk. I hadn't made any decision on where I was going yet, but Hall said they were offering me a scholarship. I said thank you, and Hall just kind of took it for granted that meant I was coming. He called in Marv Goux and Mike Giddings [two other assistants] and said, 'Hey guys, Garrett made his decision. He's coming here.'

"They all shook my hand and shook my mother's hand. Neither my mother nor I had the courage to say otherwise. We all went to Julie's for dinner, and they drove me home. I remember my mom opened the door, looked up at me, and said, 'Guess you're a Trojan, huh?' I said, 'I guess so.' It was so weird. Afterward, it sort of felt like it was divine fate."

That happy little misunderstanding proved to be the turning point in USC's return to national football prominence. As McKay's first great I-formation tailback, Garrett would set the standard. He would be the first to carry the ball more than thirty times a game, the first to show you can be a game-breaker and still be a dominant between-the-tackles runner, the first to establish a work ethic that carries on to his day at Trojan practices, where every tailback is required to run fifty yards downfield to finish every play, just as Mike Garrett always did.

Not bad for a kid who managed to make it out of the mean streets of Boyle Heights, somehow avoiding the gang violence that was, and still is, so prevalent in that low-income area of East Los Angeles. He grew up with five siblings in a four-bedroom, $36-a-month government housing project across the street from a cemetery. His father left when Garrett was a year old. He was raised by a stepfather, William Sigur, and his doting mother, Ella, who migrated to California from the South.

"I didn't know then that I was poor," Garrett says, "but I remember I put newspapers in my shoes to cover the holes in my soles. We were always fed, though, and always clean."

Garrett kept out of trouble by playing sports, especially a lot of what was then called touch football at Evergreen Playground in

Boyle Heights. "My second home," he says. "I was there all the time. My brother, John, was six years older, and he was a good athlete. I got my interest in sports from him. I think I got a lot of my talent from my mother. When she was a young girl, she could really run. I never thought much about how good I was, although I was always aware that I was one of the better players in anything I played." Soon enough, other people started to notice.

When Garrett arrived at Roosevelt High, the coach, Ray McLean, made him a quarterback. But again, fate managed to poke its head into the huddle. "Midway through that year, all our running backs got hurt, so they moved me there. In the first game after the switch against Huntington Park, I ran for fifty or sixty yards first time I touched the ball. I scored two or three touchdowns that day. Pretty soon, everyone was raving about the way I was playing. But they didn't realize I was scared to death. I was running for my life. I probably ran faster that day than any other time in my life."

Garrett's football role model was Heisman Trophy winner Howard "Hopalong" Cassady of Ohio State. "He was my boyhood idol," Garrett says. "I watched him on TV. I loved the way he faked guys out and left them standing bewildered. This was the kind of runner I wanted to become." Remarkably, it was exactly the kind of runner into which Garrett would eventually evolve, and he, too, would go on to win the Heisman.

It all started to take shape in high school, where Garrett had become an all-city halfback and one of USC's prize recruits. "I remember when I first got here, all the other freshmen were looking around and saying, 'I think I can make it.' They were hoping they could make it, but I'll never forget thinking I had no choice. What in the world would I go back to? That bottomless pit in Boyle Heights? I had no bleeping choice. No choice at all. For me, this was a gift from God, to come and play football here. . . . If it hadn't been for football, I'd have been a bum. There was no way I could have gone to college. I'd have had to work to survive, so I suppose I'd have found some job for two-fifty an hour. I'd be slugging along, hating it the rest of my life."

By the time Garrett was a sophomore, his ability was evident. But McKay, who had a definite plan in mind, wanted to find out how tough this 5–83/4, 178-pounder was. "Spring practice that year was a real tell-tale time," Garrett says. "I remember one day early, McKay ran me five, six, seven, eight times in a row. I just kept running and running and running. I guess he was testing me. I did pretty well. I knew I could play with the big boys then."

McKay knew, too. The coach was ready to implement an offense in which the I-back would be like a tailback in the old single wing, carrying the ball on almost every rushing play. "He wanted to know how tough I was," Garrett says. "It was a gut-check of sorts. I was the first, but I know he did it with O. J. [Simpson] and every back he had."

Not far into that season, Garrett carried the ball for more than twenty times in a game. "I remember that Monday, Coach kept watching me and watching me at the Monday run-through. Finally, he came over. 'How do you feel?' he asked. Well, other than a nick on my thigh, I felt fine. Carrying that many times was nothing. 'Think you can do it again?' he asked me. 'Coach,' I told him, 'really, it felt like nothing.'" That's all McKay had to hear. The first of the great USC tailbacks was ready to carry the burden and establish what would become the most glamorous position in football.

"I think the reason I was so good is that I just loved playing for John McKay," says Garrett. "He was tough, demanding, unforgiving, relentless. And that's just how I ran. I never wanted him to have a reason to criticize me." He never had to worry. McKay loved the way Garrett played, with a toughness that defined what the Trojans were trying to become. "By the time I was a senior, I weighed a hundred ninety or a hundred ninety-one pounds. I didn't take a lot of big shots. If you tackled me, you didn't get a lot of me. I had a great forward body lean, and when we ran, we attacked first. We were taught to run that way."

In practice, Garrett established what would become a USC tradition. "I would run forty or fifty yards downfield on every carry," he says. "You had to run like you wanted to break every play. As you ran into the secondary, you'd learn where people would be and how they would react. That would help you a lot in game situations. Plus, you had to be in great shape to run that much in practice. When you got to the actual games, it was easy, man. The games were always easier than our practices. Soon, running that far on every practice play became something every tailback did at USC."

McKay used to love to talk about a run Garrett made as a sophomore against Michigan State. "It was a twenty-four-yard run, but Mike had to break six tackles," McKay said. "No one else could have done it. But Mike did." Garrett would be doing that a lot. "Iron Mike," they began to call him after he ran for 833 yards as a sophomore, then 948 as a junior. But it was his senior season that would be the one to remember.

That year he carried the ball an almost unheard-of 267 times, rushing for 1,440 yards, averaging a remarkable 5.4 yards per carry and scoring thirteen touchdowns in ten games. In his college career, he set fourteen NCAA, conference, and USC records, surpassing the existing collegiate rushing mark of 3,221 yards set fifteen years earlier by Ollie Matson of the University of San Francisco. Garrett became only the second black to win the Heisman [Syracuse's Ernie Davis was the first, in 1961] and the second player from the West Coast to be so honored [Oregon State's Terry Baker was the other].

"He is the best college back I've ever seen," said Stanford coach John Ralston. "His forte was never giving less than one hundred percent, whether things were going good or bad for him," said Giddings, who was an assistant under McKay. "He worked as hard as anyone and was the complete football player mentally and physically." Goux, perhaps the Trojans' most famous assistant, said: "My regret is that I didn't play on the same team with him." Rod Sherman, a teammate who caught the winning pass in a stirring 1964 upset of Notre Dame, said: "Garrett is so good, he makes you try harder."

Garrett wasn't just a great runner from scrimmage. He could catch passes, he could block, he could return kicks, he could even play defensive back. He could do it all. He was the first USC player to lead the conference in rushing three consecutive years and was the conference scoring leader in 1964 and '65. He owns the Trojans' record for most yards on punt returns (162) and most punt returns for a touchdown in a game (2), both registered against Cal in 1965.

Aaron Brown, the Minnesota All-American, couldn't get over Garrett when his team played USC. "They were running a play to the right," Brown recalls. "Mike went the opposite way of the decoy. He was just messing around out there. I was watching him, but I was leaning outside because it looked like they might throw up the middle. The play was stopped completely, but in desperation they threw to Mike. He saw right away that I was off balance. He gave me a little fake and away he went. He was strong, too. If he got you off balance, he could run over you. He's the best back I ever played against."

But for all of his massive achievements—earning All-America honors, capturing the Heisman, setting an extraordinary list of new NCAA records—Garrett never made it to the Rose Bowl, a fact that rankles him to this day. His senior year, the Trojans were undefeated in the conference and heading to Pasadena when they played UCLA to clinch the bowl berth. Led by Garrett's ultimate workhorse performance, grinding out 210 yards in forty carries, USC outplayed the Bruins until late in the fourth quarter when Gary Beban, UCLA's brilliant sophomore quarterback, unloaded two long scoring bombs to complete one of the more shocking upsets in the history of the crosstown rivalry, 20–16.

"I still can't get over that game," Garrett says. "We whipped them in the line, in the backfield, every place. And we still didn't win. The game should have been a rout. We had all kinds of scoring chances, but something always seemed to happen. For example, on one drive, I fumbled on the one-yard line. I had never done that before in all the times I played college ball. When I got back to the dressing room that day,

I cried. I just couldn't believe it. I'll bet I've seen the game films a hundred times. Every time I look at them, I feel like crying all over again."

In typical Garrett style, however, even in the midst of his grief, he made it a point to go to the UCLA dressing room afterward and personally congratulate Beban and the Bruins. "That showed a lot of class," Beban would say later.

A week later, after USC had beaten up on Wyoming in Garrett's final home game, there was a special ceremony afterward, in front of the student rooting section. University President Norman Topping gave a speech, and Garrett, teary-eyed and emotional, thanked everyone at the school for making his experience so memorable.

"It was the end of a big part of my life," Garrett says, "perhaps the biggest. I love USC. I have loved it here from the first minute I stepped foot on campus. Never again would I be able to play for her, and yet here was President Topping honoring me, and thousands of USC students and fans in the Coliseum honoring me. When I was a little boy, I used to dream about becoming a famous college athlete, then going on to be a star as a professional. My boyhood dreams were coming true."

Years later, when USC was at the peak of its success rattling off national championships, assistant coach Dave Levy reflected on what had happened in the mid-sixties. "Without Mike Garrett," Levy said, "we might never have come to the place we are now."

Garrett was drafted by both the NFL Rams and the Kansas City Chiefs of the American Football League, and chose to play with the latter. He spent eight seasons with the Chiefs and then the San Diego Chargers, making All-Pro and playing in two Super Bowls. He was inducted into the College Football Hall of Fame in 1985. Shortly thereafter, he earned a law degree from Western State University.

In 1990, the great broken-field runner reversed his course and found his way back to his beloved university, accepting a position as associate athletic director. Three years later, he was named the school's sixth athletic director, with a promise to rebuild a football program that really hadn't been the same since the end of the McKay-Robinson era. It took him a while, and he absorbed his share of criticism from the media, especially after the ill-fated Paul Hackett tenure. But eventually, Garrett made it happen. He hired Pete Carroll in 2001, and the Trojans have begun an extraordinary run of championships and Heismans that threatens to outdo even the great eras that preceded them.

In between, Garrett has proved he knows a little about developing winning programs in all areas of athletics. In his thirteen years on the job, USC has won fifteen national titles, including championships in tennis, women's swimming, baseball, men's and women's water polo, and women's track and field, volleyball, and golf. He completely overhauled the coaching staffs at the university, firing a number of coaches and hiring sixteen new head coaches. Of that group, nine have received national Coach of the Year honors and twenty-two have been selected conference Coach of the Year.

"I was getting ripped up and down for a long time," Garrett says. "When I got here, we had eighteen coaches, and only two were any good. I had to fire a lot of them. I was depicted like I had a guillotine or something. But we got it turned around." That's not all he turned around. Garrett also began the biggest building program in the history of USC athletics, improving many of the teams' facilities and topping it all off by eventually getting the long-promised on-campus basketball area, the $57 million Galen Events Center, scheduled to open later this year.

Of all his accomplishments, the one Garrett loves to talk about is the return of USC's football program to national prominence. "It feels good to have all Trojandom excited about football again," Garrett says. "It's nice to have that pride back, to go to alumni functions and see so many people happy about what is going on, to see so many of our former great players back on campus and enthused about what we're doing. I think I enjoy that more than anything else."

He admits to being surprised that Carroll has accomplished what he has so quickly. "I thought it would take him two or three years," Garrett says. "I didn't expect him to begin winning midway through his second year."

He had faith in his choice, though. "I was convinced Pete was our man," Garrett says. "No one knows McKay was a great defensive coach before he was known as an offensive genius. I never forgot that. I wanted to build a great defense here. Pete is a fine coach. He's the closest thing we've had to McKay."

If you sense that McKay's name keeps threading its way through the story of Garrett's life, you're right. "The whole thing I do now is all McKay," Garrett says. "Unrelenting, uncompromising. You have to win. It's all McKay. I told his wife, Corky, that the day of his funeral. If not for Coach McKay, I wouldn't have that philosophy. It shaped my entire life."

Now the first Heisman Trophy winner, the great All-American who established the tailback tradition, the athlete who shaped USC's past, will concentrate on continuing to build for the future at the university he loves. When he talks about it now, in that steely, determined way of his, you can almost hear John McKay's voice reverberating in the background.

"We will not lose much anymore," Mike Garrett says. "Not in anything."

THE TRUEST TROJAN

Don't look for his name on any of the glistening trophies in Heritage Hall. You won't find him listed on any of the Trojans' all-time teams or see his picture hanging up there with the Garretts and McKays and Allens. He certainly didn't have any fancy nicknames. He wasn't "the Juice" like O. J. Simpson, or "the Noblest Trojan of Them All" like Morley Drury.

No, Marv Goux was not the noblest Trojan. He was just the truest.

No one embodied what it meant to be a part of USC football more than this onetime player who went on to become the loudest, most profane, most intimidating, and, yes, most beloved assistant coach in the history of the school. Goux, who died in 2002, bled cardinal and gold. He loved the university, its tradition, its storied history, and, obviously, its players with every fiber of his being.

"There is no one else like Marvie," John McKay used to say. Anybody who spent time around the football program knew he was right. There was no one else who could scream out his kind of tough love on a practice field. No one else who could make those impassioned, expletive-filled pregame speeches. No one else who could make playing in a three-and-a-half-hour game against Notre Dame sound like the most important thing a young athlete would do in his lifetime.

"Goux was a football man for the ages," said John Papadakis, who played linebacker under him in the early 1970s. "Football was his religion, and USC was where he worshipped. It was his cathedral. The 'Fight On' spirit of the last half-century was a direct result of Coach Goux's gladiator approach to the game. He didn't say, 'Let's win,' he demanded annihilation.

"Goux created an intense modern-day mythology by convincing every player that every game was the chariot race in *Ben Hur*. First and foremost, he was a great communicator.

He passionately called on all the ferocity of the human heart and got to the gut of the guys. Cardinal, he said, was our blood—what made us real—but never show it to our enemies. Gold was what every player longed for and fought for. Gold made us rich. He was the most real and valuable man USC will ever have. He is the red brick of the buildings. He is the mortar in the walls of Troy. I will always hail Marv Goux."

Goux would go up to kids who had never seen anything like him and shout into their helmet ear hole. "I want to see how much gold you can get on that cardinal helmet," he'd scream. "I want to see you go big man on big man." And the kids would get this wild, glazed look in their eyes, like they could run through a locker room wall for USC. Goux would smile and wink at the head coach, as if to say: "OK, I got 'em ready to play now."

And he almost always did. Goux, who started at USC for three years and was a captain in 1955, often said he'd have given up ten years of his life to have a chance to play just one more game for the Trojans. And the more you watched him coach, the more you believed him. He coached attitude more than anything else. If the Trojans weren't the biggest, strongest, or toughest team on the field, he made them think they were. In his twenty-six years at USC, his teams won four national championships, went to eleven Rose Bowls, and won eight of them. He coached more All-Americans than you could count.

But he always treated everyone the same—like dirt. At least at the beginning. It became part of the ritual. If you wanted to be a Trojan, you had to endure Goux's drill-sergeant-like fury. Sometimes only once, but often a lot more than that.

Gary Kirner, an offensive lineman on the 1962 national champions who went on to have a six-year career with the NFL San Diego Chargers, recalled one of his first run-ins with Goux. "I remember that at the start of my first day of spring practice, I had to urinate," Kirner said. "I told Coach Goux about the problem, and he told me they didn't have time for that. He said to just go in my pants." That story is so Goux. To him, nothing came before football, absolutely nothing. Not girl friends, not parents, not even bodily functions.

"Then we were doing a drill where Coach Goux would stand about ten yards away and hold a football in his hands, about where a quarterback would drop back to throw a pass," Kirner said. "When he moved the ball to the right, we had to stutter-step to the right. When he moved the ball to the left, we had to stutter-step to the left. If he pointed the ball down, we had to drop to the ground and come up immediately and stutter-step in place. If he raised the ball over his head, we had to rush the passer with our hands up in the air to block the pass. I was stutter-stepping to the right and left and hitting the ground, coming up in the wink of an eye and stutter-stepping in place.

"It was hot, about a hundred degrees. When Coach Goux raised the football, I dutifully charged him with my hands held high. As I was running toward him, he threw the ball, and it bounced about thirty yards off my head. I was momentarily shocked by what had happened. Coach Goux told me not to stand there but to get the ball. I charged after the ball, grabbed it, and tossed the ball back to him. The ball sailed over his head. He said he wanted the ball brought back to him, not thrown at him. That was my introduction to football at USC."

John Robinson, the USC coach who had Goux on his staff both with the Trojans and later with the Los Angeles Rams, always understood how the fiery assistant could get away with treating players the way he did. "He could do it," Robinson said, "because even with all the yelling, the players knew he cared. The more he yelled at them, the more players loved him."

To this day, if you ask any former Trojan about his days under McKay or Robinson, almost to a man, they will talk more about Goux than they will the head coach. Most of them will bring up the pregame speeches, especially those who were around back in the early McKay years, when practices were held on Bovard Field and the locker room was downstairs in a cramped area in the old P.E. Building. It was in that often stifling, odor-filled atmosphere, in the hallway adjacent to the locker room, that Goux would gather the entire squad, including coaches and players and even a few members of the media, on the Friday before the Notre Dame game and present the wildest, X-rated, emotion-filled talk imaginable. "I've been in the game a long time," Robinson once said, "and I've still never heard anything like that."

Goux was like a football version of a Southern Baptist preacher—except for the harsh language, of course—and his tired but mesmerized flock, most of them still in perspiration-soaked pads, would hang on his every word. A few of the players' parents would sneak in to hear him at times, too. Some were not quite as impressed, especially by the language he used. In fact, it was the father of one of the Trojans' more talented receivers of the 1960s who threatened to pull his son out of school if Goux's X-rated rants didn't stop. Not long after, McKay, who didn't want to lose any players because of those speeches, put an end to them. It's too bad. There hasn't been anything like them since.

Not surprisingly, Goux, given his communication skills, was a tremendous recruiter. Ask Lynn Swann, who was all but locked up for Stanford when Goux got ahold of him for a few hours. Next thing anyone knew, the future All-American and Pro Football Hall of Fame receiver had signed with the Trojans.

Longtime USC supporters are still saddened that it was Goux who had to take the brunt of the NCAA infractions against the university in 1982. He was cited for selling complimentary tickets after the team was put on probation, and he subsequently was asked to resign. But those close to the athletic department whispered that Goux had "fallen on his sword," accepting the toughest penalty to prevent the university from incurring more serious sanctions from the NCAA. Goux never complained, though. Even after he left the school to join Robinson with the Rams, he never whined about the incident or claimed that he got a raw deal, even if most of his friends knew he had.

It was so typically Goux. Loyal and true to the end. As a memorial to the great assistant who died in 2002, USC players wore a gold football-shaped decal on their helmets reading "Goux" that season. Better yet, the university eventually named the entrance to Howard Jones Field, the team's daily practice facility, "Goux's Gate." There is a picture of the fiery assistant on a plaque just outside the door. Present enthusiastic coach Pete Carroll makes it a habit to sprint to practice, but he always stops in front of the plaque. He rubs his hands over the bronze face of USC's most loyal and animated employee, then reaches up, touches the gate, and walks on the field.

To those who knew him best, it seemed almost eerie that Goux passed away just thirteen months after McKay, the man he worked for and worshipped for so long, had succumbed. The two will be linked forever in Trojans history, the great coach and his trusty zealot of an assistant.

"Let me tell you something," Goux used to say, "we worked hard, but we loved it. We loved every damn minute of it." And they did. When McKay died, it was as if a large piece of Goux had gone with him. "Ladies and gentlemen," a choked-up Goux said at McKay's USC memorial, "the man is gone, but he's still here. He will always be here."

So will Marv Goux, who should forever be remembered in USC lore for what he was and always will be:

The Truest Trojan of Them All.

O. J. SIMPSON

O. J. stands for "Oh, Jesus, there he goes again."
ROGER VALDISERRI
Notre Dame sports publicist

O. J. Simpson is talking about attitude and how it helps win football games.

"I have a little story I like to tell about our game at Notre Dame in 1967," says Simpson, winner of the 1968 Heisman Trophy and a member of the college and professional football Halls of Fame. "Some of the members of our team have forgotten about it, but when I bring it up, yeah, they remember and laugh."

Notre Dame had handed USC its worst defeat in history the previous season, a 51–0 embarrassment at the Los Angeles Coliseum, and Trojans coach John McKay was uptight, to put it mildly, going into the 1967 game at South Bend.

McKay remembered a South Bend game two years earlier, when the Trojans were told to take the field, then stood for ten to fifteen minutes waiting for the Fighting Irish to make their entrance while the crowd heaped abuse on his USC team. As Simpson tells it, the Trojans took their warm-up drill, then returned to the locker room to await a call to go back to the field for the game.

"A guy shows up and tells us it's time to take the field," Simpson says. "My locker was right close to McKay's, and I hear him say, 'No, Notre Dame goes first.' The guy leaves, then comes back and says again, 'Coach, your guys have to take the field first.' McKay says again, 'No, we're not going first, Notre Dame is.' Pretty soon, the regular game officials show up. They tell Coach McKay if we're not out there first, there will be a forfeit. Coach McKay turns to us and says, 'OK, men, take off your uniforms, we're leaving.' I swear to God, he said we were leaving. And when nobody on the team starts taking off their uniforms, he yells, 'I said to get dressed. Now, get your uniforms off.' So, guys start slowly taking off their jerseys. The officials leave, and after a little bit they come back and say Notre Dame is going out first. What Coach McKay did was set the tone for us—we weren't going to take any crap from anybody that day."

That attitude carried over to the football field, where the Trojans intercepted seven passes and, with Simpson leading the offense, defeated the Fighting Irish, 24–7, USC's first victory in South Bend since 1939, a period of 28 years. On the plane ride home, Simpson wore a badge that said, "Kiss me, I'm Irish."

Simpson is told something he never knew, that McKay ran what was called a "gut check" on him seven months earlier on a cool, April day at Cromwell Field, where the track stadium was located. Members of the press who regularly covered the Trojans were advised several days in advance to be there. McKay wanted to know whether his 6–1, 207-pound super athlete, a world-class sprinter, could take the pounding the coach's I-formation tailbacks were forced to endure.

McKay could be ruthless in moments such as these. Thus, it was no surprise when he gave Simpson a third-string offensive line to vie with such ferocious All-America defenders as Adrian Young, Tim Rossovich, and Mike Battle. This was akin to throwing a snowball into a blast furnace and expecting it to emerge as hard as a rock. Obviously, McKay wanted a quick answer to his question.

Young remembers an element of the scrimmage as though it were yesterday. "We used a 50 defense, and I was playing right linebacker," he says. "A little pitch was thrown to O. J. in the flat, and he was swinging left toward the sideline. I had a pretty good angle on him. One of the reasons for the success I had as a linebacker was that I had a good sense of angles. Anyway, I forced him into stuttering and stopping, and by that time, some others caught up to him and tackled him. I remember [assistant coach] Dave Levy running over and yelling at O. J. Levy pointed at me and said, 'You see that guy? He couldn't run with you in a million years. Don't ever stop like that again. Just keep running.' After that, whenever O. J. saw me, he just went into that good glide and ran past me. I helped teach him a lesson—just keep running because no one will catch you."

Bob Jensen, a reserve sophomore linebacker, also remembers the Simpson test. "They ran a swing pass out to the west side of the field, and he was my read. I tackled him for a loss and thought to myself, 'I just made the team.' It was our first full scrimmage with cameras and towers on the track-football field, and it was fast and furious. Both offense and defense were substituting continuously. I remember O. J. held his own with all three lines. He took a tremendous amount of punishment that day. I think Coach McKay really wanted to see if he could play at this level, not just junior college, where he came from. I tell this story about my tackle against O. J. at full speed, and I can still visualize every second of it."

Reminded of the circumstances, Simpson recalls bits and pieces of the scrimmage, although he had never heard it called a gut check. "I remember McKay giving the ball to me eight times in a row in practice," he says. "I wondered what the heck was going on. On about the eighth carry, I was running right up the middle and there's Tim Rossovich standing in my way. I just sort of exploded into his chest and knocked him down. After that, Coach McKay called me over and said, 'Go run track.'"

When McKay reached the locker room after viewing Simpson, he said to members of the press, "Gentlemen, we've found ourselves a tailback."

Without question, even though, as Simpson tells it, he had no idea he would become a tailback in the power-I when he opted to attend USC. "At City College of San Francisco, we played a split-T, and I played receiver as much as I ran the ball, maybe more," he says. "It was sort of like Reggie Bush's first two years as a Trojan. I caught maybe ten or eleven passes a game. Never in a million years did I think I would be carrying the ball thirty-five to forty times a game. The tailback spot was reserved for power runners. I thought of myself as a scatback, the breakaway type."

When McKay told Simpson to "go run track" after the April "gut check," he had only seen O. J. for a couple of weeks, but he knew what he had and he knew Simpson, who recorded official 9.4 times in the 100-yard dash and a wind-aided 9.3, was anxious to see what he could do in the sport as a major-college athlete. In fact, about a month after Simpson left the football team, he teamed with Lennox Miller, Fred Kuller, and Earl McCullouch in the NCAA track and field meet in Provo, Utah to establish a world record in the 440-yard relay. Since the sport switched to meters instead of yards not long after, the world record still stands.

"If I had come into school as a sophomore in the spring of 1967, I think I might have taken 1968 off from football to try to make the U.S. Olympic team," Simpson says. "The guys I was running against were thirty to forty pounds lighter than I was, and I figured if I could take off ten pounds, that would give me that tenth of a second or two I needed to make the Olympic team. But when we won a national football championship in 1967 and I was going to be in contention for a Heisman Trophy, there was no way I was going to take the year off for track. But the Olympics had always been my dream."

Simpson will be identified forever by his performance in USC's 21–20 victory over UCLA that gave the Trojans a national championship in 1967. Earlier in the game, Simpson had scored on a thirteen-yard run that Bobby Dodd, the eminent coach at Georgia Tech, described as "the greatest run I've ever seen." Simpson remembers the run as a blown play that ended successfully. "It was 29 Pitch, which was known as Student Body Left," he says. "Even as the ball was being pitched to me,

I could see out of the corner of my eye that the play had broken down. So, instead of going wide, I cut upfield almost before I got the ball. UCLA had totally read the play. I was just trying to get positive yards, so I kept churning my legs. I was able to break a few tackles and get into the end zone."

But the play with which Simpson is most closely identified is a sixty-four-yard run in the fourth quarter that yielded a 21–20 victory for the third-ranked Trojans over the top-rated Bruins.

USC faced a third-and-eight situation at its thirty-six, and Toby Page was at quarterback in place of Steve Sogge because McKay believed Page was a superior passer.

"I was tired, and I told Toby I needed a blow," Simpson recalls. Page explains why he couldn't give Simpson a rest. "Coach McKay gave quarterbacks authority to change the play if they saw an opening, and that's what I did," says Page. "I noticed that the Bruins' linebacker, Don Manning, moved to the outside to assist in pass coverage on our receiver, Ron Drake, who was supposed to get the pass. I knew the linebacker moving out left the middle unprotected, so I changed the play and yelled 'Red,' which meant I was changing the play. Then I yelled 'twenty-three,' which meant the play was Twenty-three Blast. That play was O. J. Simpson going through left guard behind Steve Lehmer's block." Page, who coincidentally had the team's highest grade-point average, guessed correctly.

He says, "O. J. went through Lehmer's hole and cut to the outside. I can still visualize how he was running along the north sideline at the Coliseum and cut back toward the middle at about midfield. I knew then he was gone because the only guy fast enough to catch him was McCullouch, and he was on our team. He just kind of escorted O. J. into the end zone. Rikki [Aldridge] kicked the extra point and we hung on to win [21–20]."

Whoa. Stop. Just a minute. There are other accounts of what transpired.

First, Simpson reveals what he thought when he heard the audible: "I'm thinking, 'Toby, that's a horrible call. I'm too tired to run.' And I was expecting a pass, so I almost went in motion when the ball was snapped."

The Lehmer version from the player who was said to have made the key block: "I missed the audible, so, when the ball was snapped, I stood up to pass block. Manning saw me stand up to pass block and took off to get into pass coverage. That left an opening for O. J. to go through. Hey, look at the films; you'll see what happened. When the play was over, I ran to the sideline and said to Coach Levy, 'Coach, I blew the call, I blew the call.' He said, 'Forget it. We just scored a touchdown.'"

And now for Manning's rebuttal: "Toby Page lived off that audible for five years. The truth is, I didn't move at all into pass coverage. Simpson just gave me a good move and I missed the tackle."

Simpson's version: "The hole opened up between Steve Lehmer and Mike Taylor. Our fullback, Danny Scott, was on their linebacker, Don Manning, so fast before Manning realized it was a run that Danny was on him about seven yards downfield. When Danny hit Manning, I kind of leaped on Danny because I wanted to make sure we got a first down. That was my one thought—get a first down. Then I swung to the outside, and things opened up for me to go all the way."

All-America tight end Bob Klein recalls something else: "I learned soon after O. J. came to school that after you made your first block, you had better be ready for more action, because he might be coming back the same way," says Klein. "So, on that play, I made a block, got up, and then remember chasing down the field after O. J."

When told the Trojans threw only six passes in the game and completed one, for thirteen yards, Simpson laughs and says, "You mean we played for the national championship and threw only six times? Well, I can tell you, there were times when I couldn't tell which guys on the other team were linebackers and which ones were safeties. They were all so close to the line of scrimmage."

How Simpson got to USC in the first place was a virtual comedy act. He finished his freshman season at City College of San

Francisco, where he displayed blistering speed and moves to match, but his grades weren't adequate for him to enroll at USC, his favorite from the beginning. However, Jack Stovall, who owned some motels near Disneyland in Anaheim and was helping Arizona State recruit, persuaded Simpson to go to Tempe and enroll.

"We were in the San Francisco airport, and Stovall went to make a phone call," says Simpson. "While he was gone, the Utah coach comes along, sees me, and tells me he'd like for me to come to Utah for a visit. So, when Stovall returned, I told him I was going to visit Utah. Truthfully, I didn't want to go to Arizona State in the first place. Anyway, I got on the plane to Utah, and as I recall, I announced on TV I was going to attend Utah, and I believe I signed a conference letter of intent with them.

"Someone up there called Coach McKay and told him USC had better get someone on me right away. I had to go back to San Francisco because I didn't have any extra clothes, so, while I'm at my girlfriend's house, Marv Goux shows up for USC. He said I had to put in another semester at junior college and then I could get into USC. He showed me a national championship ring he had from 1962 and said, 'You'll have an opportunity to get one of these. We're not going to offer you a car or anything. We'll just give you an opportunity of being a Trojan. Don't you think that would be worth waiting for?' I said, 'Coach, I'm going back to junior college.'"

After his sensational break-in season in 1967, Simpson was an odds-on favorite to win the Heisman Trophy in 1968 and captured the honor by the greatest landslide vote in the history of Heisman balloting. The announcement of his victory was made on November 26, and the trophy dinner was scheduled for December 5, 1968.

"I had spent half a week in New York with the Kodak All-American thing, and believe me, the Downtown Athletic Club, which presents the trophy, keeps you busy about twenty hours a day with various things. So, the night the trophy was going to be presented, I was overwhelmingly tired, and then I got a call that my wife was in labor with our first child. I'm standing there waiting to speak—it was on radio—and the guy tells me they're running short and I'll only have two minutes for my acceptance speech. As I'm getting ready to go to the podium, a guy hands me a note telling me I'm the father of a seven-pound, fourteen-ounce daughter [Arnelle]. I walked up to the podium and said, "I've gotten a bigger award tonight than the Heisman Trophy. My wife just gave me my first child.' I was in a daze, and I wanted to get out of there and back to Los Angeles."

Simpson admits he was opposed to the hiring of Pete Carroll as head coach of the Trojans but also concedes he made a terrible mistake. "Pete is the perfect type of personality for college kids," he says. "The decision to hire him was the best ever, ever made at the school. As long as Pete is at USC, our tradition will stand tall."

He says he was not among those who thought USC's days were over because, as it was said, changes in the number of scholarships and other NCAA regulations made it impossible to repeat the Howard Jones and John McKay successes.

"You heard all the reasons it couldn't be done, but I was living in Miami and seeing the players they had, and the winning they were doing. I said, 'Sure, you can still do this.' I think what hurt USC for a while was that parents in Los Angeles were wanting their kids to get out of the L.A. area. I like John Robinson, but he didn't do us a favor by recommending Ted Tollner for the head-coaching job. Ted is a nice guy, but I remember hearing him say after one loss how the guys played real hard and put in a good effort. Sort of like a moral victory. Well, I remember my senior year we beat Northwestern at Evanston by 24–7 and Coach McKay chewed our butts out for not doing better and not playing harder."

If there's a bitter memory of his days at USC, it would be the Trojans' 3–0 loss to Oregon State at Corvallis, the only defeat of a 1967 national championship season.

"It rained all week in Corvallis, and they hadn't put a tarp on the field," he says. "I think Oregon State kicked a field goal about the first time it had the ball, and we kicked what we thought was a good field goal about the first time we had it. The rest of the game was played between the forty-yard lines."

Simpson is a Reggie Bush admirer but believes Bush attempted to do too much in the national championship game against Texas at the Rose Bowl. Sort of what Simpson was doing when the Trojans fell behind in the 1968 season opener at Minnesota. "Reggie was trying to break a run in the Rose Bowl. You can't do that. You have to get positive yards and then see what happens. At Minnesota in 1968, Coach McKay came to me during the game and said, 'Jay, just turn up field and accelerate.' I think I did that for the last three touchdowns and we won."

For those who wonder whether he or Bush would have won a match race, Simpson laughs and says, "Back in my day, I'd have been right there."

SAM BAM
INTEGRATES 'BAMA
FOOTBALL

he city was "Bombingham," aptly named because it was
rocked for years by civil strife as deep Dixie struggled to
maintain a segregated way of life.

The date: September 9, 1970, three days before the University of
Southern California was to become the first heavily integrated college football team to face an all-white Alabama aggregation at Birmingham's Legion Field.

The implications of such an athletic confrontation were immense,
as everyone knew, apparently including the man who eased his automobile up to a curb at the Tutwiler Hotel.

He stepped out, introduced himself as "General Johnson,"
recently retired from the U.S. Army, and explained he had been given
the assignment of escorting Don Andersen, sports information director for USC, and a Southern California sportswriter to a Quarterback Club meeting in Bessemer, a Birmingham suburb. The trio
entered the car, General Johnson and Andersen in front and the

sportswriter in back. After exchanging pleasantries with Andersen, the general came directly to the point.

"I hear y'all got a lotta niggahs on your team," he said to Andersen.

Taken aback, Andersen said, "What did you say?"

"I said I hear y'all got a lotta niggahs on your team," the general said again, this time making certain the confrontational nature of his words were not lost on his chosen adversary.

Andersen paused, measuring his words. "If you mean, do we have a lot of black players, the answer is yes. And, I might add, we're mighty proud to have them."

Without turning toward Andersen or taking a moment to digest what had been said, the general quickly replied: "Have it *your* way."

At that moment, the sociological and political implications of a mere football game scheduled to take place on Saturday night at Legion Field in Birmingham assumed even greater proportions than previously predicted. By extension, the general's conduct confirmed the fears of several black members of the USC football team, all of whom had read over the years of Birmingham's race-related bombings, particularly one at the Sixteenth Street Baptist Church in 1963 that claimed the lives of four young black girls.

They also were aware of the lawless acts of the city's commissioner of public safety, Bull Connor, who turned dogs, powerful water hoses, and club-wielding deputies loose on peaceful demonstrations by Martin Luther King Jr. of the Southern Christian Leadership Conference and his followers. Additionally, they were cognizant of Alabama Governor George Wallace's defiance of a federal edict that the doors to the University of Alabama be opened to all races, and they recalled how Wallace had stood in the doorway to the university's Foster Auditorium on June 11, 1963, and refused to let two black students, James Hood and Vivian Malone, enter and register, a dramatic scene carried live on television across America. Wallace yielded only when Nicholas deB. Katzenbach, an assistant to U.S. Attorney General Robert Kennedy, read him a court order that was backed up by the muscle of federalized troops.

Now, more than thirty-five years later, it has been learned that five black members of the USC football team were so frightened of the visit to Birmingham, so fearful lawless elements of Birmingham society might take matters into their own hands, that they acquired guns and brought them along on the trip. USC coach John McKay never mentioned the guns incident before his death in 2003. Dave Levy, McKay's chief assistant, says he also knew nothing about them. "Maybe it was just bravado," he said. No, says team member John Papadakis, who is white, there was "genuine fear" among those who brought weapons that someone might attack them in Birmingham. But, he said, there also was strong disagreement among the other ten blacks who made the trip about the wisdom of players arming themselves.

The buildup for the game was enormous, and a large press contingent prepared to descend upon Birmingham for a contest that not only brought together two of the nation's traditional powers but also offered racial-groundbreaking overtones. A reporter visiting Alabama coach Paul "Bear" Bryant in Tuscaloosa, site of the university, on Thursday, September 10, two days before the game, found the 'Bama coach relaxed and affable. He also found Bryant defensive about his failure to recruit African-Americans for his team.

"We've begun integrating our team," Bryant said. "We have one black player on scholarship now, Wilbur Jackson." One? Why not more? At that point, Bryant diverted the conversation to the Rose Bowl. "I played in the 1935 game," the Alabama coach said. "I've always wanted to go back. When are you Californians going to open it up again for teams other than those from the Big Ten? I've always said if they let other teams go to the Rose Bowl and Alabama gets a bid, we'll go to California just the way we did back in my playing days. We'll charter a train and make our way to Pasadena that way."

He laughed as he recalled an incident that occurred during Alabama's 29–13 victory over Stanford. "You know, those were hard times, with the Depression and all. Well, early in the second quarter, I was down on the ground. I saw some coins lying there—a bunch of quarters and half-dollars. I picked up the change and put it in my right hand. It was about $2.50, a lot of money in 1935. Under the rules of that time, if you left a game, you couldn't return in the same quarter. So, I was stuck with holding the money in my right hand. When I got the chance, I was going to run over to the bench and get someone to hold it for me. But on the next play, their great back, Bobby Grayson, came right at me. I think that was the only tackle I made all day. Anyway, I lost the money and couldn't find it."

At that point, Bryant suggested the reporter look at the dormitory housing his players—some called it the "Bryant Hilton." The verdict: well-appointed and spacious. The reporter asked if the black recruit, Wilbur Jackson, lived there. "No," said Bryant. "But he will next year." One cautious step at a time, he seemed to be saying. He certainly wasn't unaware that the university had 300 black students enrolled but no one of color playing on the football team.

The following evening, September 11, writers were invited to a party at the Tutwiler Hotel at which Bryant was to be honored on his fifty-seventh birthday. The coach arrived early and was immediately surrounded by more than a dozen newsmen. He was charming, at least for the moment. Then, the visiting coach, John McKay arrived, shook hands with the Bear and headed for the other end of a spacious ballroom. And with McKay went the entire press corps—with one exception.

"Don't leave, don't leave," USC publicist Andersen whispered to a reporter. "Don't leave the Bear here alone." Bryant was attempting to maintain a grin, but the strain was turning it into a grimace. Andersen had a picture taken of Bryant and the reporter, and the pained expression on the Alabama coach's face is preserved for all time. The picture is framed in the reporter's home office.

Eventually, the party broke up, and all attention was turned to the football game the following evening.

There are those who suggest Bryant had earlier sought permission from the Alabama governor to integrate his football team but was rebuffed. Other schools in the Southeastern Conference, a league that was last to approve participation by blacks in football, were bringing in minorities, although all at a snail's pace. It was further suggested that Bryant had conspired with McKay to bring his minority-laden team to Birmingham, where it would deliver a whipping to the Crimson Tide that would speed the pace of integration.

Sportswriters from California and Alabama place little credence in such speculation. Rather, a $250,000 guarantee contained sufficient inducement for McKay, as USC athletic director, to agree to come to Birmingham. "Bryant was smarter than ninety-nine percent of the coaches," says Bill Lumpkin, sports editor of the *Birmingham Post-Herald* at the time of the USC game and a Bryant confidant. "He knew all along he had to play black players. But as powerful as Bryant was, I don't think he could have challenged George Wallace. It was difficult to challenge political power at that time."

Yes, what these old friends, Bryant and McKay, were conspiring to do was stage a great college football game. As it turned out, what transpired on the night of September 12, 1970, at Legion Field in Birmingham couldn't have done more for the long-run good of Alabama football. A substitute USC fullback, 6–3, 215-pound Sam Cunningham, a black sophomore out of Santa Barbara, California, performing in his first collegiate game, turned Legion Field into his personal stage. He carried the ball only twelve times but gained 135 yards and scored two touchdowns as the Trojans cruised to a 42–21 victory that shocked a crowd of 72,175.

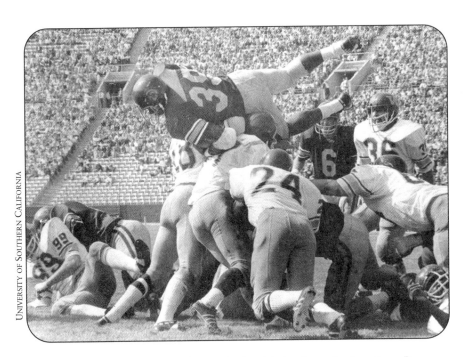

UNIVERSITY OF SOUTHERN CALIFORNIA

Fullback Sam Cunningham demonstrates his trademark play. Sam Bam became famous for diving into the end zone for a long series of short-yardage USC touchdowns. As plays go, it was almost impossible to stop.

Statistics alone do not reveal the extent of the impression Cunningham made on the partisan Alabama gathering. Once described by former USC track and field coach Vern Wolfe as physically talented enough to challenge for Olympic decathlon honors, Cunningham ran rings around the Crimson Tide. And when he couldn't run around the Alabamans, he ran over them, delivering considerable punishment to those who challenged him.

Mike Morgan, a wide receiver who was hoping to get into the game and catch his first touchdown pass, recalls that McKay demonstrated compassion for his old pal Bryant. "Craig Fertig [USC assistant] told me in the second half that McKay didn't want to run up the score on Bryant," says Morgan. "He said we weren't going to pass the ball. We did throw once, as I recall. The coaches were trying to see if a real good athlete, Skip Thomas, who was playing cornerback, could catch the ball. He caught a touchdown pass."

Cunningham's performance was so impressive that McKay, who usually employed his fullback as a blocker in his I-formation offense, gave the ball generously to Cunningham during his three seasons, 1970, 1971, and 1972. In fact, Cunningham was a hard-charging tailback as a junior until sustaining an injury, and as a senior, won 1973 Rose Bowl Player of the Game honors after four over-the-top touchdowns against Ohio State in a 42–17 victory that clinched a national championship for the Trojans. But even though he put in ten seasons with the New England Patriots and holds the club's total yardage record, Cunningham's fame evolves from that September evening in Birmingham.

There is considerable debate about what occurred after the game. One version has Bryant entering the USC locker room after the game and asking for permission to take Cunningham to his Alabama locker room, where he introduced the Trojan star with these words, "Gentlemen, this is what a football player looks like." Columnist Lumpkin offers vociferous dissent to this version. "Cunningham didn't go into the Alabama dressing room," says Lumpkin. "I talked to assistant coaches, and they told me he wasn't in there. I tried to pin that story down, but the coaches all say the same thing—he didn't come in the locker room. I haven't been able to find a single person who saw him in there."

178222

Another version has Bryant escorting Cunningham to the 'Bama locker room and introducing him to a few players in a hallway. There is no organized opposition to this account.

A third version, promoted by Lumpkin and other Alabama partisans as most likely to have happened, has Bryant entering the USC locker room, congratulating Cunningham, then leaving without him.

A couple of years before McKay's death in 2002, he told of Bryant taking Cunningham with him to the Alabama locker room. "Everybody was showered and dressed, and we were ready to head for the airport," McKay said. "Suddenly, Sam came back. We had to hold up the buses until he got out of his uniform and got ready."

Cunningham, averse to publicity from the moment he stepped on the USC campus in September 1969, wishes people would just forget the whole affair and let him get on with his life as a landscape designer in Long Beach, California. He confirms that Bryant took him from the USC locker room and headed somewhere. "But what was said when we got to where he wanted to take me, well, it's fuzzy," he says. "Someone interviewed me about it and asked me to recall that night. I couldn't. I remember I had a good game, got a lot of yards, but all that other stuff, no. As I said, it's fuzzy. About that night, the older I get, the more people think I was six-four, two hundred forty pounds, and scored four touchdowns."

Sam Bam, as he was known, has this observation: "Coach Bryant could have talked until he was blue in the face and not have changed anything. But they [Alabama fans] knew right away they couldn't play teams like us if they didn't have all the players in the state playing for them. Things changed right away in Alabama."

Cunningham says he was unused to being involved in a racial matter. "I grew up in Santa Barbara," he says. "We all played football together in Santa Barbara. It didn't make any difference what the color of your skin was. So, at the time we played the game in Birmingham, I didn't understand what an effect it might have on college football. One thing that happened was that the black colleges in the South began getting fewer and fewer good players. Also, schools like Michigan State that had been going into places like Beaumont, Texas, to pick up guys like Bubba Smith and George Webster were no longer as successful in recruiting black players from the South."

Lumpkin insists the Cunningham game had little or nothing to do with integrating Alabama and Southeastern Conference football. "That game didn't integrate Alabama football," he says. "The Tide played against Penn State in the 1959 Liberty Bowl when Penn State had a black player, and in the '63 Orange Bowl when Oklahoma had a black player. Cunningham had a great night, but he didn't integrate Alabama football. People forget Tennessee had linebacker Jackie Walker two years before that. And Bryant had five players show up for spring practice in 1970, but they weren't that good and didn't make the team. The Birmingham Barons of the Southern Association folded when they were going to have black baseball players in the league playing against whites. But they came back in 1964 with Reggie Jackson on the team. So, there were integrated sports in Birmingham long before that 1970 football game."

Perhaps a former Bryant assistant, Jerry Claiborne, offered the best rebuttal to Lumpkin's assertions. "Sam Cunningham did more to integrate Alabama in sixty minutes than Martin Luther King had accomplished in twenty years," said Claiborne. Cunningham disputes this assertion. "I just played in a football game," he says. "Those people lost their lives for what they did." Jimmy Jones, USC's black quarterback, put it concisely: "It was no ordinary day." And Papadakis, Cunningham's close friend and former teammate, viewed the Birmingham game thusly: "That game eliminated all colors except cardinal and gold," he said, alluding to USC's school colors.

It should be noted that Lumpkin ignores evidence that Southeastern Conference football teams were employing only token blacks, and it wasn't until the difficulty of competing for a national championship under these conditions was so strikingly presented to them that they went full-bore on integration.

Cunningham reveals he encountered Bryant during the mid-1970s and discussed that night in Birmingham with him. "He said the game was something he and McKay had wanted to do for a long time," says Cunningham. "They just didn't tell anyone."

Allan Graf, another of Cunningham's teammates that night in Birmingham, has evolved from stunt man to stunt coordinator to second-unit director in the movie industry, and is hoping he can get financial backing for a film about the game and Cunningham's impact on football integration. "I have a script and it's called, 'Turning the Tide,'" says Graf, who directed all football action in the film *Friday Night Lights*. Graf says it's difficult to get financial support for football movies "because it's hard to sell to foreign markets since they don't know anything about American football." But, Graf vows, "I'm not going to give up. Sam Cunningham is one of the greatest people in the world, and he deserves to have this movie made about him."

Another former Cunningham teammate, Lynn Swann, a member of both the college and professional football Halls of Fame, adds this accolade: "I'm embarrassed to be in the college Hall of Fame ahead of my old teammate Sam Cunningham. That's not right. I don't know a player in college football who should be in the Hall of Fame more than Sam Cunningham."

Sam Bam, one of a kind.

THE RHODES SCHOLAR QUARTERBACK

Usually, when you're the pure-passing quarterback of a national championship team and you lead USC to victories in back-to-back Rose Bowls, you advance to New York, where you either pause at the Heisman Trophy selection podium or move on to the NFL draft stage where you are announced as an early first-round pick.

Pat Haden was different. After all his football success with the Trojans in the early 1970s, he didn't go to New York. He went to Oxford. He wasn't immediately paid multimillions to play professional football. He was handed a prestigious offer to be a Rhodes Scholar.

In his own way, Haden, all 5–10 1/2 and 180 pounds of him, changed the image of quarterbacks forever. Sure, some were good at reading defenses. But how many were adept at analyzing English literature of the sixteenth century? While most were busy strapping on pads and a helmet, Haden was quietly donning a full academic gown in the hallowed halls of one of the world's great educational institutions.

Clearly, Haden, who was on two national championship and three Rose Bowl teams, might not be the most celebrated quarterback in USC history. But he certainly has to qualify as the smartest. So how did all this start? How did a hotshot prep quarterback from Bishop Amat High School, one who was wildly recruited by everyone from Notre Dame to Alabama, wind up at USC where he would come to be remembered as much for his academic achievements as his ability to throw a pretty spiral?

"Well," Haden says, "I am the fourth of five children in my family, and I was lucky, because my parents put a big emphasis on education. My brothers and sisters all got good grades. So did I, although I was never the smartest kid in class. I just kind of worked hard."

Don't let him kid you. Haden had a 3.8 grade-point average in high school, something that isn't easy to do when you're in all the local newspapers and the recruiters make sure your phone never stops ringing. "I thought at my size—about five-ten and a hundred sixty pounds back then—I might go somewhere else," Haden says. "I thought seriously about Stanford, and considering I grew up with a Catholic background, I think my mom is still mad I didn't attend Notre Dame."

The recruiters shouldn't have wasted their time. Haden's best friend and his favorite receiver at Bishop Amat was J. K. McKay, whose father just happened to be the celebrated head football coach at USC. When Haden's parents moved before his senior year, the quarterback moved into the John McKay home, where the recruiting advantage was obvious.

"You know, it was funny," Haden says, "whenever the recruiters from the big schools would come for a visit, Coach McKay always made it a habit to be there. He would even answer the door, startling more than a few of the coaches. I remember when Bear Bryant came out to see me, and Coach McKay and he were really good friends. I might have even gone to Alabama, except I couldn't understand one word Bear said with that Southern drawl of his."

Haden and J. K. McKay were going to attend the same college, no matter what happened. And whenever someone asked J. K.'s dad if he thought he had an unfair advantage, the coach would smile and say: "Well, in J. K.'s case, I guess I do. I sleep with his mother."

It also helped that Haden and J. K. were inseparable on and off the field. "We first met our freshmen year the first day of football practice at Bishop Amat High. I wanted to be a quarterback, but after I watched him throw the first day, I thought, *OK, maybe I should try something else*," J. K. says. Anyone who knows Haden and J. K. is aware they love to kid each other even to this day. "Pat was the same size then as he is now," J. K. says. "About five-two. We have been best friends since that day.

We're godfathers of each other's children, and we were best man at each other's wedding."

When Haden and J. K. made it official they were attending USC, no one was surprised. They starred for the Trojans' freshman team in 1971, then moved up to the varsity when USC produced perhaps the finest team in its history. Haden played behind senior Mike Rae at quarterback, then took over as the full-time starter his junior season, enjoying two productive years on the job. All the while, he continued to grind out impressive grades in the classroom.

"I was an English Lit major," he says, "and the chairman of the English department pulled me aside my junior year and asked me to apply for a Rhodes Scholarship. I'd heard about Bill Bradley when he was a Rhodes Scholar at Princeton, but other than that, I really didn't know much about it. So I just kind of let it slide. The next year, the same professor insisted I apply. So I did. The scholarship was awarded to me right before the Rose Bowl in my senior year."

Later, when he played quarterback for the Los Angeles Rams, the veterans on the team called him "Oxford." Haden didn't mind. His experience in England is one he continues to treasure to this day.

"It was phenomenal," he says. "Growing up in California, it was so different. Suddenly, I had Scottish-, German-, and Spanish-speaking friends and had a chance to travel all over Europe. The learning experience there is unique, too. You have your own tutor for each subject, and you are expected to wear a full academic gown. You sit there with a glass of sherry, and you discuss at length each essay you happened to write."

The academic honors should take nothing away from Haden's ability on the football field. He was a terrific college football player who capped his USC career with a storybook victory that led to the national championship. Haden and McKay, who were as close as brothers since those days at Bishop Amat, combined for the winning thirty-eight-yard touchdown pass with two minutes left in the Rose Bowl. "It was nothing new," J. K. said. "That's been going on since high school." Haden, with his typical sense of humor, said, "It was a great way to go out. I was hoping I wouldn't play like a Rhodes Scholar."

He didn't. Haden completed twelve of twenty-two passes and threw for two touchdowns against the Big Ten champions from Ohio State. McKay caught five balls for 104 yards and was the game's leading receiver. "I had some really strong feelings," Haden says. "It was my last game with J. K., and we'd been together for so long. And it was my last game for Coach McKay. He's been awfully good to me, and I wanted to play well for him."

As theatrical as the touchdown pass from Haden to McKay was, it only brought the Trojans to within one point of the Buckeyes at 17–16. Now McKay's dad, who never played it conservatively, decided to go for the two-point conversion. Not surprisingly, the play-call was another pass to McKay. But J. K. was double covered, so Haden rolled out and spotted Shelton Diggs, firing a bullet that cemented the 18–17 victory.

"Pat Haden was one of those great kids you knew would be a success in whatever he tried," says Dave Levy, a longtime McKay assistant at USC. "You didn't have to mess with kids like that. We didn't have to counsel him. He was delightful to coach from the first day. He never caused problems, he spoke well, presented himself well. You'd look at him and think that's what we want our kids to be like."

Levy says he could play a little, too. "He was a very good passer who threw a tight, accurate spiral. He was obviously intelligent but also very competitive. John [McKay] had an affinity for him, definitely. He'd coach him personally. But we all knew what Pat and J. K. were going to be even when they were sophomores."

When Haden returned from Oxford, he signed with the Rams and played six years in the NFL. He was the team's Rookie of the Year in 1976 and a Pro Bowler in 1977, when he was also named NFC Player of the Year by the Washington, D.C., Touchdown Club. For someone who had trouble even seeing over most of the 6–5 linemen on both sides of the line of scrimmage, he was remarkably effective and always popular in Los Angeles, where he'd become something of a folk hero.

As you would expect from a young man with his intellect, Haden wasn't satisfied just to play football, so he attended Loyola Law School at night, eventually earning a Juris Doctor in 1982. He also was inducted into the national high school and Rose Bowl Halls of Fame. Besides being a respected and erudite football broadcaster who has been working the Notre Dame games for NBC the past five years, Haden has been a partner in Riordan Lewis & Haden, a successful private equity firm, for the past eighteen years.

"Pat has been so successful in everything he's done, I'm not surprised," says J. K. McKay. "When he sets his mind to something, he achieves it. He was also better in school than I was. I operated on the theory that if I got an 'A,' it meant I spent a little too much time on that subject."

Still active in USC alumni events, Haden remains the ideal Trojans spokesman in many ways. He has evolved into a role model for alumni to point to, hoping their children will grow up someday to follow in his steps. He is what many would like to think of as the university prototype, reaching the pinnacle both on the football field and in the classroom.

If he never won the Heisman Trophy, Pat Haden won something better. He won the right to be remembered as USC's ultimate student-athlete.

"I'd never say this in front of him," says J. K., "but he's the most well-rounded person I've ever met. As a friend, a father, a good guy, and a good human being, you just can't beat him."

Then the former Rhodes Scholar's best friend for life pauses, and with that perfect timing his father possessed, smiles, and adds one more thing about Haden:

"If he were taller, he'd be perfect."

THE ROBINSON
YEARS

I t was the year of The Big Turnover in Los Angeles. Two of the most revered sporting legends in the history of the city had moved on after their 1975 seasons, and the reverberations could be felt from the sun-splashed beaches of Santa Monica to the picturesque mountains of Lake Arrowhead. John Wooden had retired after ten national championships as the highly decorated basketball coach at UCLA, and John McKay, who had returned USC to a perennial national power in football, was leaving to accept a lucrative NFL head-coaching offer at Tampa Bay.

How do you follow those acts? Everyone knew it would be difficult, if not impossible. At UCLA, they swallowed hard and then brought in Gene Bartow, who at least could include being the head coach of a Final Four team on his resumé.

At USC, they held a major press conference to announce the school had hired John Robinson, and the immediate reaction across the Southland was exactly the same: "John Who?" People were expecting a big name. What they got, instead, was a no-name.

Robinson had been an assistant under McKay before moving on to join the coaching staff of the NFL Oakland Raiders. But he wasn't one of those high-profile guys who had "future star" already scribbled on his young forehead.

Big-time USC alums didn't know what to think. Many of them had been lobbying for Dave Levy, McKay's No. 1 lieutenant whom many considered the smartest assistant coach in America. Others were hoping for Marv Goux, whose fiery personality had burned a cardinal-and-gold hole through many a pregame rally or routine weekday practice. Levy was as intellectual as Goux was emotional, and either would have been a popular choice among the Trojans backers.

But nobody knew what to make of Robinson. USC could have hired John Travolta and it wouldn't have been any bigger surprise. Most of the people, including many in the media, who flocked into that introductory press conference that day weren't even sure what Robinson looked like.

"The whole thing was a huge secret," Robinson says. "I think a lot of it came down to Dr. [John] Hubbard [USC Chancellor]. He was a huge football fan, and he used to come to practice all the time when I was an assistant under McKay. I think he'd made some decisions about the type of coach he wanted if McKay ever left. Anyway, I was with the Raiders when he called me from an airport in Washington, D.C., and he says, 'Do you want this job?' I couldn't say yes quick enough. 'All right,' he says, 'just keep your mouth shut, and I'll talk to you when I get back to L.A.' We didn't even discuss salary. Hell, I'd have paid them to take the job.

"They flew me down to introduce me, and you could tell it was a shock to everyone. All those coaches on the staff thought they had a chance. Levy would have been as good as anybody. It is tragic that he never did get a shot at being a head coach." At the press conference that day, Goux was ashen-faced. Levy, some said, greeted Robinson warmly, then sat down, put sunglasses on, and quietly wept. This was one of the more coveted positions in sports, and some of these men had just seen their life-long dreams shattered. But Robinson was undaunted. He had his own dreams, and part of what made him so appealing to administrators was his ability to always say the right thing, especially in public. He was smooth and personable, but his first few weeks on the job were more difficult than he had imagined.

"The most complicated thing was hiring a staff," Robinson says. "Most of the assistants from McKay's staff were angry with way it all happened, although they were not necessarily angry at me. Wayne Fontes decided to go with McKay to Tampa. Levy took a job as assistant athletic director, and Goux stayed on my staff, and that proved to be very important. Marv and Dave Levy are two of the best men I've ever known in terms of honor and loyalty. I hired John Jackson, and Don Lindsey, who had been on the staff, decided to stay. Those were really key people."

Across town, Bartow never could overcome the pressure of trying to follow in Wooden's giant footsteps. At USC, Robinson reveled in the same kind of situation. "I evaluated it," he says, "and I came to this conclusion: This man [McKay] had carried the flag here for fifteen years. Now it was my turn to pick it up. I was very careful not to change any of the tradition. I didn't want to take anything away from what had been. What I did do was try to change some of the little things. They were not coming off one of their best seasons. It seemed like, as with all successful programs, maybe they had drifted to a plateau where they had begun to think everything was fine. They didn't think they had to tinker with what they were doing."

Robinson was tinkering, almost from the beginning. "We hired a new quarterbacks coach in Paul Hackett. They had been struggling with the passing game a little, and we thought we could improve it," he says. "I hired Hudson Houck, Norv Turner, and Bob Toledo, all young guys who were just starting their careers." Robinson was new, but he was also calculating. He began preparing for this job, or a job of similar magnitude, back when he was just breaking in as a graduate assistant at Oregon, where, it turns out, his favorite coach on Len Casanova's staff was a bright, wisecracking guy named McKay.

"He was like my idol," Robinson says. "I'd go into his office and talk football all the time. When John Madden and I were growing up together in the Bay Area, we always talked about being coaches someday. McKay knew I was really interested. When he left to go to USC, I became a full-time assistant and eventually the offensive and

John Robinson tries to encourage the troops. Following McKay was not easy, but the personable Robinson was known as a players' coach.

defensive coordinator at Oregon. I called and wrote him all the time. We incorporated a lot of his philosophy into what we were doing. He'd been at USC about ten years when he became a little dissatisfied with some of the things they were doing. He called and asked me if I wanted a job. I was in my car in two minutes.

"I fit into a nice slot when I got there. A lot of the other coaches were already entrenched, and McKay didn't share a lot of his private thoughts with them, I don't think. He brought me in as a way to revitalize things. He told me to go in the film room and stay in there and study film all day. He'd come in at three or four in the afternoon, and we'd talk. He'd ask me questions, and then he made the decisions. It was great stuff. I got there in 1972 and walked in on one of the best teams ever. We had Lynn Swann, Charles Young, Richard Wood, Mike Rae. Pat Haden was just a backup quarterback, and Anthony Davis was just starting out."

It wasn't long before Robinson became one of the guys at USC. "You knew you were OK," Robinson says, "when practice would be over and McKay would say, 'Johnny Boy, come with me,' and you'd head over to Julie's and sit there with him and the other coaches and maybe a couple of newspaper guys and drink from six to eight o'clock. Then I'd go back to watch film for a while more, and two or three hours later I'd come back to Julie's, and McKay would still be holding court. The writers would leave, and I'd stay and we'd drink and talk some more. Then I'd drive him home. We won the national championship in '72 and then we won it again in '74, and by that time, I was well on my way to becoming an alcoholic."

He's kidding, but you get the idea. Robinson soaked up everything he could from McKay, like a young aspiring director would if he were able to spend hours every day with Steven Spielberg. But while all of McKay's other assistants stayed, Robinson decided to move on to the Raiders. This wasn't some random decision. It was yet another example of a man who understood the way his business worked.

"I'd felt I'd done well at USC and the more I stayed, the more immersed I'd become," Robinson says. And although he won't admit he was already projecting ahead to when McKay would leave, he does add, "Sometimes those who do the hiring see people better when they're at a different level. McKay talked to me midway through his final year at USC, and he wanted me to go to Tampa with him." Most coaches would have gone. Robinson didn't, maybe because he was thinking he had a shot at another job, the one at USC. "Oh, sure," he says, "I thought about it." USC, it turns out, was thinking about him, too.

Everyone was thinking about him on the eve of his first game in 1976. In spring practice, he hadn't won many converts by naming Vince Evans, a gifted athlete who had been an erratic passer, as his quarterback. The previous season, there had been bumper stickers around the L.A. Coliseum that read, "Save USC Football—Shoot Vince Evans."

Yes, they take their football seriously at USC. Not surprisingly, they were eager to see what this unknown coach would do to their football team. What they found out, before a relatively sparse crowd of 49,535, that first warm September night was not encouraging.

Robinson probably should have realized things wouldn't turn out well before he even made it onto the field that evening. "I'll never forget it," said Paul McDonald, who was a young backup quarterback on that team. "Coach was so fired up, so emotional, and then we were all running out of the tunnel at the Coliseum, and he stumbled and half the team ran right over him. If you go back and look at the game tape, you can see the grass stain on one leg."

As memories go, Robinson feels much worse about the way his team was run over. Missouri beat up the Trojans, 46–25. "I thought our team was ready," Robinson says. "Maybe we were overprepared. We made some colossal mistakes in that game. It was ugly." So was the reaction to Evans, who didn't play well. "At one point, Vince was hurt, and I went out on the field to see how he was," Robinson says. "When he got up, he and I were walking back to the sideline together, and the whole place started booing. You could feel it in your bones, it was so loud."

The postgame media briefing and the appearances in front of alumni groups the next week were not pleasant. Neither were the next day's columns in the L.A. newspapers. At the Cardinal and Gold Club two days later, the new coach startled the disappointed members by saying, "This is my fault. This will never happen again." If nothing else, they had to give the coach points for not making excuses.

"I really felt like it was an anomaly," Robinson says. "I thought that game was a one-time thing. I felt confident we'd get everything straightened out." His confidence proved well founded. On the second play from scrimmage in the game the following week at Oregon, Ricky Bell burst up the middle for a long touchdown. The Trojans won, 53–0, and never lost another game the entire season. They finished 11–1–0, winning the conference and capping a splendid first season for Robinson and a great year for Evans with a 14–6 victory over Michigan in the Rose Bowl.

"In our big game against UCLA, we were leading, 17–0, and we ran a quarterback draw, and Evans ran through their whole team for a touchdown," Robinson says. "I remember we hugged each other after that play, and this time eighty thousand people were screaming at how wonderful he was. Evans went on to make key plays in that Rose Bowl and be named the MVP of the game."

Not long after that, Robinson shared a memorable moment with an old buddy. "John Madden and I had been great friends since we were in the fourth grade," Robinson says. "Two weeks after our Rose Bowl victory, he and the Raiders played the Super Bowl in Pasadena and won. I went to that game, and afterward, he came out of the locker room and we just looked at each other and smiled. As he described it later, 'Who would have ever thought, two goofs from Daly City doing this?' It was pretty amazing."

That first season bought Robinson some credibility in Los Angeles. He would need it a year later, when his Trojans would stumble some, going 8–4 and being relegated to the Bluebonnet Bowl, where at least they outpointed Texas A&M, 47–28. That's one thing Robinson would prove to be great at throughout his career—winning bowl games. His overall record at USC was 7–1. "It seemed to me we didn't have the same kind of passion in 1977," he says. "We changed a lot after that. People were learning how to defend

UNIVERSITY OF SOUTHERN CALIFORNIA

Paul McDonald was the crisp-throwing, poised quarterback on USC's 1978 national championshhip team. Today, he's the color analyst on the Trojans' popular radio broadcast.

against the I-formation, putting eight men in the box. We made some innovative changes, I think. We were one of the first teams to put a guy in motion, have him stop, turn around and go back through [the appointed hole]. Paul McDonald was a brilliant quarterback for us in 1978. He was extremely efficient."

That whole team was full of future NFL players, including a future Hall of Famer named Ronnie Lott. "We had some incredible athletes that year," Lott says. "We had Anthony Munoz, who played baseball. We had Charlie White, who ran track. We had Dennis Smith, who high jumped. I played some basketball one season. We had an enormous amount of talent, but more than that, we had a lot of guys on that team who wanted to be great. More, I think, than on any team I've ever been associated with, even in the pros. Even when you look at those great teams we had with the Forty-Niners from 1984 to '88, if you look at our USC team in

1978 and go man for man, we were pretty darn close. That's how good that team was."

One of Robinson's favorite memories that year was going to Alabama and beating up on Bear Bryant's team, 24–14. "It was huge for us, beating Bear," he says, "He was like one of those gods of football. At the end of the game, he came up to me, shook my hand and said, 'Y'all just beat the bleep out of us.' I mumbled back, 'Thank you, sir, thank you,' and kind of ran off in a daze." The only blip on that season's radar screen came in the middle of October when the Trojans were upset, 20–7, at Arizona. They rebounded the next week with a resounding 38–17 victory against Oregon State and were never stopped again. By the time they defeated Michigan once more in the Rose Bowl, 17–10, they had gone 12–1, and that was good enough for USC to claim its first national championship in four years. As things turned out, it would be the Trojans' last for some twenty-five years.

UNIVERSITY OF SOUTHERN CALIFORNIA

John Robinson talks to one of his assistants in the L.A. Coliseum press box. Robinson went 7–1 in bowl games he coached at USC.

"A lot of what happened in 1978 was unexpected," says McDonald, the smooth-throwing left-handed quarterback of that team. "We had a lot of talent, but we were young. Every week, momentum seemed to build. I think going down to Birmingham, the way we smoked Alabama, we all kind of looked around and said, 'Wow, we might be pretty good.'" McDonald remembers Robinson most for his attitude. "He was passionate, and he loved USC," the former quarterback says. "He loved to go on about the mystique and the history of the school. He was always into what it meant to be at USC. He was also very much of a teacher. He loved to roll up his sleeves and teach every aspect of the game."

Quarterbacks were never Robinson's favorites, though. "He loved the tough guys," McDonald says. "He loved the Charlie Whites and the Marcus Allens who were the real football players. The only time I ever talked to Robinson was on game day, during TV timeouts. He was good at that. He'd pull you aside, put his arm on your shoulder, and try to lighten the moment. He always made sure you realized there was a fun aspect to the game. I think what he was really trying to do was relax me. It probably relaxed him, too."

Maybe Robinson's most memorable moment in that respect was caught on national television. USC was trying to come back to beat powerful Oklahoma in 1981. The clock was ticking down in the fourth quarter, and the Trojans were driving near the Sooners' end zone. A capacity crowd was screaming, the pressure was building, and Robinson called his quarterback, John Mazur, over to the sidelines. The coach put his arm around the startled player and smiled. "Look around," he said, pointing to 90,000 or so in the stands. "Man, isn't this great? Isn't this what you came here for? This isn't pressure. It's fun. So don't worry, just go out there and enjoy yourself." Mazur trotted back out and threw the touchdown pass that won the game.

After the 1980 Rose Bowl, after Charles White ran for 247 yards, 71 in a final, scintillating drive to beat Ohio State, 17–16, in one of the most dramatic games in the history of Pasadena's famous old saucer, a flushed Robinson addressed the media. "Before anyone over-analyzes what happened out there," he said, "I think we should all sit down and say, 'That was a great football game, one of the greatest you'll ever see.' I don't know what they charge to get in here, but damn, it's worth it."

In 1979, Robinson's team was every bit as strong as the championship 1978 squad, cruising through the season without losing a game, although a 21–21 tie with Stanford probably cost the Trojans any chance of a second consecutive No. 1 finish. That year was topped off by the aforementioned Charles White-led Rose Bowl victory over Ohio State. Nobody knew it at the time, but that was the pinnacle for Robinson at USC. He had two eleven-victory and one twelve-victory seasons in four years, and whatever else would happen, he'd clearly established himself as a coach who, at least for that period, was on the same exalted level as McKay.

"The best quality John Robinson brought to our team was his ability to tell everybody—the media, the alumni, everybody—that it was his fault when we lost," Lott says. "I thought that was an amazing quality. He never criticized any of the players, and that made you want to play for him. The other big thing he did was teach us how to compete. I remember he always talked about Lynn Swann when he was at USC, and how he had the mind-set to go after every ball. He'd find a way to catch the football if he had to climb the goal posts to do it. He always said that's what made the truly great players. Their ability to compete and compete hard was what made them special. He said the fourth quarter, that's when the game is going to be won. When you're tired and it's tough, you have to have the will to get it done. John was at his best teaching that."

Meanwhile, that 17–16 victory over Ohio State taught Robinson something. "When I got back to my office a few days later, I was flooded with messages and phone calls," he says. "At the end of that game, we had the ball down there at the Ohio State one-yard line. I chose not to go for it. We had the game won. What I didn't realize is that I guess we didn't cover the spread, as a result. I didn't care, but a lot of people apparently did. I don't think coaches are aware of the magnitude of gambling. I know I wasn't before that game."

What happened in 1980 is difficult to explain. The season started as if the magic was still there. USC won its first five games and climbed to No. 2 in the national polls before a 7–7 tie at Oregon stopped the momentum. The Trojans lost twice in the next five weeks, to Washington and UCLA, and were banned from any postseason bowl because of a Pac-10 penalty. That 8–2–1 season was followed by 9–3 and 8–3 years that would be considered solid at other schools, but not at USC, where the students and alums had been spoiled by years of success. The fact Robinson's 1982 team had been banned again from postseason activity because of an NCAA penalty involving players selling tickets didn't help the overall image of the program, either.

Comedian Bob Hope welcomes a pair of Heisman Trophy-winning tailbacks on his popular TV show in December 1979: Oklahoma's Billy Sims, left, and USC's Charles White. If not for Sims, White might have won two Heismans.

"I don't know if complacency set in, or what," Robinson says. "Maybe you just can't keep something going at that high of a level. I know Washington and UCLA were both very good, Top Ten-caliber teams those seasons, and that made it difficult. Maybe we just didn't do our jobs as well. You tend to find the same solutions to problems, and sometimes they don't always work. The ticket thing is something that was pretty standard in college football. Players selling tickets was nothing new. But they focused on us, maybe because we'd been so successful. We were guilty of it. Goux took a big hit because of it, and I don't think it was fair. He wasn't allowed to recruit for a year, but he kept his job."

The shock is that Robinson didn't keep his. He resigned in a move that was almost as surprising as the announcement of his hiring seven years earlier. "It was like everything else in life," he says. "It was time to go. A lot of people were shocked when I left. Some people in the NFL had talked to me the year before, but that isn't what was behind my decision. I just got caught up with some influential L.A. people who wanted me to be involved in politics. I think that was a big part of it. I was forty-six years old, and I had a need to change. I think you have to have a certain type of personality to do the Joe Paterno thing, to stay around on one job that long. I became a vice president of the university. It wasn't a phony job, like some people thought; I was in charge of fundraising. But it was never going to be a permanent thing for me; it was going to be more of a bridge. I really did think I wouldn't coach football anymore, though."

A few months into his new world, Robinson quickly changed his mind. "I realized how different it was not to be involved with football," he says. "The pace of everything was not the same. In football, if there was a problem, you tried to fix it the next time you were out on the practice field. In the academic and business world, they would drag out problems, and if you weren't used to it, it was difficult to deal with. It wasn't too long before I realized I had made a mistake."

He was still a football coach, and you knew eventually he would get back into it. In 1983, the Los Angeles Rams came calling, and Robinson brought the same enthusiasm and emotion with him to Orange County, where he took the franchise to the NFL playoffs in six of his eight years on the job. His knack for developing great runners continued when Eric Dickerson arrived in the NFL draft and eventually broke Walter Payton's NFL rushing record. Running behind a typically physical and dominating Robinson-coached offensive line, Dickerson rushed for 2,105 yards in 1984.

Later, after several All-Pro seasons, Dickerson was traded following an ugly dispute with management over his contract. The next year, Robinson's old USC friend, Charles White, found his way back to Southern California and a pro career that had seemed disappointing had a one-year resurgence when White, too, won the NFL rushing title with 1,374 yards in 1987.

Somewhat as it did at USC, Robinson's run with the Rams ended. He was fired, partly because of lagging energy but more because of poor front-office decisions and bad drafts that prevented him from gathering the kind of personnel he needed. At one point, the Rams had a chance to reunite Robinson with Ronnie Lott, the great former USC star who went on to become a Hall of Fame safety. He was a free agent after leaving San Francisco, and the Rams were desperately in need of a leader on defense. But as in most cases with the

Georgia Frontiere-John Shaw regime in Los Angeles, the Rams were outbid, this time by the crosstown Raiders, with whom Lott spent several effective years, including one in which his highlight was a late interception to beat the Rams at the Coliseum.

Robinson moved on to do some television work, keeping his options open until, again much to his surprise, USC came calling. "In 1993, I'd been away from football for a couple of years, and Steven Sample, the USC president, called," Robinson says. The Trojans' program was reeling after Larry Smith, who had enjoyed several strong years taking USC to Rose Bowls, finished the 1992 season with a loss to Fresno State in the lowly Freedom Bowl. After the game, Smith made it a point to say that parity and limited squad sizes were making it more and more difficult for the major schools to dominate the way they once had.

USC alums didn't want to hear that. With their tradition and resources, they thought the Trojans should be a national power year-in and year-out. If Smith didn't feel that way, Sample and others felt it was time to part ways. Robinson, it seemed, was the perfect antidote. He could come in immediately and "stop the bleeding," as he described it then. He was still associated with the glory years, with national championships and Heisman Trophy winners. He was the one, they felt, who could return the Trojans to power.

Somehow, it didn't quite work out that way. Robinson improved the situation, upgrading the image, and even took the Trojans to the Cotton Bowl in his second year, then back to the Rose Bowl, beating the Cinderella team from Northwestern in his third season. But he couldn't sustain the momentum. Part of it was his own fault, and part of it was circumstances. He didn't hire the same kind of quality staff he had in his first turn with the Trojans. In fact, it wasn't even close. There were some that also grumbled about his failure to work as hard as he should have. Whatever the reasons, Robinson ran into some of the same problems Smith had grappled with, and after a couple of disappointing seasons, he was unceremoniously fired by Mike Garrett, a relatively new athletic director who wanted to bring in his own coach.

"I made a big mistake in miscalculating what happened at USC while I was away [after his first coaching stint]," Robinson says. "The school had changed. Certain entrance requirements had changed. They had stopped investing in the program. I clearly miscalculated that. I look now at what Pete Carroll has done. He came in and was able to make a dramatic improvement. He changed things. He used his leverage. We did all right at first, building things back and then going to the Rose Bowl. People don't realize that Northwestern team we beat was really a good team. You know, I only lost one bowl game in all my years at USC. I'm proud of that. Unfortunately, we couldn't keep it going after that.

"At the end, I have to be honest, we weren't doing that good of a job. Mike Garrett and I were not on the same page. We just stopped communicating with each other. But the fact remains, we weren't on the way up. We weren't close to competing for a national title. You know, sometimes things don't always go your way. Coaching can be like that. And when that happens, you become vulnerable. It is part of the business."

Even though things didn't end the way he would have preferred, Robinson has no regrets about his years at USC. "Overall, it was fabulous," he says. "The relationship with fans, alumni, the media. I think we advanced the image of USC while we were there. I give Marv Goux a lot of credit for being the standard-bearer of USC tradition. I was proud to have him on my staff. I think one thing we did was make it fun and accessible. You know, schools such as Ohio State and Notre Dame and USC, they exude a certain spirit, a tradition. It is something that enhances our country, that is part of the American culture. It is difficult for the schools that don't have that. I feel like I was one of the lucky ones. I will always feel fortunate that I was able to coach at a special university like USC."

Once, late in his second run at USC, he won a game with a mediocre Trojans team that held off an even less impressive Notre Dame squad in South Bend. Uncharacteristically, he was late coming back to the locker room to meet reporters. "I'm sorry," he said, upon arriving. "But I wanted to stay out there and listen to the band and soak up all the atmosphere and everything. This is such a special place, and you never know when you're going to be back again. This is what college football is supposed to be about."

Looking back, it also proved to be what John Robinson was about.

Heisman III
CHARLES WHITE

Toughest player I've ever been around.
JOHN ROBINSON
former USC football coach

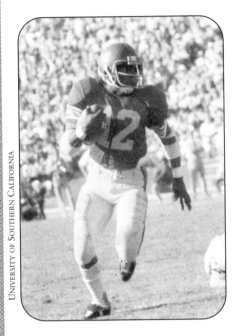

UNIVERSITY OF SOUTHERN CALIFORNIA

It has been more than a quarter of a century—January 1, 1980, to be precise—since Charlie White was standing on the eastern sideline at the Rose Bowl, blood pouring from a broken nose and dripping onto his USC football uniform.

It was getting late in the game—only 5:21 remained—and No. 1-ranked Ohio State held a 16–10 lead over the third-ranked Trojans.

USC coach John Robinson recalls walking over to White and asking, "Are you OK, Charlie?"

White stared straight ahead and said with a low growl, "Just give me the damn ball."

Robinson says he looked again, not certain what to do. "Are you sure, Charlie?" he inquired.

Same stare, same reply from White, USC's All-America tailback and winner of the 1979 Heisman Trophy. "Just give me the damn ball."

Robinson says he shrugged and said, "OK, Charlie, I'll give you the damn ball."

And what a ball White had with the damn ball. "We had been trying to pass the ball, probably too much, and I just decided to give the ball to Charlie and let him run behind Anthony Munoz, our great offensive tackle," Robinson says.

Robinson's decision turned out to be a haymaker that flattened the Ohio State defense. First play, White went off right tackle for thirty-two yards. Next play, he got twenty around right end. He took two plays off, then was given the damn ball at the Ohio State eleven and scored in four plays, the last from the one-yard line, and Eric Hipp's conversion gave USC a 17–16 lead it preserved for the remaining minute and thirty-two seconds.

White was declared Player of the Game, hardly a surprise, given his Rose Bowl-record 247 yards and his seventy-one yards in six carries on the game-winning march.

Nothing White achieved under the stress of this game or any other contest surprised Robinson, whose relationship with White would last another fifteen years. "I'll tell what Charlie did when he came into our program from San Fernando High in 1976, my first season as head coach," Robinson says. "He was a great track athlete in high school, a hurdler who was number one in the country at the three-thirty hurdles and was Los Angeles City Player of the Year in football. But he's about fourth string or fifth string for us when he starts fall practice. Well, he didn't stay there for long. After a couple of weeks, he was second team behind our All-America tailback, Ricky Bell, and he gets to play quite a bit because Ricky was hurt in three or four games."

But Robinson, now in retirement in Arizona after nearly three decades as a head coach for USC, the Los Angeles Rams, and Nevada-Las Vegas, offers a compliment for White that goes beyond yardage and touchdowns.

"Charlie's the toughest player I've ever been around," says Robinson. "You know, he isn't big, but he's solid as a rock and his body fat is ridiculously low. I think it's one-point-five or something like that. He loves to run into people. I'll tell you what we used to do. On plays in which the ball was faked to

Charlie and given to someone else, he just didn't run off and hide. He'd look for someone to hit. Maybe a guy standing around gawking or something, and, *whop*, he gets leveled by Charlie. We used to put together films of what he would do when he didn't have the ball and show them to the rest of the team. Charlie didn't take any plays off."

Turn Robinson on about White and he can't stop.

"When we had him at USC, he was the best football player in America," says Robinson. "He was a fierce competitor who was both elusive and powerful as a runner, had great balance and vision, and was an excellent receiver. And he was the most durable player I've ever coached. Other runners get tired. Charlie doesn't. I think he could have played a doubleheader.

"Another thing about Charlie—he could have been an outstanding defensive back. There was only one problem with him—he didn't like school. John Jackson [an assistant] had to fight him to get his schoolwork done, but he would always do it if John stayed after him."

Other coaches marveled at White's durability, including Michigan's Bo Schembechler, who said, "I am a tremendous admirer of White because he's so durable. I can't believe the guy could run three hundred seventy-four times without getting hurt."

Alabama's Bear Bryant also was an admirer. "I'm trying to think back, but I don't remember ever playing against a tailback that can run like that White," said the famed Alabama coach.

One of Bryant's players, All-America linebacker Barry Krauss, raved about White after playing against him. Said Krauss, "White is the best back I've ever played against. When we hit him, he still had momentum, and, believe me, it was hard to get a good lick on him. He's quick, he's agile, and he's powerful, and he explodes so fast it seems like he can break a long run at any time."

White laughs when asked what persuaded him to enroll at USC. "Well," he says, "Anthony Davis pulled up to the campus at San Fernando High School in his Rolls-Royce one day and picked up Kenney Moore, Kevin Williams, and me to take us to lunch. He had just signed a big bonus contract with the World Football League and bought the car with the money. When I saw what A. D. was driving, I said, 'Where do I sign?'"

Davis was a San Fernando graduate before going to USC and destroying Notre Dame with eleven touchdowns in three games against the Fighting Irish. By inducing White to sign with the Trojans, Davis helped set up his old school for a dynamite run of four years, capped by a 1978 national championship and White's selection as the 1979 Heisman Trophy winner.

White's achievements are legendary. A Heisman winner in 1979, unanimous All-America choice in 1978 and '79, three times an all-conference selection, 1996 College Hall of Fame inductee, Rose Bowl and USC Halls of Fame, Maxwell Award winner as the nation's leading player in 1979, and Trojan captain as a senior. White also is one of four players to be selected Player of the Game in two Rose Bowls.

Everything except a Rolls-Royce.

Despite carrying a heavy workload for the USC offense week after week, White missed only one of forty-nine games because of injury in his four-year career. In thirty-one of those games, he surpassed 100 yards in rushing. Next closest in the USC record book? Marcus Allen with twenty-one 100-yard games; O. J. Simpson and Anthony Davis, each with seventeen; Ricky Bell with sixteen, and Mike Garrett with fourteen. During the 2005 season, LenDale White and Reggie Bush moved into double figures for career 100-yard games, with fourteen and eleven, respectively. Morley Drury, known as "the Noblest Trojan of Them All" during his years, 1925–27, had seven.

Listed at a height of six feet during his football career, White admits he might have added a couple of inches to the correct figure. "I'm five feet, ten inches," he says.

He also confesses that he fumbled short of the goal line on a three-yard dive that was ruled a touchdown during a 17–10 victory over Michigan in the 1979 Rose Bowl, a victory that gave the Trojans a national championship.

What? Immediately after that game, a reporter ran as fast as he could in order to be first to talk to White about the controversial play. Asked whether he had fumbled short of the goal, White, with a straight face, replied: "No, you only have to get the ball to the goal line. I was flying through the air and looked down. I saw I was over the goal, so I just dropped the ball."

Asked if he intended to stick with that story, White responded: "Until the day I die." He is amused when reminded what he said to the same reporter a quarter of a century earlier. "I've seen film since then, and it's clear I wasn't over the goal line when I fumbled," he says.

As noted earlier, White left nothing to chance a year later when he led a game-winning touchdown drive that defeated Ohio State in the 1980 Rose Bowl.

The Rose Bowl seemed to offer special inspiration for White. As a freshman, he expected to be enjoying a leisurely day as Ricky Bell's backup in the 1977 Rose Bowl game against Michigan. "I didn't think I'd even get in the game because Ricky was healthy and this was the Rose Bowl," says White. But Bell suffered a head injury early in the first quarter and was held out of action the remainder of the game. USC, which had lost its opening game of the season and then won ten in a row, appeared to have sustained a fatal blow, but White stepped in like a veteran. Bell had missed all or part of other games because of injuries, so White wasn't a raw rookie. But being thrust unexpectedly to center stage in a Rose Bowl game might have affected a player of lesser confidence. White rushed for 122 yards and had a seven-yard touchdown run as the Trojans triumphed, 14–6.

In the Bluebonnet Bowl in Houston a year later against Texas A&M, White shredded the Aggies for 187 yards in twenty-one rushing attempts. His average per carry in a 47–28 victory was 8.9 yards. White demonstrated again that he was a big man for big games.

He remembers Notre Dame games as "something special," and he usually served up something special for the Fighting Irish, none more memorable than his forty-four-carry, 261-yard performance against Notre Dame on October 20, 1979, in South Bend.

As the Heisman favorite, White was a target of Notre Dame fans seated behind the USC bench, some of the catcalls becoming intensely personal. But White laughed them off as the Irish came at him in waves, attempting to intimidate the USC tailback. Bob Crable, a Notre Dame linebacker, seemed obsessed with intimidation tactics, straddling White after a tackle as a fighter might a downed foe. White would laugh and hop to his feet, then come back on the next play with more wallop than the last.

"Yeah, I remember that linebacker, Bob Crable, getting on me," White says. "But it was just good, hard football."

All these years later, Robinson remembers a play during that Notre Dame game that demonstrated White's toughness.

"He was running down the field and turned into the sideline," says Robinson. "He's running along the sideline, and three Notre Dame guys come flying over to try to knock him out of bounds. Just as they're going to hit him, he turns right into them, and bodies go flying all over the place. Who's the first guy to jump up? Yeah, Charlie was the man."

White didn't have any rushing attempts against the Fighting Irish as a freshman, but he scorched them for 135 as a sophomore and 205 as a junior. That's a three-game average of slightly more than 200 yards against what generally is one of the tougher defenses in college football.

Robinson concedes that White was aided by the presence of such great linemen as Brad Budde, who won the 1979 Lombardi Award as the nation's top college lineman; Anthony Munoz, who went on to professional fame and is in the Pro Football Hall of Fame; Keith Van Horne, an All-American; Chris Foote, a great center; Roy Foster, an All-America guard; and others of considerable skill. To give you an idea of the skill level possessed by the Trojans in 1978, thirty-seven players on the roster that year would go on to play in the National Football League.

"Yes, he had a lot of help, but Charlie was terrific," Robinson says. "All great runners have help, have good linemen. I saw him do a lot of things without help, too. As for toughness, think about having guys like Charlie, Marcus Allen, and Ronnie Lott. You put guys like that in a little cluster."

White also was fortunate to have a quarterback with the skill of Paul McDonald, who could keep defenses honest, and a great receiver such as Kevin Williams. In a 1979 game against Louisiana State at Baton Rouge, the No. 1 Trojans battled crowd noise and a good LSU team and were in danger of losing to the twentieth-ranked Tigers when White started them rolling down the field in the final minutes and McDonald threw a winning touchdown pass to Williams with thirty-two seconds remaining. But two games later, unranked Stanford rallied to achieve a 21–21 tie with the top-ranked Trojans. The tie dropped USC to No. 4 in the rankings, and the Trojans were able to regain the top spot, despite a 17–16 triumph over No. 1 Ohio State in the Rose Bowl.

White often talked about the good blocking and strong passing attack the Trojans had. Usually, after a game, he would make a point of mentioning the great blocking he was receiving.

"Those are the guys who make it possible for me to gain yardage," he said. "They open up the holes, and I just run through them. Without them, I'm nothing. They're the ones who make it possible for me to be interviewed by all the reporters."

And, yes, there were plenty of teams other than Notre Dame that attempted intimidation tactics. "They would jump up and down, yelling over me, particularly if I got thrown for a loss. And sometimes you could hear them chanting on defense, 'Stop Charlie White! Stop Charlie White!' But I never talked back to a tackler. I just threw the ball to the referee and ran back to the huddle. A champion doesn't talk. We weren't attempting to intimidate people. We were trying to play football."

He finished his college years with a Pacific-10 record of 6,245 yards, and concluded his career as No. 2 all-time in the National Collegiate Athletic Association with 5,598 yards (the NCAA didn't count bowl-game yardage).

White said his intensity when he was playing was a result of his hatred of losing. "I was playing pool with a girl one time and she beat me. She just kept talking about it and talking about it, so there was no way I was going home until I beat her. I had to stand in line behind three other guys—and she beat them all—to get another chance. But I finally beat her."

After completing his USC career, White was the twenty-seventh selection in the NFL draft, taken in the first round by the Cleveland Browns, and he remained with the club for five seasons. "It wasn't the happiest time of my life," he says.

But John Robinson was with the Los Angeles Rams by this time, and he knew what White could produce if given a fair opportunity. White joined the Rams in 1985 and had four good seasons with them. In fact, White led the National Football League in rushing in 1987 with 1,387 yards, and also scored eleven touchdowns.

When Robinson returned to USC as head coach in 1993, he hired White as a running backs coach. White remained on the staff until Robinson was fired after the 19097 season. Since leaving the football staff, White, forty-six, has worked as a computer consultant in Administrative Information Services at the university.

Charlie White, putting up numbers? Always.

"WHY RICKY?"

Ricky Bell was plainly bothered. He was fidgeting with his food at a USC football training table in one of the school's dorms near Figueroa Avenue, and his thoughts seemed to be drifting in space. He leaned over to a writer interviewing him about his impending debut as the anointed one at Tailback U. and said softly, "Let's get out of here. There's something I want to tell you."

Bell and the writer left, climbing into Bell's ten-year-old Chevrolet and heading toward Heritage Hall on the other side of the campus. As the drive began, the writer asked Bell what he wanted to talk about. "I just need to tell somebody how scared I am about tomorrow night," he said, referring to USC's 1975 season opener against Duke at the Los Angeles Coliseum. "Think of all the great tailbacks this school has had—Frank Gifford, Jon Arnett, Mike Garrett, O. J. Simpson, Clarence Davis, Anthony Davis—and *I'm* supposed to do what *they* did? I'm just frightened down to my toes that I'll be a big flop. I mean, my knees are shaking, and I've got a funny feeling right in the pit of my stomach. The closer it gets to the game, the more nervous I get."

As they reached a parking area near Heritage Hall, where Bell was scheduled to attend a meeting, the writer attempted to assure the burly junior tailback that all the running backs probably felt the same unease on the eve of their debuts at the key position in the USC offense. "Thanks,"' said Bell, "I just hope I don't fumble the first time I touch the ball tomorrow night."

Converted by coach John McKay from fullback to tailback the previous spring, Bell performed like a champion from the first time he touched a ball, which he didn't fumble, as he had feared. By the time he left the game midway in the fourth quarter, he had carried the ball thirty-four times for 256 yards, his yardage total surpassing anything achieved by those superstars he feared following. Bell received a huge ovation from a crowd of 56,727 that thoroughly enjoyed his eye-popping performance and a 35–7 victory over the Blue Devils.

McKay wasn't surprised. He had remarked a year earlier, after seeing Bell shoot through a hole for a long gain against Washington State while running from the fullback position, that "Ricky's going to wind up at tailback someday."

The coach had an eye for tailbacks, as Bell demonstrated during the remainder of the 1975 season. Although the Trojans went into a late-season slide after McKay announced he was leaving at the end of the year for Tampa Bay and the NFL, Bell kept pounding away with success. He had ten games in which he exceeded 120 yards, three in excess of 200. His teammates dubbed him "Bulldog" and delighted at the growl he emitted as he tore his way through opponents— and they loved the modesty with which he accepted success. He may have been as beloved as any player the university has had.

Bell amassed 1,957 yards in 385 rushing attempts, a 5.1 average per carry, and scored fourteen touchdowns. He finished third to Archie Griffin of Ohio State and Chuck Muncie of Cal in the Heisman Trophy balloting. Bell was in a perfect position to make a strong run for the Heisman in 1976, the Trojans' first year under new coach John Robinson. He began the season with a 172-yard performance in a shocking 46–25 loss to Missouri, the Trojans' only defeat in a twelve-game season. Bell followed with a 193-yard game against Oregon, tallied 177 against Purdue in the rain at West Lafayette, Indiana, and 118 against Iowa.

Then came an earthshaking, and equally debilitating, fifty-one-carry, 347-yard performance in a 23–14 victory over Washington State on the concrete-hard Kingdome pad in Seattle. "As far as I'm concerned, he's the best football player of all time," said Robinson after the game. "I've never seen a man equal to him. The tougher the game got, the tougher he got." But Bell was so beaten and exhausted after the game that he could barely talk, or walk. The following day, as he soaked his tortured body for hours in a whirlpool at Heritage Hall, he told a writer he "would be better off dead."

Bell seemed to lose some of his zest over the next few weeks, which seemed evident from a drop in his statistical output the remainder of the 1976 season. Bell missed all of one game and parts of others in the weeks following the Washington State contest. Only once in the last six games did he exceed 100 yards rushing, a thirty-six-carry, 167-yard performance against UCLA in a 24–14 Trojans victory. Bell gained 1,433 yards in 280 carries during the 1976 campaign, finishing second to Tony Dorsett of Pittsburgh in Heisman Trophy balloting. Clearly, the USC tailback's drop in production late in the season doomed his Heisman hopes.

In the 1977 Rose Bowl game against Michigan, Bell sustained a head injury early in the contest, leaving freshman Charles White, a future Heisman winner, to display his abilities in a 14–6 USC triumph.

Bell was twice an All-American, and his failure to win the Heisman Trophy didn't harm his standing in the National Football League draft three months after the Rose Bowl, because sitting in Tampa with the first selection was Ricky's biggest booster, John McKay. The Tampa Bay coach never wavered, despite pressure from the media to select Dorsett, who had captured huge attention for his Heisman Trophy triumph and stellar performances against Notre Dame during his career at Pitt. McKay chose Bell over Dorsett for the No. 1 spot.

He explained his reason to a Southern California writer. "We had a very poor offensive line, and I knew my tailback was going to take a real beating," McKay said. "Ricky was big and strong and tough. Dorsett was flashier, but I questioned whether he could stand up to the pounding he was sure to receive. I think Ricky proved us right."

Few would argue with McKay. Tampa Bay, which began operation with a twenty-six-game losing streak under McKay, suddenly became respectable, Bell creating his own holes to run through. Two years after the former USC star arrived in Tampa, the Buccaneers faced the Los Angeles Rams in a 1979 National

Football Conference championship game from which the winner would move on to the Super Bowl. The Rams won, 9–0, but Bell clearly had taken the Buccaneers from the depths of despair to a level of respectability.

"Ricky Bell was a physical terror," said the team's quarterback, Doug Williams. "Whatever Tampa Bay did in 1979, the bulk of the credit should go to Ricky Bell. He was a horse, and we rode him. The thing people never saw was his leadership. There were times for me, when I got booed, when I was disgusted, but Ricky was there for me. He said, 'Keep your head up. It'll get better.' He pulled me through some things mentally. That was Ricky. Quiet, but effective."

But within five years, Ricky Bell was dead. Something began happening to his body after the landmark 1979 season. His stamina wavered, and he couldn't blast his way through holes as in days of yore. Injuries that should have taken only days to heal took weeks. McKay had difficulty comprehending what had taken hold of Bell and traded him to San Diego in 1982. Bell was looking for a new start but instead soon learned he was stricken with dermatomyositis, an inflammation of the skin and muscles. A small number of patients who contract that disease also contract a degenerative disease of the heart muscle (cardiomyopathy), and Bell suffered from both. He lost huge amounts of weight and sometimes woke up screaming in pain.

His son, Ricky Bell Jr., lived with his father the last nine months of Ricky Sr.'s life. "Those were probably the most priceless days of my life," he said. He remembered attempting to massage his father's muscles, attempting to relieve the pain. One day, Ricky Sr. started crying. "I love you so much, son," he said. Bell Jr. remembers saying, "I love you, Dad."

On November 28, 1984, Bell died at the age of twenty-nine.

Five days after his death, Pilgrim Baptist Church in Los Angeles was filled to capacity as family, friends, and admirers came to grips with the loss of a special loved one. Former USC tailback Mike Garrett, now the school's athletic director, delivered one of the eulogies. He turned to Bell's mother, Ruthie Lee Graves, and said, "Be proud, you raised a man." To Bell's children, ten-year-old Ricky and three-year-old Noelle, Garrett added: "You have the blood of a king."

Bell was posthumously inducted into the USC Athletic Hall of Fame in 1997 and the National Football Foundation's College Football Hall of Fame in 2004. A bronze bust of Bell is displayed in Heritage Hall, and an annual memorial golf tournament in his name raises money to help disadvantaged students from south central Los Angeles attend college.

There are still memories among his old teammates. "I think about Ricky quite a bit," said another college Hall of Famer, Anthony Davis. "He was a great player, but as a person, Ricky was a diamond. The question always bugs you. Out of all of us out here, why Ricky? He was the good one, the jewel. Why him?"

Indeed, why him?

Heisman IV
MARCUS ALLEN

"He played Superman. I swear I saw him changing clothes in the phone booth. I even saw him fly over the stadium."

JIM WALDEN
former Washington State coach,
describing Marcus Allen

It was in the winter of his senior year in high school, and young Marcus Allen, the CIF Player of the Year at Lincoln High in San Diego, sat with a reporter outside then-San Diego Stadium and talked about his future after signing a commitment to attend USC.

UNIVERSITY OF SOUTHERN CALIFORNIA

"I'm going there to be a defensive back," said Allen, who had played safety and quarterback at Lincoln. "But, you know," he added, with that smile that would someday become nationally famous, "I wouldn't mind if somewhere along the road they gave me a chance to play tailback." Later, he would confide that tailback was always on his mind. "When I was a little kid, I used to watch O. J. [Simpson] on TV, and I made up my mind that I wanted to come to USC and play football and play tailback. You could say it was a lifelong ambition."

John Robinson, who would coach him at USC, would have to be convinced, although he knew Allen was a great athlete. "I honestly believe he could have been an All-America safety," Robinson says. But soon after Marcus began practicing with the Trojans, Robinson, the noted running back guru, couldn't resist. He quickly switched Allen to offense. There was only one problem: the tailback position was already occupied by a young man named Charles White. So Robinson decided the next best thing was to convert Allen, a 185-pound sophomore, into a blocking fullback.

Instead of running into holes with the football, he was racing into the same space without one, clearing the way for an eventual Heisman Trophy winner. It was not easy. Physically, Allen was overmatched much of the time. But as everyone at USC would soon discover, there was little on a football field this kid couldn't do. Run, block, pass, catch—you name it, and he could pull it off with the best of them. Soon enough, opposing tacklers were disappearing under the crunching blocks of No. 33, allowing White to run to Heisman glory.

Talk to Marcus, though, and he'll tell you it was hardly that simple. "I think I got my nose broken the first day of practice," he says. "The transition to fullback was very difficult. Coach Robinson shifted me to offense, but it was clear I wasn't going to play much at tailback with Charles [White] there. So he said we'd like you to play and we think you're a good enough athlete to play fullback. The only problem is that I weighed about 190 pounds, and suddenly I had to take on guys fifty, sixty, even seventy pounds heavier than me. I had to learn to rely on my smarts. I couldn't take those guys head-on. It was a matter of survival for me.

"To this day, I think fullback has to be one of the toughest positions in football," Allen says. "It's crazy, really. You have to understand it is a test of your intestinal fortitude. Pounding away at guys like that, it hurts. It's like running into a brick wall on every play."

Allen admits that was a long year. "Oh yeah," he says, "there were plenty of times when I stood back and wondered, *How did*

I get myself in this position? I came here to play in the second-ary, to hit people, and now I'm out here blocking. I had to learn that Charlie was an aggressive back, that he hit the hole so fast I couldn't hesitate. I had to initiate contact with the player I had to block. If I didn't, I'd wind up getting hit in the back by Charlie. It was hard, but in the end, I think it made me a better all-around player."

One year and many bruises later, White was gone, and Robin-son never hesitated. He shifted Allen once again, this time back to tailback. Think about that. This was not just another player accepting a new challenge. This was an ambitious junior trying to step into the most celebrated position in college football hav-ing had zero experience at running with the football from that glamorous spot. The transition was understandably difficult.

"I don't think people realize that I hadn't played tailback ever before," Allen says. "I mean, I was a quarterback who ran a lot in high school, but that's not like playing tailback at USC. I really hadn't played running back since I was eleven years old. I think it took me one year of playing there before I understood what it was all about."

Early, Marcus developed a nagging habit of slipping when making his cuts, and he would often lurch into holes he should have been powering into, lunging instead of bulling his way through. In Los Angeles, where Trojans fans had been spoiled by a long succession of brilliant tailbacks, the media critics were not kind. Some said he wasn't built for the position. Oth-ers questioned whether one of the other great athletes on Robinson's roster would be better suited to play tailback.

"I realized there were still some things I had to learn about our offense, the position and myself," Allen says. "We believed he was going to be The Guy," Robinson says. "We thought he was a great player. What we didn't know was how he was going to handle the responsibility of the position."

Former Heisman Trophy winner Mike Garrett knew. He took the young tailback aside and talked to him. "What Mike said is that it depends on how much you want it," Allen says. "Some-times I was inconsistent. I wanted it, obviously; I wanted it bad.

But sometimes your attention level is inconsistent. You can be high and then you can come down, and that can hurt you . . . sometimes, within the same game. So it does have its benefits to maintain a high intensity level."

Robinson would soon find out how high Allen's intensity level had risen. By the end of that same season, his confidence in Allen had been more than rewarded. Marcus finished with 1,563 yards rushing, an impressive total for someone who had taken so much early-season heat. If he hadn't been as consistent as he hoped, that junior year provided the foundation that would vault Allen to the next level. That "mental competitiveness" Robinson always talked about took over, and by the time his senior season drew close, Allen realized what he was capable of accomplishing. Even more than his coaches, he sensed something special was about to happen.

Trojans assistant coach John Jackson called him into a meeting before spring practice one day. "I want us to sit down and set up some realistic goals for you this season," Jackson said. Allen smiled. "OK," he said, "I want to be the first back to gain two thousand yards." Jackson understandably was taken aback. "No, come on, let's get serious," he said. Allen looked up at him, this time without a smile, and said, "I *am* serious, Coach."

If that wasn't the college football equivalent of Babe Ruth calling his famous home run shot, it comes as close as anything else in the context of this sport's rich history. Six months later, Allen began the 1981 season like a tailback possessed.

He opened by rushing for 210 yards and four touchdowns on just twenty-two carries in a 43–7 route of Tennessee in the L.A. Coliseum, and even many of his former critics were impressed. Turns out, Allen was just warming up. He followed that by running for 274 yards in forty carries in a 21–0 grind of a victory against Indiana. And after two games, he had accumulated almost 500 yards. Now the whole nation had begun to notice.

"People were making a big deal about it," Allen says, "but I wasn't really giving it a lot of thought. I was just thinking about picking up as much real estate as possible and getting the ball downfield. I was getting more confident with every game, though."

The big test would come the following week. Oklahoma, the No. 2-ranked team in the nation, was heading to Los Angeles determined to show USC's flashy tailback what a real defense looked like. With Heisman talk already stirring, this was the game that would demonstrate to America if this new Trojans running star belonged in the same class as the O. J. Simpsons and Charles Whites.

It didn't take long for the fans, or the Sooners, to find out. Allen ran for 208 yards in thirty-nine carries in a thrilling 28–24 USC victory, and it was that performance, more than any other, that made him realize how far he'd come. "Oklahoma was a great team and a lot tougher challenge," Allen says. "For some reason, the way I played in that game reminded me of how I played in high school. If one game maybe catapulted me to a new level of superiority, to thinking that maybe no one could stop me, that was the one."

After that, the Allen Express rumbled through the rest of the schedule like some kind of runaway train. Behind the blocking of future NFL stars such as Bruce Matthews and Don Mosebar, Allen became a 200-yard-per-game machine, proving remarkably durable by carrying the ball thirty-five, forty, even forty-six times a Saturday. Some of it had to do with his style. He was all feints and whirling moves, rarely allowing tacklers to get a full-on shot at him. He didn't run as straight up as O. J. or barrel into opponents full charge like White.

"I could slash, but I was also pretty slippery," Allen says. "And I could lower my head, too, when the occasion required me to. Hey, I took my share of big hits. You carry the ball that much, you're going to get hit. But you had to get up and ignore it. That's how you were taught to play the position at USC."

By now, the 200-yard games were beginning to pile up like championship trophies at USC. Allen had four, five, six, seven and, finally, a record-shattering eight. Even Robinson and his coaches were amazed. "John Jackson, Hudson Houck, and I would sit in there, watching tapes," Robinson says, "and we'd say, 'Oh my God, did you see that one?' Clearly, we were a little bit in awe of what he was doing. He was just such a great competitor. He was absolutely the best mental competitor I'd ever seen. He was smart and always knew how to get extra stuff out of any situation he was in."

Nicknamed "Young Juice" because he now resembled O. J. Simpson, Allen was, nonetheless, relaxing and being himself. This was the ability he had flashed while streaking by all those San Diego high school teams on punt returns or quarterback rollouts. It took a while for him to adjust to running from tailback, but once his vision and his instincts took over, the results weren't surprising to anyone who had watched him back at Lincoln High.

"I think, early on, everybody thought they had to teach me how to run," Allen says. "But by my senior year, I became more natural, more instinctive. I remember one early run I made. It was a three-hundred-sixty-degree move on some guy that I never would have tried my junior year. It was at that point I knew I was completely free and confident of myself."

People were noticing, too. "His is one of the most amazing turnabouts for a player I can ever remember," said Gil Brandt, the Dallas Cowboys' vice president, at the time. "He learned to run so much better in a year's time. He runs with great vision and knows where the hole is. I've even seen him turn a five-yard loss into a seven-yard gain. He's playing as well as any tailback ever has."

Dick Steinberg, scouting for the New England Patriots, had this to say: "Most college tailbacks haven't played other positions like Marcus. The thing that gives him a Heisman Trophy edge is that he thinks like a quarterback, hits like a fullback, runs like a tailback, and catches like a wide receiver. And he knows how defensive people react, because he played there, too."

Wide receiver Jeff Simmons, one of Allen's teammates, was equally impressed. "Marcus is running with a lot more confidence," Simmons said. "Last year, he was tentative. But now he's running like he owns the place. You can see the fire in his eyes. It makes the whole team feel more confident. You get the impression he's thinking, 'I'm good for another two hundred today, guys.'"

Allen's great senior season climaxed with two unforgettable moments. At Washington, on a typically damp, rainy, November day in the Pacific Northwest, he entered the game needing thirty-two yards to surpass 2,000 for the season. He got them early, officially registering that number on the Trojans' signature Student Body Right play, cutting away from a couple of tacklers, then dragging a few more on a thirteen-yard lunge into history.

Part of the excitement of accomplishing his goal was tempered by the fact that USC lost the game, 13–3, and with it any chance of going to the Rose Bowl. But a week later, against crosstown rival UCLA, Allen made it a memorable regular-season finale by rushing for 219 more yards in an emotional 22–21 USC victory.

"That was an incredible day," Allen says. "I just remember what a great feeling it was afterwards, going over in front of the student section and hearing all those cheers and then running into the Coliseum tunnel for the last time as a Trojan. It was the kind of day you just don't forget."

It was the kind of season you couldn't forget, either. "He doesn't show any signs of wear," an amazed Robinson said as the season wound down. "He's made two-hundred-yard games commonplace. He broke the national rushing record in nine games. He's set a standard so high, it's shocking. If he has a hundred-fifty-yard game, it's considered a bad day. Imagine that!"

Allen's style, seemingly running on cruise control, waiting for the perfect moment to make his cut without making it noticeable, was a combination of raw ability and obvious intelligence. "He doesn't spend time looking for daylight," said Tennessee coach Johnny Majors, an old tailback himself. "He just runs for daylight. He runs with a more slashing style than anyone since Tony Dorsett. But the most important thing about Allen is his aggressive approach to the running game. He picks his holes as well as anyone I've seen in my coaching career."

The display of durability was almost as impressive as the statistics he piled up. "I told Marcus to eat a spoonful of pure bee honey every morning, and he did," said his father, Harold "Red"

Allen. "When everyone else was tired in the fourth quarter, Marcus was still going strong. It was the bee honey."

Whatever it was, Allen wound up with a mind-boggling 2,342 rushing yards for the season, setting no fewer than fifteen NCAA records along the way. He led the nation in rushing (212.9 yards per game), in all-purpose yardage (232.6 per game) and scoring (12.5 points per game). By then, the Heisman Trophy presentation was pretty much an afterthought. Giving it to anyone else would have been almost unthinkable.

"Marcus is the greatest player I've ever seen," Robinson gushed at the time. "Now I don't present myself as a football historian, but, well, I've never seen anybody do what he's done, and neither has anyone else. My God, he has that ability to compete."

By the time his USC career was finished, Allen had showcased more wide-ranging ability than perhaps any other player of the modern Trojans era. He could run, he could catch, he could pass, and as he amply demonstrated as a junior clearing the way for White, he could certainly block. Robinson swears Allen could have been another Ronnie Lott had he kept him at safety. But things seemed to work out just fine. "I think the thing I'm most proud of," Allen says, "is that the first real year I understood what playing tailback was all about, the first year I really knew what I was doing, is the year I won the Heisman Trophy."

Allen was picked in the first round of the NFL draft by the then-Los Angeles Raiders, where he flourished as an All-Pro tailback who was the MVP in the team's Super Bowl XVIII victory against the Washington Redskins.

He had a brilliant NFL career as a tailback adept at running, receiving, and often blocking for teammates such as Bo Jackson. "Marcus Allen," his distinguished Raiders' buddy, Howie Long, would say, "is the greatest football player I've ever been around." Allen finished up in Kansas City, where he would became the league's Comeback Player of the Year for the Chiefs. In 2003, he was inducted into the Pro Football Hall of Fame on the first ballot.

At the Hall of Fame news conference at the Super Bowl, when the results were announced, Allen was quick to thank his dad. "My father was always there for me," Marcus said. "I can't thank him enough." Allen said he wanted Red to be a role model for black families, many of which don't have a strong father figure.

Marcus, himself, could be a role model for athletes at USC. Dr. James H. Zumberge, the university's president at the time, certainly thought so. At the Heisman presentation, Zumberge described Marcus as "more than an accomplished athlete; he is also a successful student and a young man with poise, personal charm, and all those human qualities that endear him to his coaches, teammates and others with whom he is in daily contact.

"Marcus Allen," Zumberge continued, "you have renewed our hope that through hard work, fierce determination, rigorous self-discipline, and deep faith, we, too, can aspire to lofty goals and singular achievements. We salute you for what you have done and for the pride that you have engendered, not only in the Trojan family of the University of Southern California, but in all men and women who recognize the qualities of a true champion. You remind us that in America, opportunity for personal achievement still exists, and you have, by your example, lifted our own expectations to greater heights. For this inspiration, we are eternally in your debt."

Allen had indeed come a long way from those depressing days as an undersized fullback blocking for Charles White, suffering a broken nose and a partially broken dream along the way. Persevering through those times couldn't have been easy. But Marcus patiently waited his turn, and when it came, he knew how to take advantage of it. Years later, he would admit he realized something special was in store well before the start of his senior year at USC.

"I can't lie," he says, smiling. "Winning the Heisman was in my mind all along. I knew I was going to win it. I knew it during spring practice."

THE DIFFICULT YEARS

Maybe after so many years and so much success, maybe after two bigger-than-life coaches in John McKay and John Robinson, USC fans had come to expect the football program to thrive, almost as if it were on cruise control. The hard lesson of the next two decades was that cruisin' was no longer in style. The times had changed, and the Trojans weren't always prepared to change with them.

When Robinson surprisingly resigned at the young age of forty-six after the 1982 season, he recommended as his successor a bright, bespectacled, but low-profile offensive coordinator named Ted Tollner, who was as stunned as everyone else when he was hired to be a Division I head coach for the first time in his life early in 1983. "Yeah, I was pretty surprised," Tollner says, "because John never mentioned getting out. It wasn't until three or four weeks before the announcement that he told me he recommended me for the job. I'd only been there a year, but obviously I was excited."

It would become just as obvious that he wasn't fully prepared for what the job of USC football coach entailed, especially after the NCAA announced the program would be put on probation that included bowl and recruiting restrictions, among other things. It is never fair when a new coach is penalized for violations that occurred under a previous regime, but that's the way it often works in college athletics, and Tollner was determined to overcome the obstacles. But he soon found it wouldn't be easy.

"One of the hardest things I had to learn was how to allocate my time," Tollner says. "The job encompasses so much. You have to deal with the media and the alumni groups, two areas that probably gave me the most anxiety. You have no idea how much time those two areas take until you tackle them head on. The football part wasn't a problem; I always had great confidence in that area. But the other things were new and took a great deal of adjustment. I never felt overwhelmed, though. Some people thought I was, but I wasn't. It was just something you had to learn on the job."

In retrospect, after his first season, Tollner admits he made some mistakes. "When I looked back after one year, I realized I tried to please too many people," he says. He would have pleased a lot more if the Trojans hadn't struggled so often on the field. Tollner's team won only once in its first four tries and closed out that discouraging first season with a 4–6–1 record, finishing fourth in a Pac-10, a league the Trojans were accustomed to dominating.

Things improved considerably in his second year, however. Seemingly more relaxed and settled in, Tollner directed USC to victories in eight of its first nine games, and although the Trojans wound up losing to both UCLA and Notre Dame for the second consecutive year, they finished 9–3 and were Pac-10 champions. In their first Rose Bowl appearance in five years, they then proceeded to defeat Ohio State, 20–17, buoying the hopes of USC fans who wanted to believe the program was back on the right track.

Unfortunately, the next derailment arrived the following year. Instead of building on that Rose Bowl season, the Trojans fell back to their inconsistent ways, going 6–6 in 1985, then 7–5 in 1986, and although the team made bowl appearances each year, it lost to Alabama in the Aloha Bowl, then Auburn in the Citrus Bowl. Even worse, the Trojans had lost the knack for winning games against their two principal rivals. In four years at USC, Tollner went 1–7 against Notre Dame and UCLA. If his job hadn't already been in jeopardy, that would have clinched it.

To make matters even more difficult, the man who hired Tollner, Athletic Director Dick Perry, had been replaced by Dr. Mike McGee. "I supported Mike, but I didn't see eye-to-eye with him," Tollner said. "I didn't trust him, and he didn't trust me." Clearly, McGee wanted to bring in his own football coach. It hardly came as a surprise to anyone close to the program when Tollner was fired following the 1986 season.

"The experience I had at USC, the people I met coaching there, far outweighed the way it ended," Tollner says now. "Just being the head coach at USC, winning the Rose Bowl, I wouldn't trade that for anything. Every time we went to Notre Dame, every time we played at the Coliseum and we got to run out of that tunnel, it was a unique and special experience. I tried to take it all in and do everything in my power to win. I honestly felt I left the program in a lot better shape than it was when I arrived. Sure, I still have some pangs when I see USC play on television. But then I think how fortunate I was to be part of the school and that great tradition. Two of our kids went there and graduated, so the school had a big impact on our family."

Tollner said their time at the university is one he and his wife "rarely reflect negatively" about. A coach who has gone on to a distinguished career as an assistant coach for several NFL teams, Tollner says he holds no grudges about his time at USC. "I'm not bitter about what happened," he says. "People think I am, but I'm really not."

McGee's choice for a new coach was no secret. Although many campaigned for someone in the Trojan family, this was an athletic director determined to do things his way. He hired Larry Smith, the former Arizona coach who was a good friend and espoused what McGee felt was the discipline USC's program needed. For the first three years, it looked like McGee was right. Smith took the Trojans, with many of Tollner's recruits, to the Rose Bowl in 1987, '88, and '89. In that middle season, his team, led by Heisman Trophy candidate Rodney Peete at quarterback, opened up 10–0 and moved all the way up to No. 2 in the national rankings. In its final regular-season game, USC played No. 1 ranked Notre Dame, in a game with clear national championship implications.

But Lou Holtz had the Irish ready, taking control of the game early, leaving the Trojans and an injured Peete—he separated his shoulder at the end of the first half and courageously, if somewhat ineffectively, played the final two periods—falling short of their goal, 27–10. "This is a tough loss to take," said Peete, his left arm wrapped in a sling afterward. "The seniors on this team have to leave never having beaten Notre Dame. That's really tough to take right now."

In the Rose Bowl, a few weeks later, USC lost again, this time to Michigan, 22–14, turning all the enthusiasm and excitement of a 10–0 start into a 10–2 finish that left everyone more than a little disappointed. But Smith's teams weren't done yet. His Trojans came back the following season, without Peete and minus future All-Pros Junior Seau and Mark Carrier, to go 9–2–1 and win the Pac-10 crown, and defeat Michigan, 17–10, in the Rose Bowl. At that point, it would have been blasphemy to suggest USC football wouldn't be rolling right along, winning Rose Bowls and competing for national championships in the next couple of years. But somehow, it didn't quite turn out that way.

It is difficult to know exactly where things began to go wrong, but part of it had to do with Smith's style. "He was a real disciplinarian, and he was very strong on academics," says Mike Salmon, who played safety on Smith's teams from 1990 through '92. "He was a Woody Hayes type. You had to be on time, handle your commitments, learn to be a man. I liked what he stood for. He was kind of a throwback. But coaching in L.A., he had his share of enemies. I got along with him fine, but I probably didn't learn as much on the field. I did learn more about how to be a man, though."

Some of those enemies surfaced when Jon Arnett, the great USC running back of the 1950s, co-authored a nine-page letter with a business associate calling for major changes. The letter wasn't supposed to go public, but it did, citing a "lack of an attack philosophy, unimaginative play selection," among other things. "I wrote Smith a letter apologizing," Arnett says. "Not about what I said, but that the whole thing went public. The letter was the result of many people talking to me, saying, 'Why don't you help us do something?' I felt sorry for Larry. I have great compassion for people, and I don't like to bring harm to anyone. At the same time, when you pick a profession like that, you put yourself in a fishbowl. The bigger the program, the more you'll be scrutinized."

Smith didn't help himself by exuding a style different from most USC head coaches. He didn't enjoy mixing with the media or mingling with alumni, although both are important facets of the job. John McKay had his own private booth at Julie's, the popular hangout just off campus. Smith didn't even have his own parking spot there. McKay would go drinking with writers after practice. Smith would spend his post-practice time behind closed doors with his assistants.

Smith also had his own ideas about the celebrated position of tailback at USC. Always before, especially under McKay and John Robinson, Trojan tailbacks were large, physical runners who would power between the tackles as effectively as they would race around the ends. The O. J. Simpsons and Marcus Allens and Charles Whites would often carry the ball thirty or forty times a game. Ricky Bell, another USC prototype, once carried it fifty-one times in one game. Smith wanted no part of that. He wanted his tailbacks small and wiggly, not large and muscular. He preferred them to cut back, not power ahead. He had a string of Ricky Ervins and Steven Websters who were all about 5–10 and barely weighed 180 or 190 pounds, and he got by with that fine—until the Trojans started to lose games they used to win and Smith encountered problems with some key players.

Quarterback Todd Marinovich, always controversial because of the unusual methods his dad used to groom him as an athlete, was a wonderful passer who had trouble fitting into Smith's often-less-than-creative offenses. "The whole thing got out of hand in that Sun Bowl fiasco," says Salmon, referring to the 17–16 loss to Michigan State that ended an 8–4–1 season in 1990. "After a lot of four-letter words were exchanged on the sideline, Todd was yelling at Coach Smith. Well, then Coach [Clarence] Shelmon got involved, and the thing got physical in the locker room. I remember I was just kind of standing there, and I ended up getting knocked down and both of them were on top of me. I heard a lot of stories about what really started it, later, something about Todd was supposed to throw to one guy and ended up throwing a bomb to someone else for a TD. But the thing was a mess."

That incident was followed by the real low point of the Smith era, a shocking 3–8–0 1991 season that ended without a bowl bid. In 1992, Smith's Trojans opened with a lackluster tie against San Diego State, of all schools, finishing 6–5–1 and being banished to the lower-tier Freedom Bowl, where they were badly embarrassed by a revved-up Fresno State team, 24–7. But it was after that rain-soaked bowl game in then-Anaheim Stadium that Smith sealed his fate, angrily reacting to questions about the loss. "Shocked? No, I'm not shocked," Smith said. "You people are, because you don't understand it. Disappointed? Yes, I'm very disappointed." Then he blurted out the statement that stunned everyone in the room:

"I don't think there are any Davids and Goliaths in college football today," he said. "I keep saying it, but nobody believes it. The names and logos, they don't mean anything." It was almost as if he signed his own dismissal papers with those words. At USC, the name and the logo mean *everything*. This is a university with as much proud football tradition as any in America, and boosters who already were depressed about the Freedom Bowl result were seething when they read Smith's comments in the newspaper the next morning. It didn't help that McGee, who had been Smith's biggest advocate, was about to depart to take the athletic director job at South Carolina. Not long after the Freedom Bowl fiasco, Smith was fired, and no, he did not go quietly into the night.

Even though he received a $750,000 buyout, he was quick to strike back at his critics. "In my mind, I thought I'd get at least one more year," he told writers. "If we'd won eight games [in 1992], it would have been a phenomenal job by the coaches. I was pointing for 1993 and, really, 1994. I had three years left on my contract. If I'd been 6–5 in 1993, then OK. But I didn't think that was it."

Not long after, Smith was hired as the University of Missouri's new head coach, and at that press conference he continued to defend his record at USC. "When I first got to USC, somebody in

the athletic department told me I'd better build my political base,"
he said. "I said, 'Hey, I'm just a football coach and I coach through
technique and expertise.'. . . But not being a politician cost me. The
emphasis changed. I'd been told academics were not as important as
winning. Were they? Judge for yourself. I know they say I didn't
mix with the alumni as much as I should have, and my players were
too demonstrative on the field. But if you want to get rid of somebody, you'll find something. I know I can go back on that campus
and find a lot of friends. I came to terms with everything because I
know I left that program in better shape than I found it. That's in
terms of winning and everything else."

Smith said the problem with going to the Freedom Bowl was that
none of his kids wanted to play in the game. "We lost to UCLA and
we lost to Notre Dame, then the next morning I had to tell those
kids, 'In three weeks we have to line up against Fresno.' The next
minute they're in my office saying, 'We don't want to play this
game.' I understand. The motivation definitely wasn't there. Nothing
against the Freedom Bowl, but the challenge just wasn't there. Most
programs would be happy going to any bowl, but not USC."

Smith was right about one thing. USC wanted more than the
Freedom Bowl. It wanted much more. It wanted some of the old
feelings back, some of the rich tradition it seemingly had forgotten.
It needed someone who could reconnect to the glory days. The
Trojans didn't have to go far to find him. John Robinson, who had
left the university in 1983 to coach the NFL Rams, wasn't as young
and energized as some might have liked. But the announcement of
his return, the second time around for the man they called
"Robby," served one major purpose for school officials: it stopped
the bleeding.

Robinson had won three Rose Bowls and a share of the 1978
national championship with the Trojans, so he brought that legacy
with him. He also brought the personable, public-relations role he
was so adept at, the same one in which Smith never seemed to feel
comfortable. No one had to tell Robinson what to say at the stand-
ing-room-only press conference on campus celebrating his return.
"I'll find someone who can carry the ball thirty times a game," he
promised. "I'm going to put up a stand right where those other

Heisman Trophies sit, and I'm going to get somebody to fill it." Mike Garrett, the interim athletic director who would be named to the position full time two weeks later, smiled and said: "It's good to have the legend back."

It was good, for a while, anyway. Maybe not as good as it had been in the 1970s, but still better than it had been in the Smith years when no one seemed to be having much fun. Robinson's redux team went 8–5, losing to Notre Dame and UCLA, but advancing to . . . guess where? That's right, the Freedom Bowl, where the Trojans opened up a big lead, then hung on to beat Utah, 28–21. In 1994, the second year of his second run as coach, he finished 8–3–1 and took the Trojans to the Cotton Bowl, where their stylish passing game buried undersized Texas Tech, 55–14.

The peak of Robinson's second tenure came in year three. Led by All-American Keyshawn Johnson at wide receiver, the Trojans went 8–2–1 overall and 6–1–1 in the conference to lock up their first and only Rose Bowl bid in the 1990s. Johnson topped off a spectacular two-year career at USC by being named the MVP in Pasadena, dominating the game with his catches to help the Trojans defeat a gritty Northwestern squad, 41–32.

But things slid downhill from there, with Robinson going 6–6 and 6–5 the next two seasons without any bowl bids to mask the obvious difficulties. What the coach who had been so successful in the 1970s realized is that the landscape had changed. So had his hunger and energy level. The new staff he had put together was not nearly as strong or experienced as the one he had his first time around with the Trojans.

His relationship with Garrett, who was anxious to prove his own worth as AD, began to deteriorate and slowly grew worse. The end was unseemly, to say the least. After that second consecutive disappointing, bowl-less season in 1997, Garrett left Robinson and his staff dangling through the holidays before finally announcing his decision to fire the head coach. The bitterness was not hidden when Robinson called his own farewell press conference at a downtown Los Angeles hotel, followed by Garrett and USC President Steven Sample, who held their press conference on campus.

Part of the problem was that Garrett was trying to find a suitable replacement and couldn't dismiss the present coach until he was sure he had hired a new one. "Mike told John it could still go either way," says Darryl Gross, who was assistant athletic director at the time. Lou Holtz was offered the job weeks earlier but, after much deliberation, decided to turn it down. "We thought Holtz was our new coach," says Gross. "He pulled out at the last second. We were that close. Then we made overtures to Jeff Fisher, and Jeff was interested. But then we got a call from Bud Adams, who was Jeff's boss with the Titans. "He said, 'You can't have my guy. He's already under contract.'" Then indirect overtures were made to Denny Green, Dave Wannstedt, Norv Turner, and Gary Barnett."

At that point, Paul Hackett's name surfaced. "Mike reviewed his file and called Paul," says Gross. "We interviewed him, and it sort of went lukewarm. But Paul had been part of USC before; he was a smart guy, a quarterback guy with a good background. We thought he was a high-percentage guy with a seventy-thirty chance."

The fact was, though, Hackett's only head-coaching experience had been an unimpressive, losing stint at Pittsburgh. As an offensive coordinator, he came well recommended. As a head coach, he remained very much an unproven commodity. The Hackett regime began with a passable 8–5 season that started with a lively victory over Purdue and quarterback Drew Brees. The key was a highly touted freshman who came off the bench for Hackett and sparked the winning rally. The kid's name was Carson Palmer. He was obviously talented, but like USC's teams in the next couple of years, Palmer's unlimited potential wasn't fulfilled as a sophomore or a junior. He grappled with Hackett's thick, pro-like playbook, and the Trojans stumbled to 6–6 and 5–7 seasons in Hackett's second and third seasons, with games pockmarked by the same kind of mistakes and turnovers every week.

"I think the main problem with Paul Hackett's program was the recruiting," says Palmer, who obviously made a huge improvement when Pete Carroll and Norm Chow eventually took over. "When you compared recruiting classes, well, it was obvious. We didn't have many players who were getting drafted. Maybe we couldn't let in some of the kind of athletes we had in the past, I don't know. But I know some of them were going to Oregon State and beating the snot out of us. I remember looking at one of the recruiting magazines at the time, and not one blue-chip player from out of state had USC at or near the top of his list. Now they all do.

"Those were tough times under Hackett," Palmer says. "The expectations were still high because we were USC. Every year, our fans thought we would win the Pac-10 and go to the Rose Bowl. But I remember thinking we were not that great."

He wasn't the only one thinking that as the disappointing 2000 season plodded on. The team clearly was regressing, not progressing, and the fans at the Coliseum could be heard chanting "Good-bye Hack-ett. . . . Good-bye Hack-ett. . . ." The final loss, 37–21, to a less than overpowering Notre Dame team was the last cardinal-and-gold straw. The Trojans had two punts blocked, a couple of interceptions and a fumble, giving them an almost unbelievable thirty-six turnovers in twelve games. "For our football team, the story was turnovers, as it has been all year," Hackett said that night. "Our quarterback turned the ball over three times. You can't do that against a quality opponent."

It wasn't the quarterback's fault, as Palmer would prove as a senior, winning the Heisman Trophy when provided with the right kind of coaching and playbook. The offense, the defense, even the special teams struggled week after week. That was not because of the players. It was because of the coach, and this was one of those times when everyone in Los Angeles knew, as Paul Hackett trudged sadly through the Coliseum tunnel, he had just worked his final game as the head coach at USC.

Now it was time for Mike Garrett to make another decision, a decision that would, one way or another, dictate the fate of USC football for years to come.

USC'S NO. 1 FAN

You can debate who the best USC football player is, or the best coach, or even which game was the greatest the Trojans have ever played. But you can't argue about the team's No. 1 all-time fan.

It was Giles Pellerin, and no one else is even close.

For all the other memorable streaks associated with this program, none is more amazing than Pellerin attending 797 consecutive USC football games, from the mid-1920s through 1998. That's right. That is no typo. He really did attend 797 in a row. That means at home and on the road, in the sunshine and in the shivering rain or pelting snow. It means attending seventy-five different stadiums in more than fifty cities, including Tokyo. It includes watching eight national championship squads, more than 120 first-team All-Americans, four Heisman Trophy winners, and eleven different coaching regimes.

"God must be a Trojan. I've been lucky," said Pellerin at one point. He died, at age ninety-one, in the parking lot of the Rose Bowl during the 1998 USC-UCLA game. Interestingly, it was at the same stadium where he saw his first USC game. He watched the Trojans beat Penn State in the 1923 Rose Bowl game.

This is how dedicated Pellerin was about USC football: He pushed back his honeymoon eight months so he could celebrate it at a USC game in 1935. It is estimated that he traveled some 650,000 miles to watch the Trojans play, making his way by plane, train, automobile, and whatever else was handy at the time. Someone once calculated that he spent nearly $100,000 watching USC over the years. But money, clearly, was no object when it came to his life-long obsession.

"Giles lived and breathed USC since 1926," his late brother, Oliver Pellerin, said.

"I never played the game, but I love it," Giles once explained. "There's just a certain spirit about college football. I've always said that going to USC games is the thing that has kept me alive, young, and happy. It keeps me alive looking forward to the next season. I don't think I'm a nut. It's been fun. I could have spent a lot more money on other hobbies. A guy can spend as much money playing golf or poker. Some people think I'm crazy for spending as much money as I have traveling to see these games. They don't understand that I do more than just watch a game when I visit these cities. I've met a lot of nice and interesting people on these trips. Sure, I could sit in my rocking chair and grow old. But I don't intend to do that. You've got to have something to look forward to."

The USC coaches and players looked forward to seeing and greeting Pellerin both at home and on the road. After a while, he was allowed to travel on the team's chartered plane. The players all called him "the No. 1 Trojan." Pellerin and his late wife, Jessie, had no children. "I think of all the USC players as our family," Pellerin said.

When your streak gets up that high, there have to be some close misses here and there. Giles certainly had some. In 1993, after attending a road game at Penn State, he was leaving his hotel when he suffered a ruptured aortic abdominal aneurysm. He was hospitalized in Harrisburg, Pennsylvania, for twelve days. Under ordinary circumstances, he would have missed the Trojans' next game. But as fate would have it, USC had a bye the following week. After he signed a waiver absolving hospital officials of any liability, Pellerin was released in time for the next game at home, against Washington State. Now, that's a close call.

There was the emergency appendectomy five days before one game in 1949, and the car that blew a water pump the day before a Notre Dame game in South Bend. He was even bedridden six weeks following surgery for a stomach tumor in 1969. But in every case, he figured out a way to get to the next game, whether it meant doling out a few extra bucks or sweet-talking some doctors and nurses into letting him out early.

As the years went by and the streak continued to build, Pellerin began to gain national notoriety. There have been stories about him in *Sports Illustrated* and *USA Today*. He was interviewed countless times on radio and television. In 1996, he was named the recipient of the first annual Sears DieHard Fan Award as "America's NCAA Division I DieHard College Sports Fan." He was also a finalist in a nut maker's contest to designate "America's Nuttiest Sports Nuts." Pellerin enjoyed the kudos almost as much as he enjoyed watching USC play all sports, not just football. He was known to be a regular at every Trojan basketball game, as well.

A USC graduate with a degree in electrical engineering, he was a retired telephone company executive who lived alone in a Pasadena townhouse at the time of his death. He and his wife, Jessie, donated more than $1 million to endow three football scholarships and a swimming scholarship through the years. When he died, the more than $2 million in investments he had accumulated was given to the USC Athletic Department. His townhouse also was donated to the university.

Pellerin's brother Oliver had told people that Giles always considered himself USC's No. 1 fan, and that's how he wanted to be remembered. Those closest to him, although obviously saddened by his death, weren't surprised that he was watching USC play UCLA the day he succumbed.

They knew he had died doing the one thing in the world he loved more than anything else.

Somebody should circle the number 797 in bright cardinal and gold and put it over the entrance to the Los Angeles Coliseum, where the Trojans play their home games. For all the other seemingly unbreakable records in USC history, that one, that truly extraordinary streak of consecutive games racked up by Giles Pellerin, might be the most enduring of them all.

THE ARRIVAL OF PETE CARROLL

Landing the coach who would lead USC's beleaguered football program back to the glory days of old was not as simple as it seems. It took a couple of crazy bounces, like a punted ball that squirts unpredictably first in one direction, then another, before being downed inside the twenty-yard line. And even then, the best way to describe the process that brought Pete Carroll to Los Angeles is that it was equal parts brilliant decision-making and dumb luck.

Carroll might not have been the first choice at the time, or the second, or maybe even the third. But when some of the other possibilities fell through, Athletic Director Mike Garrett somehow had the foresight to hire a man who had never been a head coach in college and had zero experience in both coaching and recruiting in the Pac-10. He and his then-assistant, Darryl Gross, won't admit it now, but it was a gamble, a huge gamble at the time. However, in Las Vegas parlance, you could say it has paid off in boxcars.

"Really, Pete was my first choice all along," says Garrett. But circumstances and some politically complex issues interfered.

"What happened," explains Gross, now the athletic director at Syracuse University, "is that that Mike said he wanted a college coach. The reason he said it is that we thought that it was ninety-five percent sure we had landed Dennis Erickson, who was at Oregon State at the time. I mean, we thought it was a done deal. To this day, I'm still shocked Dennis didn't take the job. And when I run into him now, he tells me turning down the USC job was the dumbest thing he ever did in his life. When Dennis fell out of the running, the picture all changed."

But in another way, a new, brighter picture came into focus. Garrett always had Carroll's name frozen in his mind. "I remember watching the Forty-Niners and being impressed with their defense and learning that their defensive coordinator was this guy named Pete Carroll," he says. "I kept looking at him and thinking that's what [John] McKay was. I wanted a defensive coach. I've always believed defense wins championships, offense sells tickets. When it came down to make this hire, in reality, I knew Pete was our guy. But I was getting killed in the press, and I knew if I hired Pete over the other candidates, I'd take some even bigger hits. Erickson was the safe play with me. We only offered the job to one other guy, and that was him. But all along, I figured if he turns us down, then I can go after Carroll. That's what happened. Erickson said no, and I got the guy I really wanted."

Maybe it wasn't quite that easy. Erickson did turn it down, but two more coaches from the state of Oregon apparently were still in the mix. There was Mike Bellotti, whose University of Oregon program was thriving at the time, and Mike Riley, who had proceeded Erickson at Oregon State, setting the foundation for what had become a solid program again, before moving on to the San Diego Chargers, where he had not been as successful. Still, Riley was a former USC assistant under John Robinson in Robinson's second turn with the Trojans, and he had the reputation of a brilliant offensive coach who was hugely popular with the players. Keyshawn Johnson, the All-America receiver of that era, was a particularly strong advocate of Riley.

Garrett insists Bellotti never was offered the job. "I know people wrote that, but it never happened," he says. "I did interview Bellotti and Mike Riley. I really liked him [Riley]." Some think Riley was close to getting the job at one point. Maybe as close as a simple car ride from San Diego to Los Angeles. "I was about to get into a car to drive to Los Angeles and meet with USC President Steven Sample to hopefully seal the deal," says Riley, who was still head coach of the San Diego Chargers at the time. That's when his cell phone rang. It was Dean Spanos, president of the Chargers, calling to tell him if he made that trip, he no longer had a job in San Diego. "I had not been told anything firmly yet by Mike Garrett and USC," Riley said, "so I couldn't afford to take the risk, with a family and all."

So, Erickson turned down the USC job, Riley couldn't afford to risk that one final interview, and Bellotti—well, maybe we'll never officially know if Bellotti was offered the job or not. But Garrett swears he always knew whom he wanted. "When Erickson turned us down, Darryl and I actually danced," he says. "We were so happy we could now get Pete."

This was Garrett's decision, make no mistake about that. But he also is quick to give his assistant a share of the credit. "Darryl had a lot of influence," the athletic director says. "Lots of times at USC, I'd go to Mike's house after church on Sunday to watch NFL games," Gross says. "I'd always tell him that while I was a Jets scout from 1999 to 1991, there was this coach with the team who was charismatic, intelligent, a hard worker, someone who could relate to players better than anyone I'd ever seen before. He'd meet with pro players for an hour and make it feel more like fifteen minutes, he was so full of enthusiasm. It always struck me how good he was. I'd seen them all come through, and there was no question this guy was a terrific coach. When I left, I told Pete someday we'd be working together."

When John Robinson was fired, before Hackett was hired, Carroll's name had come up. But he was head coach of the NFL New England Patriots at the time and presumably not interested in making the move back to college football. Eventually, Carroll, who also had been head coach of the Jets, even got fired in New England. He was out of a job when Hackett was dismissed, and originally didn't seem to have the same luster to his name. "That's why Mike went after Dennis [Erickson] first," Gross said. "Dennis had just taken

Oregon State to the Fiesta Bowl, and he was the hot coach of the moment. But after he turned us down, we had a list of guys to look at, and Pete was on that list."

Turns out, he was at the top of the list, and that proved to be the kick-start to an era even the staunchest of Pete Carroll believers couldn't have imagined. First, though, there was the process of negotiating with Carroll. "I got hold of Pete," Gross says, "and he was really interested. Immediately, he seemed so on top of it, so organized." Now the list of candidates included Sonny Lubick, the highly respected coach at Colorado State, and Bellotti, among others. Nobody had been tendered an offer at that point, according to Gross. "Eventually, Pete came in for an interview," Garrett says.

"It was in a suite at the Marriott Hotel near LAX. Pete was dressed to a T, in a pinstripe suit that made him look very professional," Gross says. "Well, on a scale of one to ten, his presentation was a ten. He had it all figured out—the staff, what kind of style he would play, the personnel, the recruiting, everything. He had it all covered. And when I say he was a 'ten,' the next closest person in those interviews was like a 'six.' Pete basically blew away Mike and me."

After they hired him, Garrett had no doubts. "I knew we'd done the right thing," he says . "Pete and I both had experience in the pros, but that's not all it's made out to be. There is a difference in dollars, maybe. But the peace of mind you can get coaching here, you can't get there. Every three years your roster turns over there. Here, you can coach twenty years and be successful. He can have a constant flow of talent. All he has to do is out-recruit everybody. To me, Pete is a more refined John McKay. Except McKay was shy; this guy's not shy."

Years later, Gross thought back to before the Carroll hiring. "One day, when Paul Hackett was still our coach, Pete calls me from out of the blue. He told me his daughter was considering coming to USC, and that he was going to come out and check things out. So he did, and while he was here, he came out to practice and we chatted briefly. Quietly, I told him he may want to follow what happens here. I said things could get a little shaky, and you never know what the situation might bring. Pete asked, 'Do you think you can win here?' But I think he answered his own question after seeing the campus and the environment at USC. It's funny. You look back now and wonder, if Erickson had taken the job, would he have been a good fit? Probably. But it's hard to believe he could be as good as this guy."

The good fortune for USC is that it caught Carroll at the perfect moment. "I was in Massachusetts at the time, going through a ten-month period where I was trying to figure out what I wanted to do with my life," Carroll says. "We had a lot of ideas. We had a group together trying to create a football television network. We thought that was a cool idea. I was investigating a lot of options, including creating a media company." The only thing wrong, he said, is that the business world frustrated him. "I didn't like the pace of it," he says. "It was too slow-paced for me."

Then, one fateful day, Carroll was invited to New York to visit a friend at an investment firm. "We went to see him, and I remember going up the elevator and the door opening, and the entire floor was full of people at cubicles, shouting on the telephone and running around selling stuff. The whole place was so full of energy. I distinctly recall thinking to myself, *This is way better.* I realized I need a bunch of chaos going on. I missed that high-energy environment. Working in your house is OK, but it's so quiet. I'm not real good with quiet. I knew I had to be more active, more energized. That's what football was."

Just about that time, the USC job came open, and Garrett told Gross to call Carroll. "I told them I was interested right from the start," Carroll says. "I didn't campaign for it, or anything. They came to me. I flew to L.A. for the interview with Darryl and Mike. I was ready for the challenge. I thought it was an extraordinary opportunity. I knew Mike Garrett was a great competitor. I knew he loved football and wanted this to be a great program."

Carroll knew some other things, too. He had attended the Kickoff Classic that featured USC against Penn State at the Meadowlands in August 2000. "I didn't want to look like I was sniffing around," Carroll says. "But I saw them play. I talked to some people and honestly didn't know how good they could be. I kept hearing that the Pac-10 had all evened out, with the Washington and Oregon schools getting a lot of the recruits USC used to get. It looked like the emphasis had changed, that the eighty-five-scholarship rule had caught up to it. At the same time, a lot of people thought SC was a sleeping giant. Guys in Oregon, [Jeff] Tedford [now the Cal coach] and those guys, they thought it could still work here."

Carroll was about to find out. He was hired as the Trojans' new coach in late December, and immediately much of the Los Angeles-area media criticized Garrett's choice. To many who studied Carroll's resume, he looked more like a recycled Paul Hackett, except that he emphasized defense more than offense. Like Hackett, most of Carroll's success had been as a coordinator, not as a head coach, although he did direct New England to the NFL playoffs twice. The knock on him in the pros is that he wasn't tough enough. He was too rah-rah. "Peter Prep School," is what they called him. Others insisted his high-energy style would be a perfect fit at the collegiate level. Either way, it seemed like a major gamble to pay him a reported $6 million over a five-year contract.

Carroll knew all this, realized the media was skeptical, but that didn't stop him from standing up at his introductory press conference and making a fervent pitch for himself. In typical Carroll style, he was enthusiastic to the point of appearing almost manic, refusing to stand still, moving from one end of the room to the other to make his points. "For a guy like me, the things I like to do, this is a golden opportunity," he said as the lights from the TV cameras flickered in his eyes. "I just don't think I could be more prepared for this." Others certainly thought so, but that didn't stop Carroll. "I don't need anyone to fire me up or give me pep talks," he said. "I think I bring all the things this place needs right now. . . . I hope they give us a chance to see what we turn out."

Garrett stood nearby looking ecstatic. Gross, the ever-ambitious assistant athletic director, couldn't wait to talk about the man he had helped recruit. "It wasn't so much my relationship with Pete as it was watching this coach in action [with the Jets]," Gross said at the time. "I remember the looks on the faces of his players, how they wanted to go charging through the wall for this guy. I saw that."

It didn't take long for others to see the same thing. Carroll won his opener in 2001, beating overmatched San Jose State, 21–10.

More significant, perhaps, was the crowd count that day in the Coliseum. It was 45,568, a clear indication of how far USC football had fallen in the L.A. sports market. That opening victory was followed by four consecutive losses, three of them in the Pac-10. While the critics began writing "we told you so," Carroll swears he saw hints of encouragement.

"At the Oregon game, I knew we had a chance to be really good," he says. "We lost in the final few seconds. Two weeks later, we played up at Washington, and they were really good. We lost again on a kick right at the end. I remember going up to Rick Neuheisel [the Washington coach] after the game and telling him, 'It's not going to take us very long.'" In the locker room before the Arizona State game the next week, I told our kids: 'We don't have to lose anymore.'"

If those sounded like brash statements from a coach who had opened up 1–4, Carroll didn't care. He proved he was right by winning five of his next six games, including a 27–0 crosstown statement victory over UCLA. "That was a big deal," Carroll says of the game against the Bruins. "That was our first big night at the Coliseum. That was huge. It was the first time you could really feel the Coliseum rock."

The amazing part is that Carroll was doing it with whatever bits and pieces left over from the Hackett years. There was some talent on hand, particularly on defense where players like Troy Polamalu were around to hit every opposing jersey in sight. But offensively, Carson Palmer was still adjusting to yet another new system, and the running backs were so bruised and battered that Carroll eventually had to call on a walk-on surfer dude named Sunny Byrd to carry the ball for him late in the season.

"Sunny didn't average the number on his jersey," Carroll says, smiling, "but he was big for us. He gave us an aggressiveness we didn't have before. Against Arizona State, I remember telling him to get in there and he'd carry the ball ten times in the second half. He wound up carrying it about eighteen times. He only averaged about two yards a shot, but that was OK. He sort of set a tempo for us that was really important."

Along the way, Byrd became something of a folk hero to USC fans. "Everybody keeps telling me they can't remember the last time we had a tailback who just ran straight," Byrd said. "I go, 'Yeah? Cool.'" Byrd had no speed. He had no moves. But he had no pretensions, either. What you saw is what you got. "Hey, out here, there are defensive linemen who are faster than me," he said. That would have been a funny line, except he wasn't kidding. "It's so great," Sunny gushed. "All these people keep coming up to me and saying they can't believe I'm starting."

He couldn't believe it, either. "If anyone had come up to me two months ago and told me I'd be the starting tailback the second half of the season, I probably would have bet them my car they were wrong." That was easy for Sunny to say. His car was a 1984 Toyota pickup. "Every once in a while," Byrd said, "I still think they're pulling my chain." Dude, you wanted to tell him, that's what makes this whole thing so cool. They're not.

Unfortunately, all those warm, fuzzy feelings generated by Carroll, Byrd, and the Trojans evaporated when they traveled to play against Utah in the Las Vegas Bowl. It was a long, ugly Christmas Day reminder that the Trojans still had a lot of work to do. A smattering of 22,385 people pulled themselves away from the gambling tables and thousands more back in Southern California were sitting there, aghast at what they were watching on television. In a performance that must have made all those bronze Heisman trophies in Heritage Hall blush, the Trojans were outrushed by Utah, 222 yards to one. That's right, the school once noted as "Tailback U." rushed for one yard.

The wonder is that the final score was just 10–6, considering the way Ron McBride's team not only stopped the Trojans' running game, it blitzed on almost every down against a confused, ineffective quarterback in Palmer. "Yeah, we weren't really expecting that," Palmer said afterward. "They had three or four weeks off between the last game, and they made a lot of adjustments for us. They did a good job."

USC didn't do a good job. "We were awful," Carroll says, looking back now. "It was a disgraceful performance by us." The Trojans were flat and uninspired, finishing with a minus–eighteen yards in the first quarter against the 7–4 Utes. By halftime, Utah had outgained them, 172 yards to fifteen.

What nobody knew at the time is that the Las Vegas Bowl would serve as some kind of large, glittering neon sign, much like those on the nearby Vegas Strip. Its blinking message to Carroll was that something serious had to be done. "The best thing about losing like that is that it made us decide to change the offense," the coach says. "I figured this could the last shot I ever have to be a head coach, and I'm not going to go down that way. So I spent all summer tinkering with the offense. I kept thinking let's just get us to be an average running team.

"I hadn't had an average running game as a head coach. I had Curtis Martin with the Patriots, but he was injured and missed a lot of games. So I'd never had a really solid running game. That was my first goal, to run well. Then I wanted to change the rhythm of the passing game. We play in L.A. I always liked the Lakers in their 'Showtime' era. I decided that's what I wanted. I wanted a product so good, people would want to come see us and be around the program."

It would have been hard to predict after that long, discouraging Christmas Day in Las Vegas, but that's precisely what Carroll would begin to produce only one short season later.

CARSON PALMER

Carson started what all this is going to be. His senior year is what got it all going. He and his team started it. We've just been carrying the torch.
MATT LEINART
former USC quarterback
and Heisman Trophy winner

Carson Palmer was one of those kids who had "it" from the beginning. You know the type: the great natural athlete who stands out even on the grammar school playground. The kid who is an instant leader, the one everybody else looks up to before they even get to middle school or high school.

UNIVERSITY OF SOUTHERN CALIFORNIA

"When Carson first started playing football in the fifth grade, he was already bigger and stronger than all the other kids," says Bill Palmer, Carson's father. "He never played any other position than quarterback. He wanted to play it. He wanted to throw the ball. He was the same way in baseball. He was either a pitcher or an outfielder. From the beginning, he could throw the ball farther and harder than other kids."

Bill Palmer is 6–5 and weighs 265 pounds. So naturally, all his children come in the large, economy size. Bill played high school basketball and tried to walk on at the University of Arizona, long before the Lute Olson era. If his personal athletic dreams were never quite fulfilled, he was determined to do whatever he could to help his kids achieve their goals.

"I knew how enthused Carson was about football," his dad says, "so I began looking in the newspaper for ads about a football camp. I read the one about Bob Johnson's camp and decided to give him a call." Johnson is one of the most successful high school football coaches in the history of Orange County, California. His oldest son, Bret, played quarterback at UCLA and Michigan State. Another son, Rob, starred at USC and went on to play with several teams in the NFL.

Coach Johnson has established a reputation as kind of a high school quarterback guru. He runs a camp each summer that draws most of the top high school quarterbacks from around the country. "When I called Johnson, Carson was just in the seventh grade," Bill Palmer says. "Bob explained to me he usually only works with high school kids. But he said to bring him over, he'd check him out. Well, when he saw him, he said he'd let him work with the other kids."

And in a way, that's how the Carson Palmer legend began. The word began to spread about his talent before he even enrolled at Santa Margarita High. "Bob knew all along Carson could play," says Bill Palmer. "I wasn't sure." By the time Carson was a junior, there was little doubt among the recruiters from around the country. "Oh yes," says his dad, "they started calling regularly."

By the time Palmer finished his senior season, he was the top quarterback recruit in America. Anyone who didn't think so wasn't at his final game, one of the more storied events in the recent history of Southern California high school athletics. It was Palmer and Santa Margarita High against DeShaun Foster and Tustin High in the CIF Southern Section Division V Finals. Foster, who would become a candidate for All-America and Heisman honors at UCLA and then a Super Bowl star for the Carolina Panthers, was the great runner. Palmer, obviously, was the brilliant passer, and the two of them put on an offensive show that had people in the stands at Cal State Fullerton's Titan Stadium rubbing their eyes in disbelief.

Palmer logged 255 yards passing, while Foster ran for 191 yards—and that was just in the first half. A 200-pound senior who ran with speed and power, Foster had piled up 139 yards rushing by the end of the *first quarter*. By the end of the wild evening, you needed a calculator to keep up. Foster finished with 377 yards rushing and six touchdowns. Palmer had 419 yards passing and five touchdowns and scored another on a one-yard run. Palmer's Santa Margarita team was bigger, deeper, and better balanced and eventually prevailed, 55–42, but only because Foster, who was playing both ways, was exhausted and hooked up to an oxygen tank by the end of the night.

Both were going to be big-time college players, but even back then, there was no doubt which one had the higher ceiling. Mechanically, Palmer was as advanced as any high school quarterback in recent memory. He looked more like the NFL Pro Bowl star he would eventually become than a high school senior. The technique, the footwork, the powerful arm—he had it all. And when he wasn't throwing fastballs deep into a receiver's stomach, he was showcasing a wonderful touch on balls he lofted to all areas of the field. Flushed and excited as he was being mobbed by his happy teammates afterward, Palmer told reporters that night he already had narrowed his college choices to two. "It's Colorado or USC," he said, and you imagined coaches from both those schools pounding the phone lines for months after that game.

"The first school to offer him a scholarship was the University of Miami," says Bill Palmer. "On the first day you could offer, they did. Carson had plenty of offers. He went to Notre Dame's football camp and liked it there. But eventually, it came down to USC and Colorado. He liked SC a lot, but the thing that made it tough is that they were between coaches. They had fired John Robinson and hired Paul Hackett, but we'd never met Hackett. The guy who probably convinced him to stay with USC was High Jackson, who'd been the offensive coordinator under Robinson and was kept on Hackett's new staff. Funny thing about that is, Jackson is now the receivers coach with the Cincinnati Bengals and still works with Carson. Strange how those things sometime work out."

So, Carson signed with USC, and the hype began. He was the quarterback who would begin a whole new era for the Trojans. He was Kid Carson, the can't-miss prospect with a future as bright as his silky blond hair. The fans, who were understandably restless after the disappointing end to Robinson's second tenure on the job, couldn't wait to see him in practice and chirp about the young quarterback on the radio sports-talk shows. Palmer didn't disappoint anyone once fall drills began.

Mike Van Raaphorst, a redshirt sophomore, had won the quarterback job in Hackett's first spring practice, long before Palmer arrived on campus. But one look at the large, strong-throwing freshman, and everyone at USC knew. Palmer was the reason John Fox, the previous year's opening-game starter, switched positions to H-back and tight end. He was the reason Quincy Woods, one of the highest-rated prep quarterbacks in the country two years earlier, left camp for a few days and came back as a wide receiver. And Palmer was the reason another blue-chip quarterback prospect from Southern California, Jason Thomas, decided to redshirt and eventually transferred to UNLV.

"Your typical, normal freshman always seems to have a lot of other things on his mind, and understandably so," Hackett said. "But Carson, he is really focused on football. You have to love that."

There was some politics going on at USC that Hackett had to juggle. He'd made a commitment to Van Raaphorst in the spring and wanted to keep his word. But he could see the difference in talent between the incumbent and the young freshman. Everyone could. "I'd say early in the season, 'Van Raaphorst will do most of the playing,'" the coach said. "'When I feel like it's time for Carson to come in and play, I'll tell everyone.'"

It sure didn't take long for him to shout it out. With the Trojans struggling in the season opener against Purdue and another young quarterback named Drew Brees, Hackett wiped the perspiration from his face on that blistering hot day and quickly called Palmer in from the bullpen. After nervously throwing a wobbly duck of an incompletion on his first attempt, Carson drilled Mike Bastianelli with a nine-yard dart. Then, moments later, stepping up to avoid the rush and with a Purdue tackler breathing down his facemask, Palmer made the biggest play of the day. He found Larry Parker with a forty-two-yard sideline bomb that set up the Trojans' tying touchdown.

Before his memorable debut was over, Carson had produced seventeen of USC's points in the 27–17 victory, and the real tip-off to what the future might hold came with 3:54 left in the game, when, after removing Palmer earlier, Hackett ordered him back in. Carson threw a twenty-eight-yard completion to Billy Miller and drove USC to the touchdown that finally put the game away. "I thought Carson had played well enough to go back in again," Hackett said, with a straight face. Good enough? The kid was just short of sensational. "I wasn't expecting to happen what happened," Palmer said after that game, "but it was just a great feeling."

There were plenty of good, good, good vibrations, as the Beach Boys might have put it. But the bittersweet saga of Carson Palmer's career at USC wouldn't continue on the sharp upward spiral it seemed to be traveling. It would, instead, plunge to a series of depressing depths before it could be turned around again some four years later.

There was the second season that was rubbed out early after Palmer sustained a shoulder injury at Oregon. If nothing else, because it happened in the first few weeks of the schedule, it allowed him to petition for another year of eligibility. Palmer was elated when it was granted, but not so thrilled at how it things turned out in his redshirt sophomore season.

By early in 2000, it was clear Hackett's program was not progressing. It was regressing. So, unfortunately, was Palmer. Bravely, the twenty-year-old tried to take most of the blame, but what was happening to USC football, in general, and the Trojans' offense, specifically, was more about a lack of coaching than a lack of performing. After a difficult 31–15 loss to

Arizona, when the Wildcats' defense spent the afternoon throwing Palmer around like a tackling dummy, the quarterback finally allowed himself to vent. "I'm frustrated with myself," he said. "Dropped passes happen, but I threw some bad balls, and I had that fumble."

He also didn't have much help. Hackett, in his third season, still hadn't developed anything close to a quality offensive line. He hadn't recruited a tailback with the style or the instincts that could take some of the pressure off his quarterback. And if the design of his offense was supposed to be an NFL-like, high-tech sky show, it had fallen terribly short. The danger for Palmer in all of this was that he might start losing confidence. "You have to remember Carson is still an outstanding football player," said Matt Nickels, the walk-on from Palmer's Santa Margarita High School who had become a reliable possession receiver that year. "Before this is over, he's going to make some plays."

It soon became clear they weren't going to come under Hackett. A depressing 5–7 record finally led to the coach's firing, and Pete Carroll, a man Palmer knew little about, was picked to take over. "When they fired Hackett, Carson was upset," says his dad, Bill. "He wondered, 'Now what?' I was very much opposed to Pete Carroll, based on what I knew about him. But the first time Carson met Pete, he was wowed by him. And he absolutely loved Norm Chow [the new offensive coordinator]. What Norm did was call Carson into his office, and they talked for three hours, never once talking football. I remember he completely impressed Carson. To this day, Norm still calls him three or four times a month."

Looking back, Carson remembers being confused by everything that was happening. "This was going to be my third offensive coordinator in three years," he says. "Paul Hackett told me it would take three years to learn his offense. Then he wasn't even here three years later. In the end, it gave me a chance to play in three different offenses. But yeah, it was tough.

"The thing about the Hackett era, I think, is that we just didn't have the players. We didn't have any guys who were getting drafted by the NFL. There were a lot of local guys who wanted to come to USC. But we either wouldn't let them in or we didn't recruit them. I remember reading a recruiting magazine back then called *SuperPrep*. They listed all the top high school prospects in America, and not one of them said he wanted to come to USC. Something was wrong with that. Look at USC now. Everyone wants to go there these days."

The Carroll years didn't start so well, either. A transition was taking place, and until this coach who would become one of the all-time great Trojan recruiters got rolling, things were tough. After an opening victory against San Jose State, there were four losses in a row. It wasn't until an early-November game against Oregon State that the first glimmer of a turnaround could be seen for both the Trojans and Palmer.

Struggling to beat a 3–4 Oregon State team at home, Carson faked a handoff and rolled to his left in the pandemonium of overtime at the Coliseum. He turned the corner on a naked bootleg and completed the lumbering four-yard run with a dive into the end zone. This wasn't the vintage Palmer everyone had projected when he came out of high school as the nation's top quarterback. No, in the ninth game of a dreary junior season, this was more the beleaguered Palmer. He wasn't so much trying to win as he was trying to survive.

After that less than overwhelming victory, Palmer stood in front of his cubicle and sounded like a young man who had been forced to grow up the hard way on the football field. "I'm the quarterback at USC," he said. "You're expected to win every game. When you don't, you're a bum. When you do, you're a hero. It comes with the job. And you've got to expect it."

No one, least of all Palmer, expected what transpired a year later. Carroll's second season began with modest victories against Auburn and Colorado, followed by close road losses to Kansas State and Washington State. But suddenly, around the middle of October, something seemed to click. And Palmer and the Trojans took off on a seven-game victory streak that would culminate in the dismantling of Notre Dame and a resounding victory in an Orange Bowl game against Iowa.

"Pete Carroll instilled in us what we were playing for," Carson says now. "Looking back, he made us realize how hard we had to work to get to the top. Somewhere in the middle of my senior season, we all knew something was happening. You looked around and you realized there were some great players on this team. We had Troy Polamalu and Malaefou MacKenzie, and then we added Mike Williams. I remember seeing Williams as this skinny freshman kid at practice. I thought he was kind of iffy after watching him the first time. I'll never forget Pete coming up to me in camp and saying, 'Why don't you throw to Mike more. Man, this kid is going to be great.' I didn't believe it at the time. But I started throwing more and more to him, and by the second game of the season, we all knew he was going to be phenomenal."

What they didn't know is how much Palmer would heat up. Game after game, eye-opening statistic after eye-opening statistic, the nation was slowly beginning to take notice. And by early November, the magic word "Heisman" was being whispered around campus. Tim Tessalone, USC's excellent sports information director, had to wait a while until Carson found his groove. But once he did, Tessalone got busy making phone calls, sending e-mails, and producing hundreds of "The Carson Show" tickets, replicas of show tickets complete with all of Palmer's stats and achievements. The endorsements were flooding in as well. "Having coached for a long time in Florida," said new Stanford coach Buddy Teevens, "he [Palmer] is as good as anybody I've seen in that section of the country."

If he had crept to the ledge of Heisman contention before the final game with Notre Dame, Palmer made the full leap with a spectacular performance on national TV. He threw for 425 yards and four touchdowns against what is still the most recognizable school in college football. USC won, 44–13, to finish the regular season 10–2, and voters all across America were reworking their Heisman ballots. "Carson did everything he needed to do tonight," Coach Carroll said after the game. "It was a great moment to have him walk off the field [with 1:57 left]. I wish that walk could have lasted forever."

Palmer wished that senior season could have lasted forever. "It was just so much fun once we got it rolling," he says. "It was just awesome. I had waited so long, wanted it so bad. With some of the guys so low for so long, to finally get to the top of the mountain made it even more special, even sweeter."

The topper, of course, was the Heisman Trophy apparently everyone but Palmer thought he would win. When the announcement came that December night in New York, Carson looked like the most surprised person in the place. "It was just unbelievable," he says. "I never thought in a million years I would win. You know, it was my first time in New York, and I think it was the time of my family's life. To realize they were all there and it really happened, to look back now and know how my mom and dad were feeling, it was fun to watch."

Like Matt Leinart said, Carson Palmer led the way. He put an exclamation mark on his career by leading USC to a resounding 38–17 victory over Iowa in the Orange Bowl, proving without a doubt the Trojans had returned to glory, and No. 3 was indeed the finest player in the land. Palmer had helped kick off a whole new era. Because of Pete Carroll and his quarterback, the good times were back at USC, and Palmer, selected as the eventual No. 1 overall pick in the NFL draft by Cincinnati, would move on to have a glittering pro career with the best years still ahead.

The golden boy of high school football might have had more trouble than he had anticipated getting started, but in the final, sweet Saturdays of an unforgettable senior season at USC, he certainly proved he knew how to finish.

RESCUING A
DYING DYNASTY

S o you want to know how Pete Carroll rescued a dying
dynasty? Simple. Instead of bowing to conformity, he remains
California cool, something that got him run out of the
National Football League, where every coach is straitjacketed into
employing the same offense, the same defense, the same demeanor,
the same formula for eventual dismissal.

Down to what he feared would be his last head-coaching opportunity if he didn't succeed at USC, Carroll continues to make fun out
of hard work while many other coaches make hard work out of fun.

"I love living in Southern California," says the native of Northern
California. "I love representing this university. That's all truth with
me. This is a rare opportunity, with the right elements, the right
ingredients, and I'm not going to give that up." So, in his mid-fifties
and living in an area where being Cal-cool is cool, he isn't afraid to
do a little boogie-boarding or shoot some hoops or throw a football
around or dive into a pile of flailing players or display some emotion. "People find it hard to believe a guy can have this much fun

and still work as hard as we do and be as tough as we are. Guys are supposed to be grumpy doing this job. It's confusing to people."

But that's Carroll. He doesn't wear a hound's-tooth hat and mutter homilies for the ages, and he isn't a little, white-haired guy masking his shyness by emulating Bob Hope. He's just Pete being Pete, as he's been from the moment he stepped in front of a skeptical media audience for the first time as USC's new head football coach, on December 15, 2000.

Carroll didn't attempt to ingratiate himself to these strangers in the media—in truth, he sort of stuck out his chin and dared detractors to take a swing. It was a wise move. Most of those who thought Athletic Director Mike Garrett might have hired another Paul Hackett came away impressed with the new coach's verve, his moxie, although one newspaper columnist, Bill Plaschke of the *Los Angeles Times*, wrote: "I'm mad at USC for hiring him, but we should give Carroll twenty minutes."

Carroll didn't stew over his mild reception from fans and media. "I never begrudged fans or alums a second for that, because they didn't know me. I probably would have reacted the same way if I'd been them. But almost from the minute I got here, things have flowed beautifully. I always thought USC was a sleeping giant, because of Los Angeles, the recruiting base, and the program's amazing tradition. We hit the road running at a thousand miles per hour."

Carroll hasn't slowed down, particularly since he got past that first 6–6 season and a Las Vegas Bowl defeat that left him embarrassed and angry. Since that Las Vegas nightmare (one yard rushing for the Trojans), no coach in America has matched his record of success. Carroll has won forty-eight of fifty-two games, including thirty-four in a row until falling to Texas, 41–38, in the 2005 national championship game in the Rose Bowl. He captured national championships in 2003 and 2004, and came within nineteen seconds (or three inches of a first down earlier) of making it three in succession, something that hasn't been accomplished since the inception of the Associated Press poll in 1936. His Trojans have won or tied for the last four Pacific-10 Conference titles, are a perfect 5–0 against UCLA, and have defeated Notre Dame in their last four meetings, three in succession by thirty-one points.

One feature about Carroll is unique: he takes his football seriously, but not himself. Take his first practice in the spring of 2001. The annual Academy Awards show was being held at the nearby Shrine Auditorium, and limousines and fancy cars were flooding the area. "See, guys," he yelled, "one practice and already everyone wants to be part of this."

Many media people following the NFL insist this relaxed approach to the game is what cut his time as a head coach in the league to four years, one with the New York Jets and three with the New England Patriots.

UNIVERSITY OF SOUTHERN CALIFORNIA

Nobody has more fun at USC's daily practices than the effervescent head coach. To hardly anyone's surprise, Carroll is almost always the last one off the field at the end of the day.

Bob Ryan, a columnist for the *Boston Globe*, saw Carroll through his years with the New England Patriots and probably possesses the best perspective on the reason USC's coach didn't make it big in the NFL.

"His 'problem' was his personality," Ryan says. "His failing is an essential decency and enthusiasm package that just doesn't have the same effect with guys drawing paychecks as it does with college players, and that includes those who assume they will be drawing paychecks in the near future. Perhaps this is a vague and inadequate presentation of the Pete Carroll 'personality' problem, but I believe it to be real, and I think it is nothing to be ashamed of. To the contrary, it is something that he should be proud of. Is it more important to be remembered as an effective take-no-prisoners coach or as a tremendous human being who also happens to have a lot of football knowledge to impart?"

Carroll cites the difference between New England and USC. "The first day I went to practice in New England, the dormitory was a long way from the practice field and I rode my bike to practice," he says. "It was, 'What's Carroll doing? He's on a stinking bike to practice. How can he be serious? He looks like it's a lark.'"

Carroll grins. "Here, I can do whatever I can think of," he says. "I have great control, and it's very rare and difficult to get that and maintain that in the NFL. When I was talking about the job, I knew [Athletic Director] Mike Garrett was a great competitor, and I liked that. He wants to have a premier program and be highly successful. He's been extremely supportive, and that's all I really ever needed. He's kind of steered clear and swept a clear path for me, so I could go ahead and do my thing."

So what's "doing my thing" for Carroll? First, it's competing, whether it's an important practice or a football game or recruiting or maybe just a pickup basketball game, something at which he can be ultra-competitive. He admits to perpetual motion. "High energy is pretty accurate," he says. "I'm loaded with it. I expect my staff to coach with great passion and really bring the energy to our practice, which leads us to the things that we do on game day."

Former USC All-America wide receiver Mike Williams, once a great high school basketball player, tells of dueling with Carroll on a

UNIVERSITY OF SOUTHERN CALIFORNIA

Matt Leinart and Pete Carroll have a right to smile after the Trojan quarterback was presented with the 2004 Heisman Trophy at the annual dinner in New York. One year later, Reggie Bush won.

basketball court, "He plays dirty but can shoot really well. He doesn't like to lose."

Walt Harris, who recruited Carroll to University of the Pacific in Stockton and currently is head football coach at Stanford, agrees with Williams's assessment of Carroll's basketball competitiveness, especially his persistent defense. "When you die, your hands will still be moving," Harris once told Carroll after a grueling pickup game. The USC coach's competitive nature is inbred. "My father [Jim] was one of the most competitive people I've ever been around," Carroll says. From the moment Carroll was ready for serious competition— the Little League and Pop Warner ages—he and his home were the center of frenetic action.

A "ballgame" call from Carroll meant the gang was to meet, usually at the Carroll home in Greenbrae, for some kind of action—anything that involved competition, including vying for the funniest lines as they razzed visiting players at San Francisco Giants baseball games.

"All I remember is the laughter, and then someone would give me half a sandwich," says Skip Corsini, one of Carroll's close friends who attended the 2005 Notre Dame and national championship games as Carroll's guest. "I'm a Cal man, but Pete is such a good friend I have to root for USC. My Cal friends say, 'What's happened to you?' But I'll tell you how far I would go for Pete. Even if Pete were coaching at Stanford, I'd be rooting for him."

When Carroll was a freshman at Redwood High School in Lark-spur, he was too little to reach the 115-pound minimum weight for freshman football, so he apparently did what had to be done. "I think he put some rocks in his pockets for the weigh-in," says Bob Troppmann, Carroll's coach at Redwood High. "There was no way they were going to keep him away from the football field."

OK, maybe young Pete was slight and perhaps a little slow, but there were ways to compensate for those flaws: work harder and block and tackle harder than anyone else. Those were key tenets of an ethic for success that Carroll adopted and employed as a young-ster, and, forty years later, a formula for excellence he has per-suaded his Trojans to embrace in their pursuit of excellence and, particularly, fun. Yes, never forget fun. Carroll constantly is reminding players that "you're supposed to have fun," and, on occasion, he'll shout, "Are we having any fun?"

Yet, according to Williams, while Carroll was resurrecting USC from what folks in the Pacific Northwest began calling "Yesterday U.," he never made any personal demands.

"He's one of those people in a position of power that you respect, but they never have to ask for it," says Williams. "If we had to go jump off a bridge, he could sell that to our team."

Adds All-America defensive tackle Shaun Cody, now in the NFL, "I know it sounds cheesy, but his personality really is infectious. It's just impossible to be cynical around the guy. He's so upbeat." Another Trojan and NFL player, wide receiver Keary Colbert, tells why Carroll's methods are successful. "He can get on you, but that's all out of love. He expects great things out of players. Guys do the right thing because they look up to Coach Carroll."

Tailback LenDale White, the "Thunder" of a "Thunder and Lightning" combination with 2005 Heisman Trophy winner Reggie Bush, was quickly impressed with his new coach when he joined the USC squad in August 2003. "My first reaction was, 'How can you not want to play for this guy?' People say he's a players' coach, and some people say that's a bad thing. But I know, when it's time to get the job done, he'll stick his foot in your butt and make you take care of business. But I also know when it's time to have fun, he'll be right there having fun with you."

The USC coach has become comfortable with himself by being himself. "I'm absolutely convinced that the only way you can do this is to be yourself," he says. "You don't have a chance to succeed if you try to be like somebody else. You're going to fail for sure, because you're going to get found out. You're too visible. What's important is that you know who you are, so you can be authentic and be consistent. If you're unsure of that, it's a pretty difficult job."

Carroll was certainly being himself when questioned about USC's 70–17 triumph over Arkansas at the L.A. Coliseum in the second game of the 2005 season. Asked if this was the greatest offensive display by any team he had coached at USC, Carroll responded: "Yeah, no kidding." Then, asked if a "lack of familiarity" with Oregon, a team the Trojans hadn't faced in four years, would affect his team in its next game, Carroll said, "Well, uh, I guess it could be. We'd never seen Arkansas before, either."

Asked whether coaching college players was more rewarding than handling professionals, Carroll says, "I think you can take kids farther than you can take them in the NFL, as far as going through an extraordinary blossoming time in their lives. It's just different. I think it's more fun. This is more like being a parent than being a coach. It's rewarding on both levels, but I think it is just more fun with collegians because of the freshness and naïveté of the kids, and just the way they respond. It's like watching your kids grow."

Despite a schedule of coaching and relentless media-tending that would wear out an average person, Carroll has found time to meld into campus life at USC, just as he promised when he was hired. "I look forward to this different environment, to walking on campus with all the different things going on, to be able to cheer for the different teams and feel a university's mission" he says. "In the NFL, you're sequestered from the everyday world."

Just as he pledged, Carroll came forward with congratulations to men's tennis coach Dick Leach when Leach's team won the 2002 NCAA championship. According to Leach, the telephone conversation went on for half an hour. Leach was delighted at the attention and Carroll's gesture but said, with a laugh, "I couldn't get him off the line." Carroll is a regular at USC basketball games, too.

Carroll also has become immersed in off-campus activities. In 2003, he helped develop "A Better L.A.," a nonprofit group consisting of a consortium of local agencies and organizations working to reduce gang violence by empowering change in individuals and communities. He received the Courageous Leadership Award from Women Against Gun Violence in 2005, as well as being selected as a Cedars-Sinai Sports Spectacular honoree.

Strategically, Carroll struck gold with two public relations decisions—one, opening practices to anyone with a legitimate reason for being there; and, two, encouraging former USC players to become actively involved with the football program. He's had meetings and lunches with the old-timers, and on each occasion has asked that they get active in support of the team. Many can be seen along the sideline at Coliseum games and also on the road, among

Pete Carroll welcomes two of USC's all-time greats to the Trojans sideline, Ronnie Lott, left, and Marcus Allen. Former players now flock to games.

them Ronnie Lott, Anthony Davis, Marcus Allen, and an occasional interloper such as Snoop Dogg, to whom LenDale White tossed a football after scoring a touchdown. "I want former players, coaches, and those who went to USC to feel like they can come back and be part of what we have going," Carroll says.

Although most coaches, college and professional, are paranoid about open practices, fearing spies are in attendance, Carroll professes serenity. Referring to media members attending practices, he says, "You don't know what's going on. You guys don't have a clue what's going on—you really don't. So, I'm not worried about that. Now, if I knew a coach of another team was there—I mean, we're looking and watching all the time for that. I'm trying to create an environment that is extremely fun to be in for the players. I could care less about the fans, for the most part. I do it for the players. I want them to feel the energy from the crowd cheering."

It's pointed out to Carroll that Los Angeles once housed a coach whose paranoia was boundless, George Allen of the Rams, who had guards, led by Ed Boynton, dubbed "Agent 007," patrolling the practice area at Blair Field in Long Beach. Allen was correct about NFL teams employing spies. Two of his assistants were once caught in a tree viewing a Dallas practice.

"That's a different way to send a message to your team," Carroll says. "You're so thorough and attentive, you won't let anyone even see what you're doing. I can understand that and don't see anything wrong with it. When we go to Notre Dame, there's a little high school field we practice on the day before the game, and we shut that down. I don't want anyone there we don't know. I don't know where a camera is coming from. So, we use that same mentality at times."

Pete Carroll uptight? That just demonstrates that Notre Dame games can do strange things to USC coaches on the eve of games in South Bend. John McKay once tore a phone off a hotel lobby wall in Elkhart, Indiana, the night before a game against the Fighting Irish.

Carroll was a Pop Warner football star as a youngster, played defensive back in high school, and went from there to College of Marin, a junior college, before landing at University of the Pacific for his last two years of college eligibility. He won All-Pacific Coast Athletic Association honors both years as a safety and acquired a passion for defense that has remained with him throughout his coaching career.

But Bob Troppmann, Carroll's high school coach, senses Carroll still has quarterback ambitions. "I've seen him throwing passes at [USC] practices," the coach says. The eighty-three-year-old Troppmann was a special Carroll guest at the 2005 game at Notre Dame and the national championship game against Texas at the Rose Bowl. "We had field passes at Notre Dame," Troppmann says. "We saw the pass Dwayne Jarrett ran to down near the goal line, but we weren't able to see the touchdown. It was a thrill being there."

Troppmann first came to the public's attention at the 2004 BCS Championship Game between USC and Oklahoma, which the Trojans won, 55–19. He was seated at home when the phone rang. It was Carroll, via cell phone, asking, "Should we kick or receive?" Troppmann laughs when he's reminded of the incident. "We lost the toss, so it didn't make any difference what my choice would have been," he says. "Pete calls from a lot of games. It's strange. The television will show Pete talking on the phone, and I'm sitting there looking at it, and it's me he's talking to."

A cell phone is one of the USC coach's favorite devices. While riding on the team bus to that Orange Bowl game, he was on the phone with recruits from around the nation. The phone also was in use the first time Carroll visited Notre Dame Stadium in 2001. After taking the USC job, Carroll quickly bonded with Marv Goux, the legendary former Trojan assistant whose love of the Notre Dame-USC series knew no limits. Goux described the feeling Carroll would get the first time he walked out of the tunnel and onto the field at Notre Dame. Goux, living in Palm Desert, California, and stricken with cancer that would prove fatal a few months later, was waiting for the telecast to begin when his phone rang. It was Carroll, who said, "Marv, it's exactly what you said it would be."

While Carroll has achieved success the last four years, he faced a crisis of major proportions after the 10–6 loss to Utah in the 2001 Las Vegas Bowl. Ed Orgeron, now head coach at Ole Miss but defensive line coach and recruiting coordinator at that time, recalls the torture of a drive home from Las Vegas with his wife, Kelly. "I was afraid we'd blown everything. I mean, we were so bad I was afraid we might have frightened some recruits away from us," he says. But Carroll and Orgeron put their heads together the next day and altered their game plan. USC was chosen College of the Year by the 2000 edition of the *Time/Princeton Review College Guide*, and the coaches decided to stress academics when talking to recruits in the final five weeks before 2002 letter-of-intent day.

They knew what could be achieved in a short period. Orgeron was appointed recruiting coordinator by Carroll, and they managed to put together a sixteen-player recruiting class that included two defensive linemen, Mike Patterson and Shaun Cody, both of whom would became high NFL draft choices, and 2004 Heisman Trophy winner Matt Leinart.

So, as they regrouped after the Las Vegas Bowl, they used Carroll's relentless enthusiasm and Orgeron's knowledge of recruits who might accept the revised approach. The new plan, stressing academics instead of football, worked beautifully. The Trojans landed a recruiting class ranked No. 12 by a recruiting organization then known as Insiders.com, since renamed Scout.com, and were ranked thirteenth by Rivals.com.

"Long Beach Poly had what was called the Fabulous Five," says Orgeron, referring to safety Darnell Bing, defensive tackle Manuel Wright, offensive tackle Winston Justice, tailback Hershel Dennis, and tight end Marcedes Lewis. "We got four of them—all except Lewis. Bing, Justice, and Wright all had five-star ratings, and Dennis was a four-star. Maybe we were only twelfth or thirteenth ranked for that recruiting class, but besides those Poly guys, we

Pete Carroll and quarterback Matt Leinart celebrate at the end of another big victory for the Trojans. Leinart was 37-2 at USC.

also signed Mike Williams, Dallas Sartz, Justin Wyatt, Kyle Williams, Dominique Byrd, LaJuan Ramsey, Brandon Hancock, Chris McFoy, Fred Matua, and a great punter, Tom Malone. That was really the start of something big."

Orgeron, who coached under Jimmy Johnson and Dennis Erickson in their days when the Miami Hurricanes were the scourge of college football, saw quickly what an impact Carroll was going to have on the program.

"I remember once when Coach [Paul] Hackett was here, my wife said, 'I'll bet we won't be here much longer.' I told her with the right man, USC could dominate college football. And those first two or three weeks I was with Pete Carroll, I knew we had the right man. I saw a new dimension in recruiting—about refusing to take no for an answer. He had a vision of what USC could be like. We wanted the best players in the country to come to USC to play football. He believed we could get them, and so did I. So, we went after the very best—and we got 'em."

Indeed, starting with the 2003 recruiting class, Carroll has distanced himself from the pack. In Scout.com rankings, Carroll had the Trojans in the No. 1 position, and he was No. 1 in 2004, No. 5 in 2005, and No. 1 in 2006. Rivals.com had the Trojans thirteenth in 2002, third in 2003 and No. 1 the last three years—2004, 2005, and 2006. USC's domination of national recruiting is unprecedented since specialty organizations began putting together rankings a decade or so ago.

Orgeron notes a difference in recruiting methods between Carroll and Jimmy Johnson at Miami. "Pete was completely involved in recruiting, which is different from previous staffs I've been on. On those staffs, assistants were completely responsible for recruiting. I will say this: Johnson was a hands-on guy and had the same eye for talent Pete has, but Pete was more of a go-get-'em-in-the-house guy. Johnson was more of a closer.

UNIVERSITY OF SOUTHERN CALIFORNIA

"Also, Pete makes the final decision on all recruits. He says yes or no on all scholarships. His is the final say."

And, says Orgeron, "We did a better job of evaluating talent than any staff I've been around, and again, Pete was the man. Recruiting is going there and talking to players, but also it's spending time evaluating film and making sure they can play. With Pete, there's a one-hundred percent involvement in all parts of recruiting."

Matt Leinart celebrates after leading the Trojans to an overwhelming 55–19 victory over Oklahoma in the 2005 Orange Bowl. Leinart was voted the game's MVP.

Asked if Carroll will eventually wear himself out with the ninety-hour weeks he maintains, Orgeron says, "No, no, no. That's a natural thing with him. He's unique. For one thing, he has the ability to delegate."

But Orgeron, who also was elevated to assistant head coach under Carroll, believes he knows the secret to his former boss's success. "The thing Pete does best is focus on things that are important. He doesn't worry about things that aren't important to winning."

Most coaches hate recruiting, but not Carroll. "Coaches who don't like recruiting have never recruited at USC," he says. "When you recruit for this university, recruiting's a blast. We're recruiting the top kids in America." And, says Carroll, "I like to recruit during May, because hardly anyone else is out there."

Oregon State coach Mike Riley describes himself as a "grinder" in recruiting, someone who's out among recruits through all periods open for talking to players. Who does he see most often? "Pete Carroll," Riley says. "I've run into him at Vegas and other places. There are a lot of players in Southern California. If you go from one end of the area to the other, over the course of May recruiting, I must have run into Pete six or seven times. I give him a lot of credit. I admire that in him. He's grinding it, and he's at USC."

It's true that USC is located in a unique and talent-rich area, so much so that former BYU coach LaVell Edwards, when asked whether he preferred speed or quickness in a receiver, replied: "I'd prefer both, but if a kid has both, he's at Southern Cal." Former Oklahoma coach Barry Switzer added: "A USC coach drives past more major-college prospects on his way to work than we have in the entire state of Oklahoma." Plus, former Purdue coach Alex Agase, when asked if he recruited California kids, replied: "No, if a kid is dumb enough to leave that beautiful weather, we wouldn't want him."

Troppmann, Carroll's high school coach, cites his former pupil's personal charm as a factor in his recruiting success. "If he can get inside a recruit's house, he's got him," says Troppmann.

Terry Woodley of Saginaw, Michigan, can attest to Carroll's persuasiveness. While building his 2003 recruiting class, Carroll made as concerted an effort to land Woodley's son, LaMarr, as he has for any player since he arrived at USC. He made such a persuasive presentation in a visit to Woodley's home that, after the visit, Terry Woodley commented, "Well, I don't know what LaMarr is going to do, but Pete Carroll made it sound so good I think *I'll* sign with USC. I've got four years of college eligibility left."

Alas, the son chose Michigan. When young Woodley called Carroll to inform him of his decision, the USC coach jokingly said to him, "We're going to kick your butt when we play you." Eleven months later, Carroll kept his word, as the Trojans defeated the Wolverines in the 2004 Rose Bowl game and won the 2003 national championship.

Lane Kiffin, who has assumed Orgeron's recruiting coordinator position in addition to being offensive coordinator, isn't surprised that Carroll has lifted the USC program to great heights so quickly.

Kiffin, who played at Fresno State, says it was generally acknowledged by other California schools that the Trojans could land just about any recruit they sought if the school had the right coach.

"Pete's the perfect guy," says Kiffin, who says Carroll remembers him as someone "who messed up his office" when he was a kid and his father, Monte, and Carroll were serving on the same staffs. He remembers Carroll as someone who played practical jokes, something not fully appreciated by the Minnesota Vikings' defensive coordinator, Floyd Peters. "I remember hearing Bud Grant [Minnesota coach] saying that Pete was driving Floyd nuts." But Grant also remembers Carroll as "a heck of a coach" and a "wonderful family man, the type of person we wanted on our staff."

Allen Wallace, whose SuperPrep.com and *SuperPrep* magazine are popular recruiting sources, is impressed with Carroll's approach.

"Pete Carroll has brought an extremely aggressive recruiting approach to the USC football program from the day his tenure started," says Wallace. "His very first class, though small in numbers [sixteen], contained future NFL defensive linemen Shaun Cody and Mike Patterson, and Heisman-winning quarterback Matt Leinart. The battle for Cody went down to the wire, with Notre Dame coming in No. 2.

"Carroll's second Trojan recruiting class, in 2002, was ranked number seven by *SuperPrep* magazine, the highest-ranked USC class since 1996. That class contained wide receiver Mike Williams from Florida and tight end Dominique Byrd from Minnesota.

Carroll had broadened USC's horizons by deciding to recruit elite athletes far from California, now that he had the time to put these efforts together.

"This has become a Carroll trademark as a recruiter. He's willing to go to any state, against any competition, to battle for youngsters whom he and his staff feel can give them any kind of edge in talent. Oftentimes, these recruiting battles literally stretch out until letter-of-intent day before a decision is made. Carroll has always been comfortable gambling that he can win these battles, and the results speak for themselves. However, Carroll's staff is careful in its talent-evaluation process. They are organized and persistent, but often not quick to offer scholarships.

"Look for Carroll's recruiting classes to always contain some high-profile prospects from outside of California. He will continue to focus on where he believes the best talent is and has proven he has the energy, drive, enthusiasm, and patience to be continually success-ful in these efforts."

Carroll breaks down his approach to recruiting this way. "First, we try to lock up California," he says. "We are really not recruiting against other schools in the Pac-10 Conference. We got eight of the top ten kids from California, and something like fourteen of the top twenty. Historically, the Pac-10 has taken a hundred kids a year out of the state of California. That means California kids are filling everybody's rosters. If we can get the top ten of these guys, that means nobody else is getting them. Our first year here, we were com-peting with Oregon, Oregon State, and Washington, and UCLA was getting some guys. But we don't recruit against those guys hardly ever, anymore.

"I remember the first year Butch Davis was at Miami and he went 6–5. Five years later, he had twenty-two first-round NFL draft picks in his last four years there. So, there was a time when all those guys were on the same roster. That's what we've been shooting for."

What Carroll is "shooting for" on out-of-state recruits is a group of athletes capable of being first-round NFL draft selections.

"We've been very selective with the guys we go after from out of state," he says. "Then we look at the makeup of the kid. Is he a California-type guy? From that, we can find fifteen to twenty guys

UNIVERSITY OF SOUTHERN CALIFORNIA

The scariest sight for any defender is Reggie Bush coming at you in the open field. Bush, the 2005 Heisman Trophy winner, has to rank as the most exciting player in USC history.

to go after and get five or six. And if they're not guys we project to be eventual first-round NFL draft picks, we don't go after them."

It certainly doesn't hurt to have a basketball background to capture Carroll's attention. "It's one of the first questions I ask a recruit— whether he plays basketball. I look for guys who play basketball because they generally have better hand-eye coordination. If they were good enough athletes, they would have played basketball. Steve Smith and Dwayne Jarrett are two great examples. Steve led his league in scoring and was Player of the Year for three years, or something like that. Will Harris, a freshman last year, was a basketball player, and Derek Simmons, who is coming in with the 2006 class, is a great basketball player. Dominique Byrd was a point guard, and Jeff Byers played on a traveling team in high school."

While being a basketball player can help a recruit attract USC's attention, asking questions about the depth chart is quick way for an athlete to eliminate himself from the Trojans' recruiting list.

"If they're worried about competition, they weed themselves out," says Kiffin. "We don't want players who fear competition." That's because, Carroll says, "We build our program around competition. We compete in every phase of our program and try to heighten the level of performance by the level of our practice and our off-season work. It's been instrumental in what we're doing."

Although there was little talk about a change in offensive strategy after the Las Vegas Bowl, Carroll told the authors of this book the Trojans were "so awful, disgraceful," that he "decided that we were going to change the offense."

A former member of the staff said Carroll, in effect, "junked the BYU offense" Norm Chow brought with him to USC in 2001. Carroll turned to two professional coaches for assistance—Alex Gibbs of the Denver Broncos and Jon Gruden, who was then at Oakland but moved to Tampa Bay. Denver had been known for possessing the best running attack in the NFL, and Gibbs was generally accorded most of the credit for developing it. Gruden was young, but he was known for his passing schemes and offensive brilliance. Each summer, Lane Kiffin has spent time with Gruden, who is head coach of the Tampa Bay Buccaneers. His defensive coordinator is Monte Kiffin, Lane's father.

"I had decided we were going to do the whole offense over again," says Carroll. "I had gotten real frustrated with our offense, and I always wanted to be more involved to see if the things and concepts I liked would work. But I always gave in to the coordinators I had. This time, I decided this might be my last shot at being a head coach, and I'm not going to go down that way. I'm not going to leave it all on somebody else's shoulders. So, I spent the off-season working with the offense, and we recreated everything—philosophy-wise, rhythm, and principles—and the results have been phenomenal. The first game against Auburn, Carson Palmer was poppin' that ball around, and we were running the ball better. I even told the guys, 'I don't care if we're the best running team in the conference, just get it to average.' That was how high I set my goals then."

When Chow was praised for what "his" offense was doing, the offensive coordinator would make a point of saying, "It isn't *my* offense; it's Pete Carroll's offense." But most USC followers assumed Chow was just being modest, when, in fact, he was telling it like it was. But Chow's play calling was a valuable asset for Carroll.

As Carroll states, he was determined the Trojans would run the football—effectively, he hoped. But a preseason incident threw a significant roadblock in the way of his planning. Justin Fargas, a former Southern California prep star who transferred to USC from Michigan, lit up spring practice with his jarring runs, and Carroll was depending heavily upon the tailback to be a key link in the offense.

One fall practice, however, Fargas was running near a sideline at Howard Jones Field and All-America safety Troy Polamalu was coming from the other direction. Fargas could have stepped out of bounds, but he didn't. He and Polamalu measured each other and lowered their heads like rams. The collision was so loud, so violent, so frightening, that bystanders gasped. The result: a concussion for Polamalu that kept him out for a day or two, and a hamstring injury for Fargas that hampered him for weeks. It wasn't until Game Three against Kansas State that he carried the ball, and not until Game Eight at Oregon that he was healthy enough to start and turn on power and speed that yielded 139 yards in twenty-seven rushing attempts. Besides the 44–33 win, Fargas gave the Trojans the "attitude" Carroll was seeking from his new offense. No more dink and dunk.

By that juncture, however, USC had lost two games and was out of contention for national honors. But, with their last-season surge that included a 49–17 victory over Stanford, a 34–13 waltz over Arizona State, a 52–21 triumph over UCLA, and a 44–13 smasher over Notre Dame, the Trojans played themselves into the BCS Championship Series, earning an Orange Bowl berth and a game against Iowa. After Iowa ran back the opening kickoff for a touchdown, USC dominated a 38–17 game that included 122 yards in twenty carries by Fargas, including a fifty-yard touchdown run.

Looking back to 2002, Carroll says, "We needed Fargas's attacking style. It's been obvious that's something we need in our offense. I had no idea what was going to happen when the year started, but we had a great season and Carson won the Heisman. Then, when we came back the next season with all the new guys and did well, I knew the system was working. If you can bring in a new quarterback and all new running backs, three new linemen, and receivers, and put together a national championship year, well, that was a big statement about our new system."

After watching a film of the national championship 41–38 loss to Texas at the Rose Bowl "barely once," Carroll says, "I'll have to watch it again later, but not right now. I hate that game—hate it." Asked if he was not watching the game because he was so angry, Carroll responds, "Oh, yeah. I hate that game because we had so many ways to win it. I've always said during the streak [thirty-four consecutive wins] that we wanted to make sure we made a team play great to beat us. And not play lousy, and we didn't play lousy at all. There were so many ways to win that game."

The way his teams have been winning lately, Pete Carroll has plenty of reasons to smile on the Trojans sidelines.

So, the Trojans didn't play their best? "No, we didn't. We struggled defensively against the quarterback [Vince Young]. There were so many opportunities. The ball was on the ground five times, and we only got one. There were some instant-replay opportunities that were taken advantage of, and not one went our way—stopping them on fourth-down situations, the interception that was called an incompletion. Usually, they aren't that obvious. There was a time when we could have won the game running away. We're up twelve points and the ball falls straight to us. We would have had the ball again if a fumble had been called. If not for LenDale's [White's] fumble, we would have scored every time we had the ball in the second half. The offense was just smokin'."

Carroll concedes Texas quarterback Young was "extraordinary." In fact, he says, "We've never seen anything like that. Adrian Peterson [Oklahoma, 2005 Orange Bowl] and his hype was nothing like

273

that guy [Young]. There's no player we've ever faced who could control a game like that. We baited him into doing what he did; he just outdid us. Their whole team was him running the ball and throwing downfield. He was extremely adept at taking the ball underneath in that game. He hadn't shown he was any good at that."

But Carroll says what Young accomplished wasn't a shock. "During preparation for the game, I was really worried about him. We spent a lot of time preparing for him because we knew what he was capable of. It was just more difficult to contain him than I thought it would be."

Oh, yes, there was another huge play during the 2005 season, and Carroll says the third and twenty the Trojans faced at Notre Dame in the final two minutes "wasn't a great situation."

"We were on the verge of getting beat," he says, "but what was clear was, we didn't have to get a first down, just make it manageable on fourth down. We called a timeout and talked to Matt [Leinart], and we decided to dump the ball to Reggie [Bush]. Sark [quarterbacks coach Steve Sarkisian] said all we want to do is get half the twenty, and we did. We got eleven, making it fourth and nine. We called timeout, and Matt was told of what to check for an audible. Lane [Kiffin] said, 'He's got it; he's got it,' and Sark and I were wondering if Matt was going to do the audible. Then he stepped back and we said, 'Here we go.' The crowd couldn't have been louder, and Matt gave the protection and gave the route. The entire concept of the play worked and was right. Matt threw a strike, and off Dwayne [Jarrett] went."

Two plays later, Leinart scored on a quarterback sneak for a 34–31 victory over a shocked Fighting Irish audience.

With Bush, Leinart, White, and a bunch of others gone from the squad, Carroll faces the same rebuilding job heading into the 2006 campaign that he encountered after the 2002 season. "We'll all be wondering what's going to happen," Carroll says. "We're going to be extremely talented."

Only one thing is certain about the future: it'll be fun. You have Carroll's promise on that.

MATT LEINART

Everything that kid touches turns to gold.
LINDA LEINART,
mother of Matt

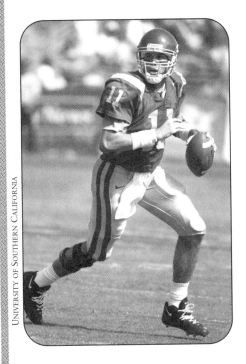

UNIVERSITY OF SOUTHERN CALIFORNIA

Matt Leinart was eleven years old, an innocent kid who had every right to be scared and crying, afraid to go into that foreboding hospital room to see his father, Bob, lying there unconscious, with tubes sticking out everywhere from his body. His older brother, Ryan, couldn't do it. His mother, Linda, was understandably distraught and shaken, but young Matt wasn't.

He was worried, sure, worried out of his skull. That wasn't only his dad lying there. It was his best friend. The man who was at every game he'd ever played, the confidant he could always talk to afterward, the head of the family. At the tender age of eleven, most kids couldn't have walked into that room, kept their composure, and dealt with the situation.

But Matt did. Maybe that was the first clue this young man is wired differently than everyone else. He not only entered the hospital room, where his dad had just undergone quadruple-bypass heart surgery, he was the stabilizing force. "Matt was a rock," said his brother, Ryan. "I couldn't go in and see my Dad. I just couldn't do it. It was too hard on me emotionally. But Matt had no problem. He's always been that way. He never got rattled, back to his early years. Nothing ever bothered him. I think that's why he was so good in all those clutch situations later on at USC."

Matt's mom, Linda, was just as amazed. "He was the one who held me together," she said. "Can you imagine that from an eleven-year-old?" Later, after he had recovered, his father was told that story. He wasn't surprised. "He has an internal strength," said Bob Leinart. "He can handle anything."

Apparently so. That inner strength has served Matt Leinart well, whether it was overcoming the taunts and teasing he endured as a chunky, cross-eyed kid growing up in Orange County, or bouncing back from being buried so far down on USC's quarterback depth chart that he seriously considered transferring at one point. The same toughness that carried Leinart through the pitfalls of his early life helped him in the heat of all those big games the Trojans had to play the past couple of years, forging the calm, poised persona that led Pete Carroll's team to unprecedented heights, to two national championships and thirty-four victories in a row.

Leinart has enjoyed a career unlike any other at USC. Bursting onto the scene as a raw sophomore, guiding the Trojans to a spectacular 12–1 season and a share of the national championship, winning All-America honors and earning the MVP trophy in the 2004 Rose Bowl victory against Michigan. Turns out, though, he was just warming up.

His junior year, Leinhart took Carroll's team through an undefeated 13–0 season, capping it off by throwing for five touchdown passes against Oklahoma in the BCS Championship Game, and winning the Heisman Trophy as the outstanding player in college football. Then, shocking everyone, he announced he would bypass a chance to be the No. 1 overall selection in the NFL draft and the opportunity to earn $40 million, to remain at USC for his senior season.

"I think college football—and this whole atmosphere of being here with my friends and teammates that I have been with for four years—is ultimately more satisfying than any amount of money," Leinart said at his SRO press conference on campus, also noting that his left arm required surgery, something else that certainly was a factor in his decision. "Besides," he added later, "I'm having too much fun."

The fun continued in a senior season that was almost mind-boggling in its scope. Leinart wasn't just another great player anymore. He was a role model for everything that was good about college football. He'd turned down the money to stay with his friends, ignoring the danger of a career-threatening injury because, as he put it, he wanted "to stay a kid" a while longer. You couldn't blame him, either. His life couldn't have been much better. He was the biggest sports star in a town that loved celebrities. He was hanging out with Hollywood types like Nick Lachey, who was Jessica Simpson's husband at the time, kicking back and going to clubs and generally accepting his status as the No. 1 sex symbol on a USC campus full of beautiful, star-worshipping coeds. Toddlers could be seen at home games wearing T-shirts that read: "I wish I could be Matt Leinart."

The thing about Leinart, though, is that he never tried to play the role. He spent more time in his off-campus residence with roommate Dwayne Jarrett, or ducking out for midweek lunches with his dad, Bob, than he did club hopping. And although he easily could have been USC's happiest free-lancing bachelor, he preferred to be seen with his then steady date, Brynn Cameron, who was a sophomore on the USC women's basketball team.

At Pac-10 media day weeks before the season opener, a relaxed Leinart was asked if he ever thought about his place in history. "I think about it," he said. "I think it's pretty cool. But when you're living it, actually doing it, I don't think you appreciate it until it's done. If I do what I'm capable of doing this season, maybe in ten or twenty years from now, people will be saying stuff. But, you know, when I look back and remember how close I came to not even winning the quarterback job here, it keeps me grounded. For two years, I was miserable. All that makes me enjoy this even more."

The 2005 season began in the tropical air of Honolulu, where Leinart and Bush gave hints of things to come, crushing poor, overmatched Hawaii, 63–17. The scary part was the Trojans stayed relatively conservative on that unseasonably warm day on the island. "I think I only took one five-step drop all day," said Leinart, whose first of three touchdown passes on the afternoon was his seventy-third, breaking Carson Palmer's school record. Palmer needed 1,569 attempts to reach that level; Leinart required only 839. A reporter asked the quarterback that if his team played conservatively and still scored sixty-three points, how many points could it score when it decided to really open up. Leinart smiled and said, "Who knows? Maybe ninety?"

He was close. The Trojans stung Arkansas for seventy points in their home opener, and the rest of the season looked like it would be one happy romp through various end zones. It wasn't. What USC and its vulnerable defense seemed to forget momentarily is that they would be a target every week. The No. 1-ranked Trojans were the biggest game on everyone else's schedule, and trips to Eugene, Oregon; Tempe, Arizona; and South Bend, Indiana; and a late home game against Fresno State would be anything but easy.

Leinart and Company overcame a poor first half to glide by Oregon, 45–13. But the next week, in the hot Arizona desert, things really got sticky. Arizona State sprinted out to a 21–3 halftime lead, and when Leinart took a big hit and seemed woozy for much of those opening thirty minutes, the Trojans' long winning streak seemed in serious peril. Fortunately, Carroll-coached teams have a knack for coming back, and powered by a thundering ground game, the Trojans did just that. Bush and LenDale White ran through gaping holes, and Leinart, utilizing mostly play-action passes, completed thirteen of sixteen throws for 145 yards in the second half, allowing USC to escape, 38–28.

All that, though, was just a prelude to the biggest game of the year and the signature play of Leinart's career. First, however, there was a major mind-set adjustment that had to be made. "Matt and I were both feeling it," Carroll says. "The expectations were so high. There was a sense that even though we were winning, we were not enjoying it. It was right after the Arizona State game, and Matt and I got together and talked about it. It proved to be a little therapy for both of us. I told Matt, 'You're a great player. Suck it up; it's really going to be all right.' It was like the weight of the world he was carrying.

"After that, he stood up and talked to the team. He told them he wasn't playing well, but he asked them to have faith. 'I'll get better.' It was an extraordinary thing for a young man to do. I think the fact I was feeling much of the same thing made him realize he should keep it in the proper perspective. It proved to be kind of a checkpoint in the middle of the season for us. After that, we were fine."

After that, Notre Dame was waiting. The Irish pulled out all the stops. Joe Montana appeared at the rally the night before, and new coach Charlie Weis broke out the green jerseys for a game Brady Quinn and his teammates dominated for much of that memorable day. But in the end, with Notre Dame leading, 31–27, and 2:04 left on the clock, it finally came down to Leinart.

The Trojans had the ball, first and ten on their own twenty-five. Guard Fred Matua glanced up at his quarterback in the huddle. "He's just looking at us with that cool smirk," Matua says. "You could tell by the way he looked that you were in good hands." Three plays later, not everyone was convinced. It was fourth and nine at the USC twenty-six. Time and the Trojans' chances seemed to be running out. But Leinart stepped into the huddle and announced: "Let's make a big play."

USC's coaches had alerted him that an audible might be necessary if the Irish were in a specific alignment defensively. Leinart strolled up to the line of scrimmage and, amid the screaming chaos that was Notre Dame Stadium at that moment, quickly noticed his coaches were right. So, he barked out the audible, also motioning with his hands. Notre Dame blitzed as expected, but that left the quarterback's roommate, Jarrett, one on one with cornerback Ambrose Wooden. That's when Leinart delivered the most impressive pass of his celebrated college career, on the play that would define him forever.

It was a perfectly thrown ball with beautiful touch that landed directly in Jarrett's hands. The sophomore wide receiver raced sixty-one yards for a first down at the Irish thirteen. The game wasn't over yet, though. A huge decision still had to be made. With fourth and one and seven seconds remaining at the Notre Dame one-yard line, Carroll and Leinart had to decide whether to play it safe by kicking the game-tying field goal and sending the game into overtime, or to gamble and go for the touchdown.

"I never had a doubt," Carroll says. "There was no way I was going for a field goal. I didn't even think about it." Leinart turned in the midst of all that frenzy and asked Bush, "You think I should go for it?" Bush, who had scored three touchdowns and rushed for 160 yards to cement his Heisman status, never hesitated. "I thought this is what college football is all about," Bush said. "I thought these are the moments you remember forever. I told him, 'Man, you go for it. You go for it."

Leinart's quarterback sneak began in the middle of the line, then drifted left when he seemed to be momentarily stopped short. But then, from behind, almost as if preordained in some kind of Heisman heaven, here came Bush at his back. "I started shoving him in," the tailback said. "I thought I felt something," Leinart related later. "I just kept saying to myself, 'You don't want to hit the ground.' You keep pushing and pushing."

And finally, he was in, with three seconds still showing on the clock. Leinhart scored the biggest touchdown in the biggest regular-season game of his career, and if his legend hadn't been validated before, it was now. USC's streak was alive, and it would stay that way through the rest of the schedule leading up to yet another date in the BCS Championship Game.

As impressive as he is now, with his movie-star good looks and the poise of a ten-year professional, it is important to remember that Matt Leinart did not always have things go his way. As much as people saw him, thriving in the glamorous environs of Los Angeles and Hollywood, and thought he had the life everyone dreams about, he had to live through a couple of personal nightmares to get to that place. The biggest one was his father's serious heart problems. But it was an earlier physical disability of his own that created his initial trauma. The young man with the dark curly hair and the smile that makes coeds swoon was born cross-eyed. Although his parents hoped the condition wouldn't be permanent, he was forced to undergo surgery at the age of three and was required to wear thick glasses until just before high school. As if that weren't enough, Matt was a chunky kid who was overweight until a growth spurt in his teenage years.

"I hated wearing the glasses," Leinart said. "I was made fun of for being cross-eyed all the time. You know how cruel kids can be. It was a terrible time for me. Not only was I the fat kid. I was the fat kid in glasses."

Through it all, the one thing that always helped Matt persevere was his athletic ability. He was a good basketball and flag-football player, but baseball was his real love. He promised his mom he'd make it to the major leagues and buy her a new house. The same strong left arm that has made him a coveted quarterback had the radar guns lighting up early in Matt's athletic career. He hit eighty-four miles per hour at age fourteen, which usually translates into someone throwing in the mid-nineties by the time he gets to college. Something was wrong, though. Something didn't feel right in his left shoulder. He thought it was only some loose ligaments, but it turned out to be a torn labrum and a partially torn rotator cuff.

If that was the end of his baseball dream, it quickly turned him to football full time. USC fans will be forever grateful. At Mater Dei High in Orange County, California, a school that regularly produces big-time college athletes, Leinart began slowly. Early in his junior season, he was splitting time at quarterback with Matt Grootegoed, who would later become his roommate at USC and an All-America linebacker. Just past mid-season, Leinart took over as the starter at the quarterback position and eventually won a Trojan scholarship after an excellent senior season.

But once he arrived at USC, there was another roadblock—a quarterback named Carson Palmer. Leinart redshirted one year and thought he might have a chance to compete for the job the next season. But Palmer came back for his senior year, and Leinart was relegated to the bench, where his attitude took a huge hit. The coaches noticed. The kid who had always been successful now walked with drooped shoulders and looked like anything but a leader when he did get a chance in practice. Whispers were that Leinart was thinking of transferring to another school, something he would later admit was true. Norm Chow, the offensive coordinator who eventually would guide him to great things, told a reporter at one point, "I don't know who our next quarterback will be when Palmer leaves, but I can tell who it won't be. It won't be Matt Leinart."

He was wrong, because, once again, Matt's inner strength was overlooked. It took him a while to shake off his lethargy. But eventually he handled the situation the way he's handled everything else in his young life. He stood up to it. He battled and competed and finally won the job in a hotly contested spring practice.

"Pete Carroll called me," said Bruce Rollinson, the USC alum and football coach at Mater Dei High. "He told me he was going to make the move. He said, 'There is something about this guy. I'm going to make him our number-one quarterback. It's going to be his job to lose.' I think that freedom, the trust Carroll placed in him, is where the confidence came for Matt."

Buoyed by his success on the practice field, Leinart arrived for his sophomore season bursting with that confidence, and his career took off. His first pass as a starter went for a touchdown at Auburn. After that, at least until midseason, he became the quarterback who seemed to be getting it together, the guy who could lead this team to great things. But then the Trojans traveled to Berkeley, where an improving, young Cal team ambushed them, taking them to three overtimes before pulling off a shocking upset.

Leinart played poorly that day, throwing three interceptions, and the whispers already had started. John David Booty, the acclaimed high school All-American from Louisiana, was waiting his turn, and if Leinart struggled again in the game the following week against Arizona State, some already were predicting a change could be made.

That October afternoon in the desert proved to be the turning point in Leinart's career. He suffered a sprained ankle at Cal the week before, and in the first half against the Sun Devils, the pain from that ankle and a sore leg forced him to come out in the second period. The score was 10–10 at halftime, and Arizona State would go ahead by seven early in the third quarter. But the real story was happening at halftime in the locker room, where Leinart was laying on a trainer's table just outside USC's door, in obvious pain. Carroll came walking in, clearly upset, saw his quarterback was agonizing where every USC player could see him. "What are you doing sitting there?" he barked at Leinart. "We need you! Get your bleep off that table. And if you limp, you're not playing."

It was an obvious ploy on Carroll's part, while other assistants whispered in Leinart's ear, telling him they needed him to suck it up and try to play. They all hoped they were convincing, but they didn't know. "We were on the sideline getting ready to start the third quarter," said Carroll. "We were going to play [Brandon] Hance and see what would happen. Then Sark [Steve Sarkisian] says, 'Look at that.' Here comes Matt trudging onto the field. Sark says, 'Let's play him.' I said, "Are you kidding?'"

Happily for USC, Sarkisian wasn't. Neither was Leinart. Once again, that inherent toughness kicked in. So, he limped out, despite Carroll's warning, and directed his team to three touchdowns and a 37–10 victory. That was the day Leinhart not only won the game, he won over his teammates. "He rose to the top when he had to, when all the odds were stacked against him," Carroll said. "It looked like he was done. But he was at his best. He was that way the rest of his career for us."

For Leinart, it took a while to grasp that was a transcendent moment. "I didn't really realize it that much at the time," he said. "But then I read the next day that some of the guys said we want to play for someone like that. I thought, 'Wow, these guys really have my back.' It was a real confidence-builder. I had a knee sprain and a huge amount of tape on my ankle, and my leg just felt dead. I was out a while in the second quarter, then they asked me if I could make it. I said, 'Yeah, I want to try.' After that, we started scoring forty points a game and piling up five hundred yards of offense. Looking back, that was a huge turning point for us."

During his first two brilliant seasons, his most significant games probably were the Rose Bowl victory over Michigan and the Orange Bowl/national championship match in which he carved up Oklahoma for five touchdown passes a year later. In the 2004 Rose Bowl, Leinart was like a little kid again, not only throwing touchdown passes but even catching one. It was his fifteen-yard reception of a floater thrown by wide receiver Mike Williams that clinched his honor as Player of the Game. The play, called "Trips Right, 18 Toss, Reverse, Quarterback Throw-back," came on a call by Chow at just the right time. "I told them, 'Just call it, I'll catch it,'" Leinart said, smiling afterward. "I was wide open, too."

For the rest of that memorable afternoon on Pasadena's historic patch of lawn, Leinart completed twenty-three of thirty-four passes for 327 yards and three touchdowns in a game USC used as its own redemption. Although rated No. 1 in the Associated Press poll, the Trojans had been bypassed by the Orange Bowl selectors, who allowed an Oklahoma team that didn't even win its conference to play LSU in the BCS title match.

After the Trojans had whipped Michigan, 28–14, while Oklahoma had lost to the Tigers in the Sugar Bowl, Leinart and his teammates felt vindicated. Shaun Cody, the All-America defensive tackle, walked around after the Rose Bowl locker room with a T-shirt that read: "Smells Like Roses, Tastes Like Sugar." Matt Leinart, quarterback of the co-national champions and the Rose Bowl MVP, saw that and laughed harder than anyone.

A year later, USC and Oklahoma would have their long-awaited showdown. The Sooners had Jason White, the 2003 Heisman winner, going against Leinart, who won the award in 2004. Oklahoma had Adrian Peterson, the most prolific freshman running back in NCAA history. USC had Reggie Bush, the brilliant sophomore runner/receiver who finished fifth in the Heisman balloting, himself.

This seemed primed to be a game for the ages. It proved, instead, to be a mismatch for the ages. Leinart and the Trojans were just too quick and too strong and too deep. On a night when USC had more heroes than it could count, Leinart rose above them all, impressing the army of NFL scouts on hand with a series of pretty passes, several of them floating fifty or more yards downfield and nestling gently into receivers' hands. He finished the night with five touchdown passes.

This was Leinart at his best, refusing to lose his poise when the Sooners rushed out to an early 7–0 lead. At that point, the cool junior trotted back in and proceeded to lead the Trojans to a twenty-two-point burst, including one seventy-yard drive in sixty-six withering seconds, that basically put the game away. The final score was 55–19. The toughest thing Leinart had to do all night was react to the joyous USC fans who were chanting at him from the stands during the postgame celebration.

"One more year!" they were yelling. "One more year!"

Leinart stood off to the side later, looked around the Orange Bowl, and smiled. "I'm just excited," he said. "Back-to-back national championship teams. I don't think it can get any better than that." It did get better, though. Leinart came back to join Bush, the new Heisman winner, to take the Trojans through their 12–0 2005 season, surviving several scares, and getting to the BCS Championship Game. The perfect ending would have been another USC rout, but this time Texas and Vince Young decided to have none of that.

In one of the greatest Rose Bowl games in the history of that classic event, the Trojans came up inches short on a crucial fourth and two in the fourth quarter, and Young rallied the Longhorns from a twelve-point deficit to win, 41–38. Leinart played brilliantly, especially in a second half that saw him go sixteen of nineteen for 218 yards, leading his team to twenty-eight points in the final two periods. But all great streaks have to come to an end sometime, and after thirty-four remarkable victories in a row, USC's time had come.

Reflecting on it later, it was clear that in the overall scheme, nothing could take away from Leinart's accomplishments. He went 37–2 in his Trojan career, losing both games by only three points. In his three BCS bowl-game appearances, all played with national championship connotations, his final combined numbers were: seventy completions in 109 attempts for 1,024 yards, with nine touchdowns and one interception. He was a three-time All-American, a Heisman Trophy winner, one of the great quarterbacks in the history of college football, and, as a high first-round draft pick, he was destined to be one of the more celebrated rookies in the NFL this fall. Back home in Orange County, they would have to build a new room onto their house if they wanted to hold his huge collection of trophies and plaques.

All of which only proves Linda Leinart was right all along about her strong, tough-minded son.

Everything he touches really does turn to gold.

Every time he touches the ball, you hold your breath.
DICK KOETTER
Arizona State coach

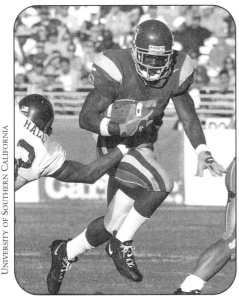

UNIVERSITY OF SOUTHERN CALIFORNIA

It all started inno-cently enough when this hyper, little eight-year-old paused momentarily from run-ning nonstop around the house in San Diego to ask his mother, Denise, a deputy sheriff at a nearby detention facil-ity, if he could sign up to play Pop Warner football. She said no. He was too young, and she didn't want him to be injured.

"So, a year later, he asked me to talk her into it," says Lamar Griffin, Reggie Bush's step-father. "I managed to do that, and then I took him to his first game. I knew he had some talent. He was always very hyper as a little boy, and he looked like he was pretty quick and all. But they lined him up at tailback and pitched the ball to him on the first play, and WOW!"

Wow! is a good word to use for Reggie Bush. Make sure to include the exclamation mark. Even throw a couple more on there, if you want. "Reggie just took off on that first play and ran all the way for a touchdown," says Griffin, a high school security officer. "I think he wound up with, like, 280 yards and three or four touchdowns. In his third game, he had eight touchdowns and 544 yards. I guess I knew then. He was just blessed. God blessed him with a gift."

It has been a gift that just keeps on giving, first to Helix High, where he became one of the most highly sought recruits in the country by rushing for 1,691 yards and twenty-seven touchdowns as a senior, despite missing four games with a broken wrist. Then to USC, where he quickly established himself as the most exciting player on the planet and maybe the most exciting ever to perform at an institution famous for grinding out fabulous tailbacks.

Trying to describe Reggie Bush is like trying to describe some rare gem twinkling in well-protected case in a museum. What he does is so unique, so breathtaking, it's difficult to put into words. There have been plenty of great running backs in the past fifty years, plenty of athletes who have showcased blurring speed and wonderful moves. But there have been none like Reggie. What he does is transcendent. Others run and then slow down to make their cuts. He seems to run and cut all at the same eye-blinking speed.

You want to compare him to somebody, but you can't. He's not as tall as Gale Sayers, but he's quicker. He's not as thick as LaDainian Tomlinson, but he's faster. He can remind you of Barry Sanders here and Marshall Faulk there. But if you're searching for a perfect fit, you won't find one. This is a once-in-a-lifetime kind of offensive player, a young man with the skill, the work ethic, and the confidence to become an all-time great.

"At nine, he came up to me and said, 'Dad, one day I might play in the NFL,'" says Griffin, whom Reggie considers his father. His birth father left the family when Reggie was an infant. "Then, another day when he was about thirteen or fourteen years old," Griffin says, "he came up to me again. 'Dad,' he said, 'one day you're never going to have to worry about money again.' It's like he had a sense of what was going to happen. Like he knew."

Pretty soon, everybody would know. What USC found out, first and foremost, is that it was lucky to have him. Bush had been impressed with Ty Willingham, then the Notre Dame coach, and was definitely leaning toward attending school in South Bend at one point. But he didn't like the cold weather or the fact it was so far from home, and while he wasn't particularly interested in USC originally, that changed when he came out and talked to Pete Carroll and watched the team practice.

"They worked so hard," Bush says. "That really impressed me." That's the thing with Reggie. He always has wanted to work hard. He always has wanted to be pushed. So he signed with the Trojans and walked out for his first day of spring practice amid four or five other tailbacks, almost all of whom could have started for most schools in the country. That's the other thing about USC. You can't go there unless you have supreme confidence in your own ability.

Bush's confidence was tested his first day of fall practice as a college football player. When he strolled through the gates that afternoon, everybody watched him, everybody whispered about him. Now he needed to prove his reputation was warranted. "I just wanted to go out and do the best I could," he says, "but yeah, I was pretty excited about it." By all accounts, what happened that day rivaled what occurred some forty years earlier, when O. J. Simpson put on such a show at his first practice that old-time Trojan followers can still talk about it for days. Bush must have been the same way.

"You almost couldn't believe it," says Norm Chow, the noted offensive coordinator who has since moved to the NFL Tennessee Titans. "The quickness Reggie had, the way he got through the smallest holes. That day, he was running over here and there was nothing there, so he suddenly pops out, reverses his field, and he's running away from everybody. He brings things to the table that are unique. I knew then this kid could be special, really special."

At talent- laden USC, Bush didn't start as a freshman. But Carroll knew what he had and began slipping him into games as much as possible. The highlight came at Notre Dame, the school that almost had lured Reggie away. In a 45–14 Trojans rout, Bush still managed to be the most exciting player on the field, busting one run for fifty-eight yards, then circling out of the backfield with some poor, slow-footed linebacker covering him, to catch another pass for thirty-eight yards. He touched the ball seven times that crisp, fall afternoon in Indiana and gained 127 yards. Afterward, he beamed in the visiting locker room.

"That was fun," he said. "I have to admit, I got a little excited when I saw a linebacker covering me on that pass." That freshman season, he ran for 521 yards on ninety carries, averaging 5.8 yards, and caught fifteen passes for another 314 yards, averaging 20.9 a catch. He scored eight touchdowns, including one on a punt return, and had no fewer than twenty-four plays of twenty-plus yards to make all the Freshman All-America teams.

That, of course, was just the beginning. Bush opened his sophomore season by preventing the No. 1-rated Trojans from suffering a shocking upset against eighteen-point underdog Virginia Tech in Landover, Maryland. Anyone who knew anything about Frank Beamer, the underrated Tech coach, realized USC might have a difficult evening. But no one thought it would be this tough. If not for Reggie, shaking free to catch touchdown passes of fifty-three, thirty-five, and twenty-nine yards from Matt Leinart, the season could have turned sour before it really got started. As it was, the Trojans escaped with a 24–13 victory.

It was a game that set the tone for Bush, who produced big plays every time USC was in danger of losing a winning streak that was beginning to grow to impressive proportions. When Stanford piled up a surprisingly large lead in Palo Alto, Reggie produced 280 all-purpose yards and a thirty-three-yard mind-blower of a punt return to set up the winning score in a 31–28 thriller. Then, at Oregon State on a cold November night, Bush came sprinting out of the gathering fog, almost like some kind of apparition, to run through the mist and most of the Beavers' defense on a jaw-dropping sixty-five-yard, fourth-quarter punt return to help Carroll's team overcome a 13–0 deficit and again survive, 28–20.

Bush finished the year with 980 yards rushing, 509 receiving and 913 more yards on kick returns, all resulting in fifteen touchdowns and who knows how many highlight reels. He was an All-American and finished fifth in the Heisman Trophy voting won by his teammate, Leinart, before both of them combined to help bury Oklahoma, 55–19, in the Orange Bowl to give the Trojans their second consecutive national championship.

Bush even traveled to New York with Leinart as an invited guest and got to take in the impressive ceremony first hand. When Leinart was announced the winner, the first thing he did was wrap his arms around Reggie, who was sitting right next to him, hugging him and thanking him. Later, Bush was asked about the experience. "It was great," he said. "I plan to be back there next year."

So, it was no surprise that the Heisman finalist would become the Heisman favorite as a junior. Bush seemed to be running free through the broken field of other candidates most of the season, leaving all of them in a cardinal-and-gold vapor trail. He topped it off by rushing for 294 yards and collecting a surreal 513 all-purpose yards to again save USC from a shocking upset, this time against Fresno State, in a game Carroll's team had to hang on to win, 50–42. Bush then rushed for 260 yards, much of it in the first half, in the 66–19 bludgeoning of UCLA.

He finished the season with 1,740 yards rushing and 478 yards receiving and scored nineteen touchdowns. In his two final regular-season games, he had two sixty-five-yard runs and three more for fifty, forty-five, and thirty-five, all from scrimmage. No wonder after the UCLA game, the crowd of 92,000 was chanting "Reg-GIE! . . . Reg-GIE! . . . Reg-GIE!" No wonder football's most exciting back was leading the Trojan band afterward, just like Leinart. No wonder Bush was smiling wider than ever in the locker room later and saying the day was "everything anyone could dream of."

After that, there was no mystery about the Heisman selection, even though Texas's Vince Young also had enjoyed a terrific year. Bush was, well, the runaway winner. Even the Trojans' great tailbacks of the past were impressed. "To me, Reggie is the best game-breaker I've seen in thirty years," said Anthony Davis. "The biggest thing Reggie has going for him is his speed," said Mike Garrett, now the USC athletic director. "He's the fastest running back I've ever seen. O. J. was fast, but you put their times next to each other, and it's like having O. J. and putting boosters on him." Charles White said Bush's best attribute is his versatility. "Playing tailback at USC now is not like it was in my day, when we'd pound, pound, pound," White said. "The game has changed. What makes Reggie so good is he does so many things. He definitely fits this offense. He reminds me of Gale Sayers, the way he can cut on a dime."

Years from now, historians will look back and recall this was the first time since the Glenn Davis-Doc Blanchard Army days in 1945–46 that two Heisman Trophy winners were playing in the same backfield. "It's been an honor to play with him," said Leinart. Bush returned the compliment by saying it has "been a blessing" to play alongside the quarterback. Although the two conspired to produce amazing results, both individually and for the team, they were distinctly different personalities.

Leinart was the glamour boy, the tall, handsome kid everyone in star-conscious Hollywood wanted to be around. He was constantly linked with this actress or that one, he appeared on all the prominent TV shows, and his every move seemed to be charted on the Internet. Bush, with his appealing little-boy smile, was much more private. For a star of his magnitude, very little was known about his personal life. There were never any pictures of him snapped dancing at clubs or newspaper stories about his social life. Quietly, he was dating a schoolteacher, slightly older than he, from a nearby Los Angeles charter school, but the woman's name never found its way into the newspapers.

Leinart stunned everyone in football after winning the Heisman as a junior by announcing he would be back for his senior season at USC, turning his back on a potential $40 million contract as the likely No. 1 pick in the NFL draft. Bush would have a similar press conference but with different results. "I've decided to forgo my senior season and make myself eligible for the NFL draft," he said, knowing he was likely to be among the top two NFL draft picks.

"It was tough. You want to please everybody, but this is something I've dreamed of since back in my Pop Warner days. It's a sad time and a happy time for me. To be able to provide for my family is something I can feel good about." While he was moving on, Reggie didn't miss the opportunity to look back. "I couldn't have asked for a better program to come to," he said. "Everyone has shown me so much love and support. USC is a special place. I'll miss everything about it. These are the best fans in America in my opinion."

And he is the most exciting young football player in America in everyone else's opinion. The plaudits never stopped coming in his spectacular final year at USC. Colorado State coach Sonny Lubick: "The thing that makes him so darned good is he's such a confident young guy and he's never out of the play, no matter how bleak it looks, no matter how much you have him surrounded." Former Trojan defensive lineman Shaun Cody, now with the Detroit Lions: "Practicing against him was great training for us. You want to improve your quickness, try chasing a rabbit around." California head coach Jeff Tedford: "He is so talented that any one-on-one situation, he's going to win. You have to pay attention to where he is." At the end of the season, Carroll might have put it best: "He's such a special player, a once-in-a-lifetime talent. All of us were fortunate to coach and play with Reggie."

There has been much discussion on what kind of back Bush will be in the pros. Some scouts downgrade him a bit by saying they question his ability to run between the tackles. But they don't understand Bush's determination, his almost steel-like will to prove his few critics wrong. "I'm waiting for my chance to be a full-time back," he says, knowing he had to share running back duties at USC with LenDale White, an All-America-caliber runner in his own right. "I think I can run inside in the pros."

He probably can, but his pass-catching ability is more likely to turn him into a Marshall Faulk-type player who is constantly being moved around to create mismatches. "I've told him,

'You're the most valuable guy on the field just by what you create with your presence,'" said Carroll. "The overriding element of his game is, he's just got such fantastic hands. You can look at the speed and all the rest, but few guys catch the ball so well. I'm talking about anybody, not just running backs." If you're expecting Bush to gain 1,500 yards rushing a season, you'll probably be disappointed. He is much more likely to be a 1,000–1,000 type, gaining as much yardage receiving the ball as running it.

Asked if he thought he'd make an impact immediately in the pros, Bush, who doesn't like to make bold statements, said, "I think so. I know there will be pressure. I've dealt with pressure all my life. I'm just going to go out and play my game, be who I am. People ask me if I'm big enough or tough enough or fast enough. Those are all questions I'll have to answer."

He has answered all of them positively up to now, even if his almost fairy-tale college career didn't have a perfect ending. But if Bush's final game at USC left a sour taste in some people's mouths, they don't really get it. Trying to extend their almost unbelievable winning streak to thirty-five games, the Trojans lost to Texas in a 41–38 shootout that always will be remembered as one of the great Rose Bowl games in history. Bush was guilty of the worst mistake of his three years as a Trojan when, after zigzagging thirty-seven yards with a screen pass in the first quarter, he attempted a lateral to a teammate trailing the play. The ball bounced free for a fumble, and Texas recovered it.

It wasn't like Bush didn't do some good things, as well. He scored on a dazzling twenty-six-yard sweep, flying through air in his trademark move into the end zone, and finished the game with 279 all-purpose yards. Texas's Young turned in a virtuoso performance, and there were those screaming that he should have been the Heisman Trophy winner. But college football's most coveted honor is judged across a full season, not by one game, and if offered a full highlight reel of Bush's collection of surreal runs during the year, it would be almost impossible to argue he wasn't deserving of the award.

ESPN certainly thought so. Throughout 2005, it couldn't show enough clips of Bush in action. Not that you can blame the network. Watching Reggie run is like listening to Ray Charles sing or watching Anthony Hopkins act. It is an experience unlike any other in the business. Just think, none of it might have happened if an understanding step-father hadn't listened to the pleas of an excited nine-year-old in San Diego.

"God does things for a reason," says Griffin, who, besides working as a security officer, preaches in a San Diego church. "You just have to pick up on it. My wife and I, we're really proud of Reggie. Not just for all he has done, but because he manages to stay in a humble area. It's funny, I remember, back in that first year of Pee Wee football, the word already was out in our neighborhood. People said, 'You better watch this kid. He might really prove to be something.' You know what? They were right."

Oh boy, were they right.

THE TOP TEN
GAMES

I t has been 118 years since a dozen male students at a school just eight years old gathered to launch the sport of football at the University of Southern California.

Surely, that first contest on November 24, 1888, must rank as a signature event in the school's history, given the enthusiasm with which USC students and fans have embraced the sport. Unfortunately, except for a 16–0 score favoring USC over Alliance A. C., there is no information about that game.

But your humble authors, who have more than eighty years of experience between them covering USC football, have warily dared to select the Trojans' top ten games of all time.

Yes, we know there will be those who will wonder how their favorite game or games could have been forgotten or missed, and they will have every reason to protest. That's the beauty of sports—everyone is an expert.

If you disagree with the authors, put together your own list. But don't expect the authors to be available for debate.

They'll be in hiding.

No. 10
USC 55, Oklahoma 19
Orange Bowl, January 4, 2005

USC LINEBACKER LOFA TATUPU was all over the place, making tackles here, there, and everywhere, and directing his team's defense like a coach on the field.

Sensing that Oklahoma was folding under pressure in the 2005 Orange Bowl game at Pro Player Stadium in Miami, Tatupu helped star Sooner tailback Adrian Peterson to his feet after one play and asked, "Aren't you guys embarrassed, getting your butts kicked by a midget?"

Yes, the Sooners were. As ABC network cameras zoomed in on the Oklahoma bench late in the Sooners' 55–19 loss to the Trojans, end Dan Cody could be heard saying, "I can't wait to get on that red-eye back to Oklahoma."

What was billed as a classic became a classic mismatch, a battle of undefeated teams in the Bowl Championship Series title game, only one was a heavyweight champion and the other a lightweight.

"You could tell early we could do what we did," said USC coach Pete Carroll, whose team recorded its twenty-third consecutive victory. "We've been in that situation so much, our guys are familiar with that feeling."

What the Trojans felt was superiority on offense and defense. Their Heisman Trophy quarterback, Matt Leinart, threw five touchdown passes, and flanker Steve Smith caught an Orange Bowl-record three of them.

On the other side of the ball, USC held Heisman runner-up Adrian Peterson, Oklahoma's highly acclaimed freshman tailback, to a meager eighty-two yards on twenty-five carries. Peterson simply was never a factor, so thoroughly schooled were the Trojans to stop him.

It was obvious Carroll was willing to gamble that Oklahoma quarterback Jason White, the Heisman winner a year earlier, would not beat the Trojans with his arm. White finished with twenty-four completions in thirty-six attempts for 244 yards and two touchdowns, but he also threw three interceptions.

Leinart connected on eighteen of thirty-five passes for 332 yards and was a beneficiary of a great night from his receiving corps of Smith, Dwayne Jarrett, Dominique Byrd, and Reggie Bush. Between them, Smith and Jarrett had 228 yards on twelve receptions for four touchdowns.

"The thing I'm most proud of is the way we answered a lot of questions coming into this season," said Leinart. "People said we were too young and had positions to fill. We had some tough times, but we battled through them."

While Bush was limited to seventy-five yards rushing, LenDale White ignored a lame ankle and ran for 118 yards, decimating the Sooners nearly every time the Trojans needed vital yardage.

Undefeated Auburn, which squeezed past Virginia Tech in the Sugar Bowl, made a lame effort to claim the national title, going so far as to hold a championship parade. But the Trojans' superiority was so clearly demonstrated that Auburn's claim didn't so much as muster weak support. Perhaps bolstering USC's claim over Auburn was the Trojans' 23–0 victory over the Tigers on Auburn's home field to open the 2003 season.

The Trojans got off to a rocky beginning, permitting the Sooners to march ninety-two yards for a touchdown and a 7–0 lead. But Oklahoma's success seemed to awaken USC, the Trojans scoring four times to take a 28–7 lead at the ten-minute mark of the second quarter. The first half concluded with USC in front, 38–10, and the final thirty minutes were merely scrimmage time.

Oklahoma permitted more points, fifty-five, than any Sooner bowl team in the history of the school.

Leinart, who was described as "overrated" in pregame talk by Oklahoma defensive end Larry Birdine, shrugged off trash talk while celebrating with teammates. "I think we proved tonight that we are the No. 1 team in the country without a doubt," said the Heisman Trophy winner. "No doubt."

Defensive end Frostee Rucker volunteered to defend Leinart against Oklahoma trash talk. "They were talking a lot of mess all month," said Rucker. "We heard it."

And answered it.

Carroll admitted the ease with which the Trojans handled the

Sooners was unexpected. "We didn't expect it to be this easy. I was a little surprised."

Oklahoma quarterback White saluted the Trojans for their effort. "They were prepared to play and came out to play, and we didn't," he said. Sooners coach Bob Stoops also hailed the Trojans. "I think they're great, and they sure proved it," he said. "We just got whupped."

USC's victory gave the Trojans their second successive national championship, the eleventh in the school's history, and sent them into the 2005 season with their eyes on a twelfth title that would move them into a tie with Notre Dame.

No. 9
USC 7, Duke 3
Rose Bowl, January 2, 1939

THERE CERTAINLY WAS NO indication from USC's performance in its season opener against Alabama at the L.A. Coliseum that the season would conclude with a game that would be a subject of conversation for many decades.

The Crimson Tide rolled relentlessly over Howard Jones's Trojans in registering a 19–7 victory before 70,000 deeply disappointed fans.

But Jones believed the opening game was an aberration, that this team assembled by such able assistants as Sam Barry, Jeff Cravath, Hobbs Adams, Julie Bescos, and Bob McNeish possessed the ability to achieve greatness.

So, after the Alabama shocker, Jones set about putting the pieces in the right places, an ability for which he was widely known.

Although Amblin' Amby Schindler was somewhat hobbled from a knee injury that kept him out of action for the entire 1937 campaign, Jones still had Grenny Lansdell to fill the key quarterback position, and, buried down on the fourth string, a kid with a rifle arm, Doyle Nave, who longed for an opportunity to throw the football to a fleet end called "Antelope" Al Krueger.

As Jones made some changes and all parts seemed to come together, the Trojans registered six successive victories, including a

14–7 triumph at Ohio State. Only overconfidence could interrupt the string of successes, with Washington upsetting the Trojans, 7–6, at Seattle. But USC bounced back, routing UCLA, 42–7, and defeating Notre Dame, 13–0, before 97,146 at the Coliseum.

With those victories, USC received a Rose Bowl invitation and chose to face Duke, which was unbeaten, untied, and unscored upon. And the Blue Devils had one of the nation's greatest players, halfback Eric "the Red" Tipton.

Duke was not a popular selection among Southern California fans. A Los Angeles sports columnist conducted a poll that showed the public wanted Texas Christian, Tennessee, Duke, and Oklahoma, in that order.

But the show had to go on, and as game went into the final minutes, with the Blue Devils leading, 3–0, on a field goal by Tony Ruffa, those who thought Duke was unworthy of a Rose Bowl invitation were feeling embarrassment. Duke's forward wall, nicknamed the Seven Iron Dukes, encountered little trouble stopping Jones's highly respected running game.

USC manufactured an opportunity when Duke fumbled a punt and the Trojans recovered at the Blue Devils' ten. After three plays, they were still at the ten, where an attempted field goal failed. Duke was unable to get a first down and punted to the USC thirty-nine, and a penalty set the Trojans back another five yards.

Quick action was needed. Lansdell got the Trojans to the thirty-four, at which point, with time running out, Jones sent Nave into the contest. Reports circulated over the years that an assistant seated on the bench faked receiving a call from assistants in the press box asking that Nave be inserted into the game. But this nonsense has been refuted by assistant Julie Bescos, who was in the press box with another assistant, McNeish, after Jones's chief assistant, Sam Barry, had left the press box and gone to the field.

Bescos and McNeish told Barry by phone that they had spotted a weakness in the Duke pass defense and had Barry tell Jones this was the spot for Nave. They also recommended a series of passes to employ.

Nave came through like a champion. Starting from the Duke thirty-four with only two minutes remaining, he threw four strikes, the last a nineteen-yarder to Krueger, who had slipped away from Blue Devils star Tipton.

In one minute and twenty seconds, Nave achieved what had seemed impossible, putting up the first points of the season yielded by the Blue Devils.

A former Jones assistant, Clifton Herd, believed he knew what happened to the Duke defense. "I feel sure neither Wallace Wade nor his players knew very much about Nave," said Herd. "If they had suspected his passing ability, they would have rushed him more than they did. It looked to me as if Wade merely spread his defense, figuring that there wouldn't be time for the Trojans to score by running the ball. He wanted to be sure to pick up the receiver somewhere."

Nave achieved instant fame with his performance. The mayor of Gordo, Alabama, sent him an authenticated appointment as acting mayor of that city for January 16, 1939. Letters from young ladies came from Omaha, Nebraska, and Fairbanks, Pennsylvania, and all points north, south, east, and west.

And, although Nave had not played the required number of minutes to win a varsity monogram, he was awarded one anyway. The team had a rule that only seniors could receive game balls.

Those teammates remaining on the 1939 Trojans took care of that shortcoming. In the first game the following season, when Nave was a senior, he was awarded a game ball. And the school gave him a lifetime pass, an honor reserved for players who had lettered all three years of their varsity careers.

A reserve who performed like a champion in the clutch remains one of USC's all-time football heroes.

No. 8
USC 18, Ohio State 17
Rose Bowl, January 1, 1975

USC'S 1974 FOOTBALL SEASON could not have begun more horrendously nor ended with such wildly soaring success.

In the season opener at Arkansas at War Memorial Stadium in

Little Rock, where USC had launched a national championship season two years earlier, the Trojans were all thumbs and left feet.

Except for Anthony Davis's kickoff return for a touchdown, the Trojans were so exasperatingly awful that coach John McKay came out of a 22–7 loss to the Razorbacks so angry with quarterback Pat Haden's four interceptions that he severely restricted Haden's ration of passes until late in the season. With Haden under wraps, the Trojans stumbled along, suffering a surprising 15–15 tie with California at the Coliseum in early November. At this point, McKay began going more often to Haden and his two ace receivers, J. K. McKay and Shelton Diggs.

Re-energized, the Trojans began to look like the champions McKay thought they would be when the season began. They polished off Stanford, Washington, and UCLA in impressive fashion, then staged a memorable comeback against Notre Dame, a game in which the Trojans rallied from a 24–0 deficit to score fifty-five points in less than seventeen minutes for a 55–24 triumph.

Their stature restored, the fifth-ranked Trojans prepared to battle third-ranked Ohio State in the 1975 Rose Bowl, which turned out to be coach John McKay's final appearance at the Pasadena stadium.

Haden recalls the circumstances. "In those days, the Rose Bowl had an ambiance and a reputation high above the other bowl games," he says. "It was the most special game on January first, more than the Orange Bowl, more than the Sugar Bowl. It meant a lot to us at USC. If you grew up in Southern California watching the game, as I did, you wanted to participate in it."

Haden got his second Rose Bowl starting assignment in two years, the first a 42–21 loss to Ohio State the previous January 1. This time he intended to succeed and chase away memories of the season opener in Little Rock.

USC had a difficult time in the first half, faced as they were by one of the best defenses in the nation, led by a pair of All-Americans, defensive back Neil Colzie and defensive end Van Ness DeCree. The Buckeyes also boasted Heisman Trophy winner Archie Griffin and a fullback, Pete Johnson, capable of plowing through a wall.

USC could manage only a field goal in the first half, its offense sustaining a terrible blow when tailback Anthony Davis, second to

Griffin in the Heisman balloting, was knocked out of the game with a rib injury. The Buckeyes scored a touchdown for a 7–3 half-time advantage.

The score remained 7–3 until the fourth quarter, when Haden fired a nine-yard touchdown pass to tight end Jim Obradovich that put USC in front, 10–7. But Ohio State received the ensuing kickoff and, starting from its eighteen, drove eighty-two yards for a touch-down that gave the Buckeyes a 14–10 edge, then added a field goal three minutes later to go in front, 17–10.

The Trojans had six minutes and thirty-eight seconds to reassemble and make a run at the Buckeyes. Allen Carter, who replaced the injured Davis at tailback, was the driving force as the Trojans began their march at the USC seventeen. They moved to the Ohio State thirty-nine, where they faced a critical fourth and one.

"I remember Allen Carter fighting, scratching his way for ten yards to get us that first down," says Haden. Ricky Bell gained six yards to the Ohio State forty-five, then in successive carries, Carter made two, one, and four yards to get the ball to the Buckeyes' thirty-eight.

J. K. McKay was on the sideline, talking to his father, who sug-gested a pass into the right corner of the end zone. "I'm not sure I can get away from Colzie," he told his father. The play was called anyway, and Haden threw an arching thirty-eight-yard pass that nes-tled neatly into McKay's arms for a touchdown that left the Trojans trailing, 17–16.

There was never any doubt what McKay, the coach, was going to do. He had always said "a tie is like kissing your sister," and he lost the 1967 Rose Bowl game to Purdue when he failed on a two-point conversion. So, McKay opted for a rollout play, which left Haden with the option of running or passing to his longtime teammate (high school and college) J. K. McKay.

McKay wasn't open, and Haden was running toward the goal line when he spotted Diggs open in the end zone. Haden threw and Diggs made a diving catch for an 18–17 lead.

There were still more then two minutes remaining in the game, and the Buckeyes reached the USC forty-five, where Tom Skladany's six-two-yard field goal fell short as time expired.

Game, set, national championship for USC.

No. 7
USC 17, Ohio State 16
Rose Bowl, January 1, 1980

CHARLIE WHITE HAD BEEN there before. As a freshman, he expected to spend a leisurely afternoon at the 1977 Rose Bowl while USC's All-America tailback, Ricky Bell, bulled his way through the Michigan Wolverines. Instead, Bell sustained a head injury early in the game, and White ran for 122 yards as the Trojans prevailed, 14–6.

As a junior, again facing Michigan, he was involved in a controversial play in which he fumbled, but officials erred in ruling he crossed the goal line before the bobble. USC won, 17–10.

As a senior, White was already the 1979 Heisman Trophy winner as USC met Ohio State in the 1980 Rose Bowl, and it evolved into one of White's most spectacular performances in cardinal and gold.

Ohio State was undefeated and ranked No. 1 in the nation going into the bowl game, and USC, a midseason tie with Stanford marring its record, held a No. 3 ranking. To the winner would likely go the national championship.

Making this contest all the more appealing was the reputation both schools had for featuring smashmouth football. Hi-diddle-diddle, right-up-the-middle. Yet each team also possessed quarterbacks rated among the elite of the nation, Paul McDonald of USC and Art Schlichter of Ohio State.

Pasadena had held an annual Rose Bowl game since 1902, except for a few years when ostrich races were featured, but never had pregame speculation produced enough hot air to fly a balloon, as this one did.

That the coaches, John Robinson of USC and Earle Bruce of Ohio State, were determined to outsmart themselves was established early. On USC's sixth play, McDonald threw a pass that was intercepted by the Buckeyes at their forty. Ohio State returned the favor on its first play, Schlichter's pass being picked off by USC's Herb Ward at the Buckeye forty-eight.

Late in the first quarter, the Trojans drove thirty-six yards, White gaining fifteen on the ground, to move kicker Eric Hipp into position for a forty-one-yard field goal that put USC in front, 3–0.

Early in the second quarter, Ronnie Lott recovered an Ohio State fumble at the USC thirty-three. Five plays later, McDonald hurled a magnificent pass that Kevin Williams hauled in just short of the goal and ran in for a fifty-three-yard touchdown. Hipp's kick gave USC a 10–0 edge.

McDonald has never let Ohio State's secondary coach forget what occurred. The Buckeye coaching victim? A fellow named Pete Carroll.

Late in the first quarter, Ohio State moved into scoring position with a first down at the USC two. But a great USC defensive stand, led by lineman Myron Lapka, kept the Buckeyes out of the end zone. Late in the second quarter, Ohio State moved into position for a thirty-five-yard field goal by Vlade Janakievski that reduced USC's lead to 10–3, but the Buckeyes weren't done. After recovering a White fumble at the Ohio State twenty, the Buckeyes scored in three plays, the touchdown coming on a sixty-seven-yard pass from Schlichter to Gary Williams. Halftime score: USC 10, Ohio State 10.

Ohio State took the second-half kickoff and marched to a position where Janakievski was able to kick a thirty-seven-yard field goal that put the Buckeyes in front, 13–10.

The Trojans moved downfield following the next kickoff, going to the Ohio State twenty-five, where Hipp missed a thirty-two-yard field goal. But the play was nullified by a penalty for roughing the kicker. The Trojans moved to the six, where McDonald passed to tight end James Hunter at the one, but offensive pass interference in the end zone resulted in a touchback that gave Ohio State possession of the ball.

After the Trojans missed a thirty-nine-yard field goal attempt early in the fourth quarter, Ohio State moved to the USC seven, largely on Schlichter's passing, where Janakievski kicked a twenty-four-yard field goal for a 16–10 Ohio State lead.

It was time for the Heisman Trophy winner to take over, and White moved the Trojans to the Buckeye twenty-four where, strangely, USC's Robinson called three consecutive passes, all of which failed, the ball going over to Ohio State.

The next time, USC gained possession at the USC seventeen with 5:31 remaining, and Robinson wisely turned the ball over to his standout tailback.

White, operating behind one of the most talented offensive lines the school ever fielded, went for thirty-two yards on the first play. Then he sailed through the Buckeyes for twenty-eight before Michael Hayes ran for seven yards and Marcus Allen for five. By this point, the Trojans were at the Ohio State eleven-yard line.

Robinson called for the obvious—White for three, White for five, White for two, and White for the final yard and a touchdown with 1:32 remaining. Hipp's kick won it, 17–16.

It was an amazing performance by White and an equally amazing demonstration of power blocking by his offensive line. White went seventy yards in six carries, tallying 247 for the day in thirty-nine rushing attempts.

"Toughest guy I've ever been around," said Robinson.

Who would argue?

No. 6
USC 20, Notre Dame 17
Los Angeles Coliseum, November 28, 1964

GRIM ISN'T A STRONG enough word to describe USC's outlook at half-time of its 1964 game against rival Notre Dame at the L.A. Coliseum.

John McKay's Trojans were trailing, 17–0, and nothing that occurred in the first thirty minutes of action lent any hope that they might be able to mount a comeback against the Fighting Irish.

Even a few days before the game, McKay, not usually given to pessimism, said after viewing film of Notre Dame's contest against Stanford he had decided the Fighting Irish "can't be beaten."

Almost everyone agreed, including oddsmakers, who installed the top-ranked and undefeated Fighting Irish as fourteen-point favorites to win the game and claim the national championship in coach Ara Parseghian's first season as head coach. "We can't run inside Notre Dame's tackles because they're too big. No team has been able to block them, and we don't have the size to handle them," McKay said. "I've decided, if we play our very best and make no mistakes whatsoever, we will definitely make a first down."

The day had gotten off to a shattering start. At the team's pregame brunch, linebacker Ernie Pye accidentally walked through a plate glass window in the dining room. Not a major injury, but Pye would be unable to play, another nail in the USC coffin.

Given all that happened that morning and in the first thirty minutes, McKay was amazingly calm when he entered the locker room to address his troops. "Our game plan is working well," he said. "Just keep pushing, and we'll get some points."

He outlined a defense the Trojans would employ in the second half to contain Notre Dame quarterback John Huarte, who would go on to win the 1964 Heisman Trophy. In the first half, Huarte completed eleven of fifteen passes for 176 yards, including one touchdown throw to end Jack Snow. "We need to put some pressure on them," McKay said.

The USC coach had noted that, despite his ominous pregame predictions, the Trojans had been able to run the ball against the Irish, but not enough to get any points. However, halfbacks Mike Garrett and Ron Heller were imposing threats. Thus, with Notre Dame forced to concentrate on Garrett and Heller, the way was open for quarterback Craig Fertig's attack through the air. Early in the third quarter, Fertig took the Trojans down the field, and Garrett ran the ball in as USC sliced Notre Dame's margin to 17–7.

One Notre Dame scoring bid was halted by a lost fumble, and a touchdown was lost when Notre Dame was called for holding on a scoring run from the one. The lost touchdown seemed to turn the game around. USC took control with an eighty-two-yard march on Fertig's passing, end Fred Hill getting a touchdown toss that narrowed Notre Dame's lead to 17–14.

At that point, McKay would say later, "I knew we had them because the momentum had swung our way." With the Coliseum crowd roaring its appreciation, the Trojan defense clamped down on Huarte, and Notre Dame was forced to punt. Garrett gave USC a mighty boost by returning the punt eighteen yards to the Notre Dame thirty-five. The Trojans had two minutes and ten seconds to negotiate the remaining distance. After a run failed to gain, Fertig hit

Hill on a pass to the Notre Dame seventeen, sending the crowd of 83,840 into a mighty roar. After a timeout, Fertig threw a pass into the flat that gained two to the fifteen. On the next play, Fertig again connected with Hill for what appeared to be a touchdown, but an official ruled the USC receiver was out of bounds.

Only a minute and forty-three seconds remained as flanker Rod Sherman conferred with McKay on the sideline. "I think Eighty-four-Z Delay will work," Sherman said. McKay agreed, and Sherman carried the message to Fertig. Sherman split to the left, sprinted ahead for a few steps at the snap of the ball, then cut sharply across the middle. Fertig's pass hit Sherman, as the Trojan flanker was pulling away from Fighting Irish defender Tony Carey, for a fifteen-yard reception and a touchdown that gave USC a 20–17 victory.

Fertig didn't see the reception. He was flat on his back after a crushing hit by Notre Dame lineman Alan Page. "But when I heard the roar of the crowd, I knew something good had happened," says Fertig.

Over the years, Sherman and Fertig have carried on a running gag about the play. "Perfect pass," says Fertig. Uh, not according to Sherman. "I had to make a leaping, stretching catch," he says.

Unfortunately, the day was not a complete conquest. The Trojans, believing their victory over the nation's No. 1-ranked team would get them a Rose Bowl bid, learned at a victory party that Oregon State had been selected to represent the West Coast.

Still, it was one of the more stirring victories in the history of USC football.

No. 5
Texas 41, USC 38
Rose Bowl, January 3, 2006

AFTER THE FIRST TWO USC football games of the 2005 season, the chances of anyone depriving the Trojans of their third consecutive national championship appeared to be slimmer than a hobo's resumé.

In the season opener, after a slow first half, Hawaii was blown away, 63–17, and the following week a Southeastern Conference opponent, Arkansas, was embarrassed, 70–17.

The Trojans looked so powerful, so unworldly worthy, that Arkansas defensive coordinator Reggie Herring shook his head and felt compelled to state, "They're the best team I've ever seen. They need to hurry up and graduate, because if they don't, they're going to ruin college football."

But in Austin, Texas, with considerably less fanfare, Mack Brown's Longhorns also were doing nasty things to opponents. They opened with a 60–3 triumph over Louisiana Lafayette and the following week went into Ohio State and surprised the Buckeyes, 25–22, shooting the Longhorns into second place behind USC in wire-service polls.

The Trojans struggled at times while getting through a twelve-game schedule unbeaten and extending their winning streak to thirty-four games, while the Longhorns had only an occasional blip on their record and never were in real danger of losing.

So, the BCS Championship Game on January 4, 2006, at the Rose Bowl in Pasadena wound up with the perfect matchup—the nation's last two undefeated teams and two high-powered offenses averaging about fifty points per game.

And one team, USC, had two Heisman Trophy winners, quarterback Matt Leinart from 2004 and tailback Reggie Bush from 2005, while the other side had a quarterback, Vince Young, who thought he should been chosen ahead of Bush.

The year's "game of the century"? Without question.

Only a minute and twenty-one seconds had elapsed when USC got its first break, recovering a fumble at the Texas forty-six. It took the Trojans just five plays to score, with tailback LenDale White crashing over from the four and placekicker Mario Danelo giving them a 7–0 lead.

It appeared USC was on its way to another score midway in the first period, but Leinart failed to convert a first down on a sneak at the Texas seventeen.

On the strangest play of the game, Bush took a screen pass for thirty-seven yards, then inexplicably attempted a lateral to Brad Walker, who couldn't handle it. Texas recovered at its own forty-five.

At this point, as quarterback Young began to demonstrate his wondrous ability to run and pass, the Longhorns kicked a field goal early in the second period to cut USC's lead to 7–3. Six minutes later, Texas scored its first touchdown on a play on which Young ran for ten yards and one of his knees appeared to touch the ground, but he lateraled to Selvin Young, who ran the last twelve yards for a touchdown that put Texas ahead, 9–7, the Longhorns missing the extra-point attempt. Texas added a touchdown two minutes later, Young running and passing the Longhorns into position for Ramonce Taylor to run thirty yards for a touchdown and a 16–7 lead.

With two seconds remaining in the first half, Danelo kicked a forty-three-yard field goal at cut Texas's lead to 16–10. The Trojans were smoking when they came out for the second half, moving sixty-two yards for a touchdown in seven plays, with White scoring from the three and Danelo adding a point that put the Trojans in front, 17–16.

The teams traded touchdowns, and USC was in front, 24–23, heading into the final period.

The Trojans took a 31–23 lead on the first series of the final quarter, Texas kicked a field goal, and Leinart threw a twenty-two-yard scoring pass to Dwayne Jarrett to build USC's lead to 38–26 with 8:46 remaining.

But Young, turning in one of the greatest individual performances imaginable, wouldn't let the Longhorns lose. In eight plays, he either ran or passed as Texas went sixty-nine yards to cut USC's lead to 38–33, but the big plays remained.

Trying to hang on, USC drove twenty-four yards to the Texas forty-five, where the Trojans gambled on fourth and two, and failed. White was stopped three inches short of a first down, and possession of the ball went to Texas with 2:09 remaining.

"We didn't want them to get the ball again," USC coach Pete Carroll explained.

With good reason. Young was unstoppable, as he demonstrated in the final two minutes. Starting from the Texas forty-four, he passed and ran the Longhorns to the USC eight, where the Texans took a timeout.

The Texas quarterback's pass was knocked down in the end zone, but on the next play, Young ran a quarterback draw into the end zone for the winning score with nineteen seconds remaining. The Longhorns added a two-point conversion to seal a 41–38 victory.

Two wonderful college football teams, possibly one of the greatest games in history and an individual performance by Vince Young that will be long remembered.

No. 4
USC 16, Notre Dame 14
Notre Dame Stadium, November 21, 1931

HOWARD JONES MADE FEW demands during fifteen seasons as the "Headman" of USC football.

But this would be a special occasion, USC's first visit to South Bend and the new Notre Dame Stadium, and eight months ahead of the game, Jones was already taking care of details for the 1931 season.

He possessed high expectations for his 1931 team, and he also was bothered by the four losses in five games he had sustained since USC's series with Notre Dame began in 1926. This time, the Headman was taking no chances.

Entering the office of Arnold Eddy, general manager of the Associated Students of USC, Jones said, "I'd like to have a special train to Notre Dame in November. We went east in 1927 and 1929 on regularly scheduled trains and found that a four-day train ride is too long a time without a workout. Schedule a special train for us so we can stop one afternoon for a workout in Hutchinson, Kansas."

Eddy explained to Jones that to make costs practicable, the train would have to include boosters, many of whom would want an occasional social drink, something the teetotalling coach abhorred.

"Well, I certainly need that train, and I'll tell you what we can do. I'll put my boys in the front two cars, and then we'll have a movie car, the diner, and the club car, and we'll put all your 'drunks' on the rear of the train."

Thus was inaugurated the first of the Trojan Specials, which became a popular form of transportation for players and fans for thirty-five years.

Jones conducted a workout in Tucson, instead of Hutchinson, and believed his team was amply prepared for the once-tied but undefeated Fighting Irish. But in front of a capacity crowd of 50,731, the Trojans began the game as though they were still practicing in Tucson.

When the third quarter closed, USC trailed, 14–0, and nothing was going its way. Brilliant sophomore Orv Mohler came on to replace injured Jim Musick, and he seemed to provide the needed spark, along with Gus Shaver and Ray Sparling.

Said *Los Angeles Times* writer Braven Dyer: "No team in modern football history ever faced a more hopeless situation and worked out of it the way the Trojans did this afternoon."

Mohler and Shaver led the way, with help from Sparling, and the Trojans scored their first touchdown, Shaver going the last yard. Johnny Baker's conversion was blocked, but that didn't discourage Jones's team. The Trojans traveled fifty-seven yards, Mohler executing a beautiful lateral to Shaver for the last ten. Baker's kick cut Notre Dame's edge to 14–13.

With four minutes remaining, USC went on offense seventy-three yards away from the Notre Dame goal. A thirty-two-yard Shaver-to-Sparling pass moved the Trojans to the Notre Dame forty, and they steadily inched their way into position for Baker to attempt a thirty-three-yard field goal.

Boom! Baker's kick sailed right down the middle of the goal posts with one minute remaining. Final score: USC 16, Notre Dame 14, marking the end of a twenty-six-game Fighting Irish unbeaten streak.

The best was yet to come. After stopping in Chicago, where team members decked themselves out in derby hats, the Victory Special headed for Los Angeles, where it arrived on Wednesday to a celebration, the likes of which the City of Angels had never witnessed.

More than 300,000 fans crowded the downtown for a parade led by USC students, and a reception was held on the steps of City Hall. It was days before the city returned to normal. Films of the game were shown at Loew's State Theater in downtown Los Angeles. There were continuous showings, all before capacity audiences. The city simply could not get enough of the Trojans, who had placed themselves in position to capture another national championship and spread the gospel of West Coast football.

Jones again had displayed a wisdom that had taken the Trojans from an average college football team to one of the nation's most celebrated aggregations. National magazines chronicled USC's successful foray into Notre Dame, declaring that a new center of power was developing in college football.

Indeed, it was. Jones had guessed correctly in choosing a mode of travel that gave the Trojans a better chance of victory, and he wasn't going to let his team get carried away with its triumph over the Fighting Irish.

He had an extra week to prepare for Washington, which USC dispatched, 44–7, and then concluded the regular season with a 60–0 breeze against Georgia.

The Headman also had the Trojans ready for Bernie Bierman's tough Tulane team in the Rose Bowl, USC winning, 21–12.

As expected, USC was declared national champion for the 1931, and followed with another national title in 1932.

The Headman was on a roll.

No. 3
USC 34, Notre Dame 31
Notre Dame Stadium, October 15, 2005

MATT LEINART WAS NO rookie quarterback being tested under fire for the first time.

This was his fifth season with USC's football team and his third as the Trojans' starting quarterback, and he had led his team to twenty-seven consecutive victories going into this October 15, 2005, game at Notre Dame Stadium. He also was the reigning Heisman Trophy winner and possessor of gaudy passing statistics.

But nothing in Leinart's past, high school or college, had prepared him for this moment—USC trailing, 31–28, third and nineteen at the Trojans' sixteen, with 1:44 remaining on the clock.

This was a point at which those who can produce separate themselves from those who can't. And Leinart is among those who can, as he demonstrated with a ten-yard pass to Reggie Bush that left USC facing fourth and nine at the twenty-six. USC called its last timeout.

Students in the Notre Dame section already were beginning to edge toward the field as Leinart stooped under center, hoping to preserve a winning streak and a chance to continue toward a third successive national championship.

Few among those at Notre Dame Stadium or watching on television around the nation and some parts of the world dared to breathe as the Trojans lined up at their twenty-six-yard line.

Radio broadcaster Pete Arbogast picks up the action:

> "Jarrett to the left, Smith and McFoy to the right. Bush is the tailback, Ryan Kalil the center . . . waiting for the call from Matt Leinart. The lines are set. Leinart changes at the line. Gets the snap, drops to pass, throws, looking for Jarrett. *It's caught by Jarrett at the forty! Thirty-five, thirty! Twenty-five, twenty! Tackled from behind at the fifteen, maybe the thirteen-yard line! I don't believe it!*"

Yes, there are miracles, and this was one of them. Sixty-one yards and a first down at the Notre Dame thirteen. Suddenly, the Trojans were in position to win, or at least get a field goal and force a tie and overtime

On first down, Leinart threw an incomplete pass. Bush followed with a run of six yards to the seven, then got five yards and a first down at the two. On the next play, Leinart dropped back to pass, swung left when he saw no one open, and took off for the goal line. He was crushed by Notre Dame safety Tom Zbikowski short of the goal, and the ball few out of bounds at the one with seven seconds remaining.

Inexplicably, the stadium clock continued to run, despite signals by the officials for stoppage. When it reached zero, Notre Dame coach Charlie Weis raised both hands in a sign of victory and students surged onto the field to embrace their players.

Finally, order was restored, students returned to their seats, and Weis, who had started across the field when the clock ran out, retreated toward the Notre Dame sideline, but never made it all the way to that spot.

He watched as the Trojans lined up for their next play, which might be an attempt to score a touchdown or a spiked ball that would allow them to try a game-tying field goal.

What would it be? USC coach Pete Carroll gave Leinart the option of going for a touchdown, but Carroll motioned for the ball to be spiked in an attempt to fool the Fighting Irish.

Leinart decided to try a sneak for a touchdown, then saw Notre Dame packing the area in front of him with defenders. He turned to Bush for help in the decision. "Go for it, dude," said Bush.

Leinart tried to surge ahead with the ball, but his path was blocked and he slid to his left, where Bush, noting the struggle his quarterback was having, gave him a shove that helped Leinart back into the end zone for the winning touchdown with three seconds left.

The Trojans received a fifteen-yard penalty for excessive celebration, and Mario Danelo missed the conversion attempt. Score: USC 34, Notre Dame 31.

But who cared? Well, Leinart, for one. He was on the bench, apparently weeping after enduring such pressure and suspense.

"I was in shock," Leinart says. "I didn't want to celebrate till the clock hit zero because who knows what can happen in three seconds. I imagine this will go down as one of the greatest games ever played."

What of the fourth-and-nine pass that Jarrett advanced sixty-one yards to the Notre Dame 13?

"Dwayne made a great move on the defensive back," Leinhart says, "and the ball just fit in there perfectly, and he just took off and did the rest. I actually thought I underthrew the ball."

He didn't—and USC's win streak was preserved.

No. 2
USC 55, Notre Dame 24
Los Angeles Coliseum, November 30, 1974

DID NOTRE DAME COACH Ara Parseghian intend to direct a second-half kickoff to USC's Anthony Davis, or didn't he?

This is a key question, since Davis had returned two kickoffs for touchdowns during his six-touchdown romp against the Fighting

Irish two years earlier at the L.A. Coliseum, and had five career kick-off touchdown returns going into the November 30, 1974, game between USC and Notre Dame.

After the game, after Davis ran back the kickoff 102 yards for a touchdown that set off a sixteen-minute, forty-nine-point explosion that propelled USC to a 55–24 victory, the Notre Dame coach waffled.

At first he indicated his kicker had been directed not to give Davis a clean chance for a runback. The fact that Notre Dame kicker Pat McLaughlin shanked his first try out of bounds would indicate Parseghian was playing it safe.

But after a five-yard penalty, McLaughlin boomed the next kick down the middle to Davis, who had seen few kickoffs come his way since returning one for a touchdown in USC's season-opening game at Arkansas.

Davis did what came naturally, following his wedge of Dave Farmer, Ricky Bell, and Mosi Tatupu until they opened a seam for him to break into the clear.

As Davis recalls, he caught Parseghian's eye as he ran past the Notre Dame bench on his way to a touchdown.

Responding after the game to another query about the kickoff, Parseghian said he thought McLaughlin would kick the ball deep enough into the end zone to discourage a return attempt.

And, in a conversation with Davis and several other football people at a 2005 College Football Hall of Fame dinner in New York, Parseghian indicated his directive was for the kicker to keep the ball away from Davis. "Everybody laughed when he said that," says Davis, whose eleven touchdowns in three games against the Fighting Irish earned him the nickname "Notre Dame Killer."

He had six touchdowns in 1972 during a 45–23 romp by USC's national championship team, one in Notre Dame's 23–14 victory at South Bend in 1973, and four on that rock 'n' roll afternoon in 1974.

Davis notes that one member of the Notre Dame team yelled at him as he headed out of the Coliseum tunnel after the halftime break to warn him the kickoff was coming his way.

Whatever Parseghian's decision, that afternoon definitely wasn't the era of Ara.

In fact, says Tom Pagna, Parseghian's chief assistant, "It was such an emotional shock. We were ahead by 24–0, but, you know, we've done things like that to other teams. We were never quite sure how or why it happened."

Farmer, a fullback who was at the point of the wedge as Davis swept upfield from the end zone, remembers the moment, recalling John McKay's halftime prediction that "A. D. is going to run the kickoff back for a touchdown."

A framed picture above Farmer's desk at his business in Aptos, California, lays out the scene. "It shows the wedge of blockers for A. D. I'm in the front left, and Ricky Bell is to the right. Mosi Tatupu and Bernard Tarver are the other guys at the point of the wedge. I hit a guy off to my left, and Ricky hit a guy off to the right. A. D . slithered through an opening and headed for the left sideline. He went all the way."

Farmer has another picture from this game. "It was a cover picture from Sports Illustrated magazine. It's A. D. scoring on 28 Pitch that put us ahead. I remember just lying on the ground after making a block and hearing the crowd respond to the touchdown. A. D. was doing that thing he did on his knees after scoring. It was dramatic, to say the least. Electrifying. Pure pandemonium."

Counting the touchdown USC managed in the final ten seconds of the first half that trimmed Notre Dame's lead to 24–6, the Trojans scored fifty-five points in sixteen minutes and fifty-four seconds, a remarkable feat considering the No. 5 national ranking of the Fighting Irish and their 9–1 record going into the contest.

Whether this game and his decision on the second-half kickoff caused Parseghian such great anguish he felt he no longer could cope with the pressures of college football isn't known. But Parseghian, a coach who ranks up there with Knute Rockne and Frank Leahy among Notre Dame's great leaders, led the Fighting Irish only one more time, a 13–11 triumph over second-ranked Alabama in the Orange Bowl. He resigned from his Notre Dame position, citing blood-pressure problems, and never again demonstrated any interest in returning to coaching.

Alabama's loss opened the way for USC to claim the national championship when it defeated third-ranked Ohio State in the Rose Bowl.

Hail Ara?

No. 1
USC 21, UCLA 20
Los Angeles Coliseum, November 18, 1967

THIS WAS A COLLEGE football game America had long awaited. No. 1 UCLA vs. No. 4 USC, two schools from the same city. A conference title, Rose Bowl invitation, and a possible national championship at stake. And, furnishing extra appeal, the two leading Heisman Trophy contenders, quarterback Gary Beban of UCLA and tailback O. J. Simpson of USC.

Whenever polls are taken concerning the most exciting game in college football history, this one is always near the top, often at the head of the list. November 18, 1967, a day to remember?

Yes and no. Did the Heisman contenders deliver Heisman-like performances? Without question. Despite suffering from torn rib cartilage, an injury that required periodic time off the field while he was receiving emergency treatment, Beban completed sixteen of twenty-four passes for 301 yards and two touchdowns. He was a champion in every respect, except for an interception that was returned for a touchdown and his inability to escape USC's pursuing defenders, led by end Jimmy Gunn. The Trojans threw him for fifty-nine yards in losses.

Simpson was incomparable, running for touchdowns of thirteen and sixty-four yards, and compiling 177 yards in thirty rushing attempts. His thirteen-yarder was described by esteemed Georgia Tech coach Bobby Dodd as the "greatest I've ever seen." And four decades later, the football world still speaks with awe about Simpson's game-winning sixty-four-yard touchdown.

But these national championship contenders also displayed their erratic sides, perhaps because so much was at stake and the participants had jangled nerves. USC was hopelessly deficient in its passing game. In the first half, the normally steady Steve Sogge threw five passes, completing one for thirteen yards.

Early in the third quarter, USC coach John McKay substituted Toby Page for Sogge at quarterback, ostensibly to juice up the Trojans' aerial game and reduce the heat on Simpson. Ugh. Page threw one pass during his twenty-four minutes in the game and—it was intercepted. Except for the early part of the game, the Bruins' running game was equally inept, as UCLA netted just forty-three rushing yards in sixty minutes.

If you didn't see the game on national television or view it as one of the 90,772 in attendance at the Los Angeles Coliseum, you might surmise it was a dull affair. Not so.

True, when the teams were wobbling around at times in what seemed like a stupor, it was difficult to view the game as a classic. But there were also moments of high drama.

Among those moments:

Midway in the first quarter, UCLA began punching holes in the USC defense with the skill of a safecracker. With Bruins fans roaring, halfback Greg Jones completed an eight-play, forty-seven-yard drive by scoring from the twelve, and Zenon Andrusyshyn, sporting a gold kicking shoe, added the extra point.

On the final play of the first quarter, Beban's pass to the deep left flat was intercepted by Trojan cornerback Pat Cashman, who returned it fifty-five yards for a tying touchdown. Said UCLA coach Tommy Prothro after the game, "I made the call, and it was a terrible call. This was the first time we ever used that play, and it will be the last time."

Early in the second quarter, Andrusyshyn missed a thirty-three-yard field goal, the beginning of a miserable afternoon for the golden-shoed UCLA kicker. Following the miss, USC flanker Earl McCullouch ran fifty-two yards on a reverse to the UCLA twenty-eight. Sogge completed his only pass of the game for thirteen yards, and Simpson ran for two yards to the thirteen-yard line, from where he scored on the next play, breaking six tackles along the way. Rikki Aldridge gave USC a 14–7 lead.

But it should also be noted that Andrusyshyn had a forty-two-yard field goal blocked by the Trojans' Tony Terry.

Two minutes into the third quarter, Beban threw a fifty-three-yard touchdown pass to George Farmer, and Andrusyshyn converted. Late in the quarter, Andrusyshyn had a forty-seven-yard field-goal attempt blocked by Bill Hayhoe. But the worst was yet to come for the Bruin kicker. After Beban threw a twenty-yard scoring pass to break a 14–14 tie in the fourth minute of the final quarter, Andrusyshyn's placement attempt was tipped by Hayhoe, causing a miss and leaving the score at 20–14, thus creating an opening the Trojans exploited. The golden shoe had turned to rust.

On the third play after UCLA's kickoff, USC quarterback Page, told by McKay to pass on third and eight at the Trojan thirty-six but given the option of changing the play at the line of scrimmage, guessed right. He switched from a pass to a play called 23 Blast, which featured Simpson running off left guard. There are several versions of why the play succeeded, but discovering the correct answer is an impossible task. But it's certainly possible to describe the touchdown run as one of the greatest in college football history, a sixty-four-yard burst that was capped by Aldridge's game-winning placement for a 21–20 lead.

The Bruins attempted to rally, but USC's defense stood its ground, the game ending on a ten-yard loss when Beban was sacked.

USC was proclaimed national champion in both wire-service polls.

Years later, when he was coaching the Tampa Bay Buccaneers of the National Football League, McKay said, "I keep a picture of O. J. Simpson at my side at all times to remind me of the days when I knew how to coach."

14

THE FIFTY GREATEST PLAYERS

(POST–1950)

he quickest way to understand how many remarkably talented football players have worn the USC uniform through
the years is to attempt the task of naming the Fifty Greatest.
If it isn't impossible, it is the closest thing to it. Yet, in any book
detailing the glorious history of the Trojans program, we would be
remiss not to include the impressive collection of gifted individual
athletes who, more than any others, have helped sculpt the rich tradition that is USC football.

So, we have tried to tackle the impossible, not only naming the
Fifty Greatest but listing them in order. Obviously, this is a subjective
process, guaranteed to ignite debates in backyards, in front of water
coolers, and inside sports bars throughout Southern California. But
that's the fun of it. Together, the two of us who have our names
attached to this book have more than eighty years of experience
watching and covering the Trojans, making us feel as qualified as
anyone to do this. The biggest problem we encountered was deciding

what to do with the pre-1950 players, as neither of us is old enough to have seen them in action. We could have gone on the word of a few other individuals we found who had watched them play, but after much discussion and consultation with others involved in the program, we decided it would be unfair, not only to the pre-1950 players but also to those who have played since, to include them in our rankings.

This is not meant to slight those players in any way, and we did want to recognize those in the pre-1950 era who have been inducted into the College Football Hall of Fame. They include Johnny Baker (1929–31), Tay Brown (1930–32), Paul Cleary (1946–47), Morley Drury (1925–27), John Ferraro (1943–47), Mort Kaer (1924–26), Dan McMillan (1917–19), Erny Pinckert (1929–31) Aaron Rosenberg (1931–33), Ernie Smith (1930–32), Harry Smith (1937–39), and Cotton Warburton (1932–34). Clearly, all of them, and probably several more, belong on any list of the greatest USC players.

But our particular list is reserved for those we have both watched and/or covered, beginning in 1950. They will be judged almost entirely by what they achieved during their college careers, although many of them went on to enjoy even larger measures of success in professional football. These rankings also take into consideration the length of players' careers at USC, with some of those who had their playing time cut short by injuries or others who left early for the NFL not rating as high as they otherwise might have. Clearly, at a school that has produced so many great athletes, more than we preferred had to be left off the list, some just barely failing to make the cut.

But after careful study and much deliberation, this is the way we have ranked the Fifty Greatest USC Players:

50. SHAUN CODY, DT

The player basically responsible for launching the Pete Carroll era certainly belongs on this list. Cody was an All-America prep star at Los Altos High School and Carroll's first major recruit. When Cody committed, it was a statement that Trojans football was on the way back, and it laid the foundation for the great recruiting classes to come. When he arrived, his performance lived up to all the hype.

He was a 2001 Freshman All-American and proceeded to only get better playing some defensive end, but mostly defensive tackle, where at 6–4 and 295 pounds, he was a force upfront as a four-year starter. It all culminated in 2004 when he was named Pac-10 co-Defensive Player of the Year and a consensus All-American. He finished his career with 130 tackles, including $31^{1}/_{2}$ for losses, twenty-one sacks, and five blocked field goals.

"It's impossible to explain how important Shaun Cody has been to our program," Carroll said. Cody was selected in the second round of the NFL draft and is currently playing for the Detroit Lions.

49. PAT HADEN, QB

This is the poster boy for USC's student-athletes. He was not only a terrific, Rose Bowl-winning quarterback, he was even more brilliant in the classroom. He never quite won All-America recognition, but he was awarded something even more difficult to attain—a Rhodes Scholarship.

A great high school quarterback who teamed with J. K. McKay, John McKay's son, to form the finest prep passing combination in America at Bishop Amat High School just outside of L.A., Haden was heavily recruited by all the major colleges. But in his senior year, his family moved, and the young quarterback lived with the McKays so he could graduate from Bishop Amat. "I guess you could say we had a slight advantage recruiting him," cracked John McKay. USC's football program has been better for it ever since.

Haden backed up Mike Rae on the 1972 national championship team, then took over the following season, and in 1974 directed the Trojans on the greatest comeback in college football history, coming from a 24–6 halftime deficit against Notre Dame to beat the Irish, 55–24. Later, he and his closest friend, J. K. McKay, teamed up for a late, fourth-quarter touchdown pass, followed by a Haden completion for a two-point PAT, to beat Ohio State in the Rose Bowl, 18–17.

A partner in the private equity firm of Riordan Lewis & Haden for the past eighteen years, as well as a noted football TV analyst, Haden remains active in all USC events and is regarded as the perfect spokesman for Trojans football.

48. LENDALE WHITE, TB

He was more than just "the other tailback" in the Reggie Bush era. He was much more. White was the primary power runner in USC's remarkable run to two national championships and thirty-four victories in a row. In three seasons, he scored fifty-two rushing touchdowns, breaking the school record, which is no small feat at USC, where there has been a steady stream of Heisman Trophy runners.

White and Bush came to be known as "Thunder and Lightning" in the Trojans' backfield, with Bush finishing his three-year career with 3,169 yards and White rushing for 3,159. Primarily running inside the tackles, White averaged 5.8 yards-per-carry, also catching thirty-one passes for an additional 331 yards and five more touchdowns.

Former USC offensive guard John Drake put it best in describing USC's great pair of runners: "Reggie is our physical mismatch, but LenDale is the law." The most important performance of White's career might have come in his freshman season against Arizona State. The Trojans were reeling, and quarterback Matt Leinart had been injured in the first half. Coach Pete Carroll went to a bruising ground game with White rushing for 140 yards and two touchdowns on just twenty-one carries. USC came from behind to win the game and turn the momentum of the whole season, if not the whole program, around.

White's impressive statistics left many to wonder what he might have achieved had he spent one season as the lone tailback. NFL scouts who have watched predict he will have a long, productive career as a professional running back.

47. JIM SEARS, HB

An old-fashioned do-everything halfback, he was a consensus All-American in 1952, finishing seventh in the Heisman Trophy balloting. He could run, he could pass, he could catch, and he even was an outstanding defensive back in an era when you played both ways in college. He won the Voit Trophy as the outstanding player on the Pacific Coast in 1952 and the Pop Warner Award given to the most valuable senior on the Pacific Coast.

He was USC's leader in passing, total offense, scoring and punt returns in 1952. It is a wonder he didn't pause between plays to show people to their seats. He played in the College All-Star Game and the Hula Bowl, then was drafted in the sixth round by the NFL Baltimore Colts and Denver's AFL team. He was a USC assistant coach in 1959 and was inducted into the school's athletic Hall of Fame in 2003. After his football career, he was an automobile dealer. He died in 2002 at the age of seventy.

46. WILLIE BROWN, TB

He was the first star tailback in the John McKay era. In 1962, when the Trojans won their first national championship under McKay, Brown starred in the same backfield with Pete Beathard and Bill Nelsen, the two quar-

terbacks who would go on to star in the NFL. He is one of those players you couldn't judge just off numbers. You had to see him to appreciate him. On another team, with less talent, he could have been a Heisman candidate.

Brown wasn't the heavy-duty runner McKay would develop in later years. He was a great athlete with multipur-pose skill, as adept at streaking over the middle to catch passes as he was at sprinting out of the backfield on a sweep that would later come to be known as "Student Body Right." In 1962, Brown rushed for 574 yards and a 6.5 average per

UNIVERSITY OF SOUTHERN CALIFORNIA

Willie Brown was the star tailback on John McKay's first national champi-onship team in 1962. He later joined McKay's coaching staff as a valuable assistant.

carry. Proving his versatility, in 1963, he led Trojans' receivers with thirty-three catches and a 13.2 average.

Brown, who was twice All-Conference, is probably best remembered for the sensational leaping catch he made against UCLA to set up a late touchdown in the Trojans' 14–3 victory that preserved an unbeaten season on the road to McKay's first national championship in 1962. He later was an assistant coach at USC under McKay from 1968–75, then worked at Tampa Bay with his former coach. He is presently an academic adviser at USC.

45. PAUL McDONALD, QB

Maybe the most underrated quarterback in USC history. He wasn't flashy, and he didn't play in an offense as wide open as the one Pete Carroll currently features. But as a smooth, left-handed passer and cool, intelligent leader, McDonald led the Trojans to the national championship in 1978 and was an All-American in 1979, when he finished sixth in the Heisman Trophy balloting.

"Paul was a terrific quarterback in a great season for us," coach John Robinson says. Even though he played in an era when USC was more famous for its dominant runners at tailback, McDonald managed to put up some excellent numbers. He led the team in completions in 1978 and '79, and his total 164 in the latter year was thirteenth best in school history. He threw for a combined thirty-seven touchdown passes and suffered only thirteen interceptions in those two seasons. He quarterbacked the team in the 1979 and 1980 Rose Bowls, was named the team's MVP in 1979, and remains eighth on USC's all-time career passing list with 4,138 yards.

McDonald was a brilliant student, as well, making the 1979 Academic All-America first team and being recognized as a 1979 National Football Foundation Scholar-Athlete. Selected in the fourth round of the NFL draft by the Cleveland Browns, McDonald played five years with the Browns and then spent two seasons with the Dallas Cowboys. His son, Michael, was a walk-on quarterback at USC in 2003–05. A successful investment banker, McDonald also has been the color man on USC's radio broadcasts since 1998.

44. TIM ROSSOVICH, DE
MIKE BATTLE, DB

It seems only appropriate to include these two as an entry, because they were All-America teammates and all-American hell-raisers who were also the closest of friends. Rossovich was a dominant defensive end and a great pass rusher from 1965 through '67, while Battle was a fearless, 170-pound defensive back who returned kicks as if every one were his last.

Some of the stories about these two might be apocryphal, but Rossovich was known for eating glass, racing through Fraternity Row with few or no clothes on, and later became nationally known for pulling such unusual pranks as setting himself on fire. Battle, they say, once drove his motorcycle off the pier at a local beach.

On the field, they weren't nearly as wild. They were simply terrific players and leaders on the 1967 national championship team. Rossovich was a consensus All-American that year and was named the Trojans' Lineman of the Year. He played in the 1968 Coaches All-America Game and the College All-Star Game. He was drafted in the first round by the Philadelphia Eagles, who converted him to middle linebacker. He played with the Eagles, San Diego Chargers and Houston Oilers in his NFL career before becoming, appropriately enough, an actor and a stuntman.

Battle was an All-American in 1968. He still ranks as one of USC's all-time best punt-return specialists and owns the school's career record for most returns (ninety-nine) and is second in yardage (1,014). An excellent defensive back who wasn't afraid to gamble, he led the team with five interceptions in 1967 and is sixth in career interceptions with thirteen. Drafted in the thirteenth round by the New York Jets, he played two seasons, becoming a mini-celebrity in New York, where they loved his penchant for doing, uh, unusual things. After the NFL, he was involved in the oil business.

43. KEITH VAN HORNE, OT
TIM RYAN, DT

Okay, we're fudging a little bit. But you really can't leave either one of these off any list of USC's great players. Both of them were just too important to their respective eras.

One of the reasons the Trojans always had tailbacks rumbling for huge chunks of yardage was the presence of great blockers like Van Horne. At 6–7 and a relatively svelte (by today's standards) 265 pounds, Van Horne was a monster upfront for the Trojans, playing on the 1978 national championship team, becoming a two-time all-conference player and then serving as captain and winning consensus All-America honors as a senior in 1980. He grew up in nearby Fullerton, California, and was on two of the Trojans' Rose Bowl teams. He was USC's Offensive Player of the Game against UCLA in 1980 and eventually played in the 1981 Hula Bowl. He was selected in the first round as the eleventh overall pick in the 1981 NFL draft by the Chicago Bears, playing with them from 1981–93, including their Super Bowl XX year. After his football career was over, he became a radio broadcaster.

Ryan was a two-time All American (consensus in 1989) who made 389 tackles in four seasons, fifty-five of them for losses. It is no wonder he was the 1989 Pop Warner Award winner as the most valuable senior on the West Coast and runner-up for the Lombardi Award that same season. He was a two-time all-conference player, USC's captain in 1989, and played on three different Rose Bowl teams.

He was chosen in the third round of the 1990 NFL draft by the Chicago Bears and played with them from 1990 through '93. After his football career, he became a building maintenance company owner and a broadcaster both of USC football and the NFL.

42. ROY FOSTER, OG

This is another one of those blue-chip blockers who played upfront with Van Horne three of their four years with the Trojans. He was a two-time All-American, making the team in 1980 and then as a consensus pick in 1981. This is how good he was in '81: On a team full of great skilled players, he was named the Trojans' Offensive Player of the Year.

He was a three-time All-Pac-10 selection , playing on two Rose Bowl teams and a Fiesta Bowl squad. He won the Pac-10's Morris Trophy in 1980 and '81, the Gloomy Gus Henderson Award for most minutes played at USC in '81, and the Howard Jones Incentive

Award (for greatest increase in grade-point average) in 1980. Played in the 1980 Hula Bowl, then was drafted in the first round by the Miami Dolphins. He played with them from 1982 through '90, then for the San Francisco 49ers from 1991 '93. He participated in Super Bowl XVII and XIX.

41. ADRIAN YOUNG, LB

Sometimes one game, one shining Saturday afternoon, turns a great player into someone who will forever be immortalized in a school's football lore. This fine broth of an Irish lad can tell you all about it. Fittingly enough, he had his career day in South Bend, Indiana, where he almost single-handedly—well, O. J. Simpson had something to do with it, too—helped defeat Notre Dame in a memorable 1967 game.

Young intercepted not one, not two, not three, but four passes that day, tying a Pac-10 record and probably becoming the most hated young man from Dublin, Ireland, ever to play against the Irish. His interceptions helped the Trojans win, 24–7, earning coach John McKay, who grew up idolizing Notre Dame, his first road victory in this famous intersectional series.

Not surprisingly, Young was a consensus All-American that season, one in which USC won the national championship. He was also the team's co-captain and was voted Most Inspirational Player after the season. He played in two Rose Bowls, the Coaches All-America Game, the College All-Star Game, and the Hula Bowl. Not a particularly big linebacker, at 6–1 and 210 pounds, he was drafted in the third round by the Philadelphia Eagles, playing with them from 1968 through '72. He finished up his football career with the Detroit Lions and Chicago Bears, and although he enjoyed some fine moments, he never had another to equal that 1967 afternoon in college football's most famous setting.

40. DAMON BAME, LG, LB

He only stood 5–11 and weighed 192 pounds, but you never would have known it watching him play. This was the finest defensive football player on the 1962 national champions, a wonderfully instinctive middle linebacker who ranged all over the field to make tackles, despite his diminutive size. He doubled as a guard on offense but was a two-time All-American because of the way he played on the other side of the line of scrimmage.

He was twice named USC's Lineman of the Year in an era when the Trojans were loaded with quality players upfront. He played in that memorable 42–37 victory over Wisconsin in the 1963 Rose Bowl and was selected to play in the Hula Bowl. He stayed in football after his college career was over, serving as an assistant coach at San Jose State, Long Beach State, and New Mexico, as well as with Hawaii of the World Football League. He later became head coach at El Segundo High, then went on to work in the industrial silver-recovery industry.

39. PETE BEATHARD, QB

You could make a case for Beathard being the most underrated player of the modern USC era. You just don't hear his name much, and you should. He was, in many ways, the breakthrough player for John McKay. He was the quarterback who made everything else work on the 1962 national championship season. Although he split time at the position with future NFL star Bill Nelsen (maybe 65–35, if you counted plays), Beathard was the better athlete and a much superior runner. It was his rollout plays that were the basis for McKay's offense in the years before he switched to the power-running tailbacks who would make the coach famous. Those plays wouldn't have worked if Beathard hadn't been a major threat running the football.

Although Ron VanderKelen of Wisconsin became famous for the furious comeback he led in the 1963 Rose Bowl, it was Beathard who threw four touchdown passes to forge a 42–14 lead and was named Player of the Game. That 42–37 shootout still ranks as one of the more exciting Rose Bowls in history. Beathard rushed for 290 yards and passed for another 948, including ten for touchdowns, in 1962, and had a rush-pass total of 2,274 yards in 1962–63. Those numbers might not sound impressive compared with players of today, but you have to remember, that was a different era.

Beathard made the all-conference team in 1961 and '62 and played in the College All-Star Game and the Hula Bowl. He went on to play with the Kansas City Chiefs (1964–67, '73), Houston Oilers (1967–69), St. Louis Cardinals (1970–71), and the Los Angeles Rams (1972) in the NFL.

38. HAL BEDSOLE, WR

He was the most decorated player on the 1962 national championship team and probably the most physically gifted. He was one of the first successful experiments of the John McKay era. An all-city quarterback from the nearby San Fernando Valley in high school, Bedsole arrived at USC as a 6–5, 221-pounder and was quickly switched to wide receiver. He was one of the first "Jumbo" receivers in college football at a time when most coaches preferred their pass catchers to be lean and speedy. Bedsole was more of a fullback than a halfback after the catch, often trampling smaller defensive backs who attempted to tackle him.

Nicknamed "Prince Hal," he averaged an almost unheard-of 25.1 yards on thirty-three receptions, scoring eleven touchdowns, in 1962, or one TD for every three catches he made. Not surprisingly, he was a consensus All-American that season. He caught two of Pete Beathard's four touchdown passes in that memorable 1963 Rose Bowl victory over Wisconsin. He still owns the USC career record for highest average per catch at 20.94 yards.

He was a two-time all-conference selection and played in the Coaches All-America Game, College All-Star Game, and the Hula Bowl. He was drafted in the second round by the NFL Minnesota Vikings and in the eighth round by the AFL Kansas City Chiefs. He played for the Vikings in 1964–66. He was inducted into the USC Athletic Hall of Fame in 2001. After his football career, he worked as a radio broadcast sales manager and in business marketing.

37. CHIP BANKS, LB

This was one of the great natural athletes of his era, a 6–5, 230-pound linebacker strong enough to play inside and quick enough to play outside. He was a four-year letterman, a two-time all-conference selection, and an All-American in 1981. In his final two years with the Trojans, he made an astonishing combined 244 tackles. He also intercepted six passes in those two seasons and eight in his USC career.

333

He was the Trojans' captain in 1981, which came as no surprise since the team went 40–6–2 in his four years on campus. He played in two Rose Bowls and the 1982 Fiesta Bowl, where he scored the team's only touchdown on a twenty-yard interception. He was picked as the third overall player in the first round of the 1982 NFL draft by the Cleveland Browns, playing with them from 1982 through '86. He then played for the San Diego Chargers (1987) and the Colts (1989–93).

36. JACK DEL RIO, OLB

Another one of those linebackers who was seemingly in on every tackle during his USC career. The difference with him is that he was thrown in there from the beginning, playing extensively as a freshman and only getting better as he gained experience. By his senior year in 1984, he was a consensus All-American.

That year he won the Pop Warner Award presented to the most valuable player on the West Coast and was runner-up in the balloting for the Lombardi Award. He was also USC's Defensive Player of the Year that season. He was responsible for 340 tackles in his four years, including a staggering fifty-eight for losses. He played in the 1982 Fiesta Bowl and was co-MVP in the 1985 Rose Bowl. An exceptional athlete, he also played baseball two years for the Trojans.

He played in the East-West Shrine Game and the Japan Bowl. He was selected in the third round of the 1985 NFL draft and played in New Orleans for two years, then moved on to the Kansas City Chiefs (1987–88), Dallas Cowboys (1989–91), and Minnesota Vikings (1992–95). A successful assistant coach in the NFL, he is now the head coach of the Jacksonville Jaguars.

35. TIM McDONALD, S

One of the great safeties in recent school history, he was a two-time All American who seemed to be all over the field in his spectacular career. He was a consensus pick in 1986 and recorded 339 tackles in his four years as a letterman. He also found time to make eleven interceptions, which is good enough to rank thirteenth on the school's all-time list. He owns USC's record for longest run with an intercepted fumble (ninety-nine yards vs. Baylor in '86). He was a two-time all-conference selection and was voted the Trojans' MVP in both 1985 and '86.

He played in the East-West Shrine Game, then was drafted in the second round by the Cardinals, where he played from 1987–92. He finished his career with the 49ers (1993–99), getting an opportunity to play in Super Bowl XXIX. After his playing career was over, he became a high school head coach.

34. DENNIS THURMAN, S

It is appropriate that he and McDonald would be so close on this list, because they're almost impossible to separate in terms of ability. Thurman, a 5–11, 173-pound playmaker, was also a two-time All-American, a consensus choice in 1976, and a rare unanimous pick in 1977. A four-year letterman who was a contributing freshman on the 1974 national championship team, he was USC's Defensive Player of the Year in 1977. He's tied for sixth on USC's career-interception list with thirteen, including two intercepted fumbles.

He played in four bowl games as a Trojan, twice in the Rose Bowl, once in the Liberty Bowl, and once again in the Bluebonnet Bowl. After participating in the 1978 Senior Bowl, he was drafted in the eleventh round by the Dallas Cowboys, and despite his lack of size, played in Dallas from 1978 through '85, participating in Super Bowl XIII. He played one year with the Arizona Cardinals, in 1986. After his playing career was over, he became an assistant coach with the Cardinals and Baltimore Ravens, as well as the World League's Ohio Glory. He came back to be an assistant at USC from 1993 through 2000.

33. JIMMY GUNN, DE

The best player on the legendary "Wild Bunch" defensive line that dominated games from 1968 through '70. Built more like a wide receiver, at 6–1 and 210 pounds, his quickness made him almost impossible to block and made the "Bunch," with teammates Charlie Weaver, Tody Smith, Al Cowlings, Williard "Bubba" Scott, and sixth man Tony Terry, maybe the most famous defensive group in USC history.

Gunn was a consensus All-American in 1969, a two-time all-conference selection, and he was USC's Lineman of the Year in '69. He was also co-captain that season. He played in three Rose Bowls and in the 1970 Hula Bowl. Drafted in the thirteenth round by the Chicago Bears, he played for them from 1970 through '75, then for the New York Giants (1975) and Tampa Bay Buccaneers (1976). He was inducted into the USC Athletic Hall of Fame in 2001. After his playing career, he became a business executive and real estate developer.

32. RODNEY PEETE, QB

He is one of the great quarterbacks in USC history, a 1988 All-American who capped a spectacular career by finishing second in the Heisman Trophy race that season. A four-year starter, his name is dotted all over the Trojans' record books, most notably with the two career total offense records he set.

He and Troy Aikman, who was at UCLA at the time, were the stars in a college football period dominated by quarterbacks. It should be noted that Peete beat Aikman, a future Pro Football Hall of Famer, in each of their head-to-head meetings in college. And it was Peete who won the 1988 Johnny Unitas Golden Arm Award given to the nation's top senior quarterback, as well as the Pop Warner Award given to the most valuable player on the Pacific Coast that same season. He was also the Pac-10's Offensive Player of the Year that season. He finished his USC career throwing for 8,225 yards and fifty-four touchdowns, and, showcasing his obvious athletic ability, he also rushed for 415 yards.

The irony is, he may have made the most memorable play of his Trojan career on defense. It was in the final seconds of the first half of a 1987 crosstown showdown with UCLA. Attempting to get on the scoreboard with his team down, 10–0, he threw a sideline pass that was intercepted by the Bruins' Eric Turner, who grabbed it inside his own five and had nothing but open field between him and the USC end zone.

Peete, completely on the other side of the field, began to race after him in a moment that almost seemed frozen in time. The blinking timer on the scoreboard slowly ticked down in seconds—

5, 4, 3, 2, 1...0. As time finally ran out, Peete caught Turner and dragged him out of bounds at the USC eleven. Instead of a 17–0 halftime score, USC was behind, by just 10–0. When the Trojans came back to outscore UCLA, 17–3, in the second half and win the game, 17–13, there was no question what the turning point had been. "I don't know how he caught him," said USC receiver Erik Affholter, "but that play changed the game around."

Peete was drafted in the sixth round by the Detroit Lions and played with them from 1989 through '93, before moving on in a busy NFL career to play with the Dallas Cowboys (1994), Philadelphia Eagles (1995–98), Washington Redskins (1999), Oakland Raiders (2000–01), and Carolina Panthers (2002–04). He is currently one of the stars on the popular Fox TV show *Best Damn Sports Show, Period.*

31. TROY POLAMALU, S

The flowing mane of hair wasn't as long as it is today, but what you see with the Pittsburgh Steelers these days is basically what you got when this guy was flying all over the field making tackles for USC. A two-time All-American, he ranks as the best defensive player of the Pete Carroll era. He bridged the gap from Carroll's first year, topped off by his twenty-tackle performance in a losing cause in the Las Vegas Bowl, to the big-time victory by the Trojans in their first BCS bowl, the 2003 Orange Bowl against Iowa, a game in which a disappointed Polamalu played only briefly because of an injury.

He was USC captain in 2001 and 2002, its MVP in '01, and Most Inspirational Player in '02. The latter award is one he could have received every season. It isn't often you hear the term "spiritual" connected to a football player, but everyone who played with Polamalu brings it up. He'd throw his body around with disregard on the field, then look up at people with soft, kind eyes and speak in a calming voice away from it. "He is an amazing football player and an amazing person," Carroll said. No wonder he was a 2002 Thorpe Award finalist.

"I believe God named me Troy for a reason," Polamalu said. "I was born to come here." That might have sounded phony coming from anyone else, but not from him. He made 118 tackles to lead the team in 2001 and probably would have had more the next season if a right-ankle sprain suffered at midseason hadn't slowed him down some. The 5–10, 215-pounder was drafted in the NFL's first round, sixteenth overall, by the Steelers, and to hardly anyone's surprise, has become an All-Pro and one of the dominant defensive players in the sport in Pittsburgh.

30. DUANE BICKETT, LB

This guy had the muscles and the brains. He was not only a 1984 All-American and the Pac-10's Defensive Player of the Year, he was a National Football Foundation Scholar-Athlete, an Academic All-America first-team selection, and recipient of an NCAA postgraduate scholarship. He had 291 career tackles, twenty-nine for losses, as well as six career interceptions.

At 6–5 and 235 pounds, he was a dominant presence on defense, winning USC's award as Defensive Player of the Year in 1984, as well as being named the Trojans' Player of the Game vs. Notre Dame in 1983. He played in the Hula Bowl and the Japan Bowl in 1985, then was picked in the first round of the NFL draft, the fifth selection overall, by the Colts. He went on to play with that franchise in 1985–93, then played for the Seattle Seahawks (1994–95) and Carolina Panthers (1996).

29. CHRIS CLAIBORNE, LB

He is USC's first winner of the Butkus Award as the outstanding linebacker in the nation. He was a unanimous All-American in that same season of 1998, making an amazing 120 tackles and intercepting eight passes, returning them for 159 yards. A former running back and linebacker in high school in Riverside, California, he was a 6–3, 250 pound terror at middle linebacker for the Trojans. There have been few, if any, linebackers at USC with his combination of size, strength and speed.

He was the 1998 Pac-10 Defensive Player of the Year and the Trojans' co-captain that same season. To no one's surprise, he was voted USC's MVP at the end of 1998. Regarded as a top pro prospect from the moment he stepped on campus, he was selected in the first round of the NFL draft as the ninth overall pick by the

Detroit Lions, for whom he played from 1999–2002. He has started at linebacker with the Minnesota Vikings since 2004.

28. TONY BOSELLI, TB

Almost as rich as the history of great tailbacks is the long tradition of large, overpowering offensive tackles at USC. Boselli was one of the latest and greatest. At 6–8 and 305 pounds, he was a rock upfront in the early 1990s.

He was a two-time All-American and a consensus selection in 1994. He was All-Pac-10 for three years, USC's Offensive Player of the Year in 1991 and the team's MVP in 1994, and also won the conference's Morris Trophy for best offensive player in '94.

He excelled in the classroom, too. He won the Howard Jones/Football Alumni Club Academic Award for highest grade-point average on the team in 1994, the year he was also the team's captain. Selected as the second overall pick in the first round of the NFL draft by Jacksonville, he played for the Jaguars from 1995 through 2001, then played for the Houston Texans in 2002 before his career was cut short by injuries.

27. FRANK GIFFORD, HB

A legendary figure in both college and pro football, he was one of the original triple-threat halfbacks—rushing, throwing, and receiving—and put up spectacular numbers for his time. He even kicked field goals. His 841 yards rushing and 1,144 yards of total offense led USC in 1951, the year he was selected to the All-America team.

A glamorous figure in college, he became even more nationally recognized when he was picked in the first round of the NFL draft by the New York Giants and enjoyed a long, productive career in New York, starring on the field and off. He played for twelve years with the Giants as an All-Pro halfback.

He was inducted into the National Football Foundation's College Football Hall of Fame in 1975, the Pro Football Hall of Fame in 1977, and the USC Athletic Hall of Fame in 1994. After his playing career was over, he gained even more fame as a football broadcaster, becoming part of the famous ABC *Monday Night Football* crew with Howard Cosell and Don Meredith. "The Giffer," as Cosell used to call him, was the play-by-play man as well as the steady hand who kept the broadcast on an even keel with two of the more colorful and unpredictable personalities in the booth with him. Gifford proved as smooth with a microphone as he was with a football in his prime at USC and in New York.

26. BRUCE MATHEWS, G
CLAY MATHEWS, LB

One of the more prominent brother tandems in USC history. Clay was an All-America linebacker in 1977, and Bruce was a consensus All-America guard in 1982. Bruce was Trojan captain in '82 and won the Pac-10 Morris Trophy on offense that season. A huge boulder of a man at 6–5 and 265 pounds, he was the more physically dominant of the two and went on to have a potential Hall of Fame career in the NFL after being drafted in the first round as the ninth overall pick by the then-Houston Oilers. He starred for the Oilers/Tennessee Titans from 1983 to 2001, proving to be one of the more consistent and durable players in the league. He started in Super Bowl XXXIV for the Titans.

Clay was a USC captain in 1977, three years after he played on the Trojans' 1974 national championship squad. He played in two Rose Bowls, a Liberty Bowl, and a Bluebonnet Bowl and was a two-time All-Pac-10 selection. He was drafted in the first round as the overall twelfth pick by the Cleveland Browns. He played with the Browns from 1978 through '93, then finished his career with the Atlanta Falcons from 1994 through '96. Clay's son, Kyle, was a walk-on safety for the Trojans in 2000–03 and another son, Clay III, is currently a linebacker at USC. Clearly, the Mathews clan has to rank as one of USC's main football families.

25. MIKE WILLIAMS, WR

One of the dominant players in USC history at his position, there is no telling how high on this list he might have finished if he hadn't left the program after just two extraordinary seasons. Williams arrived in 2002 without as much hype as some players at USC, but he quickly became quarterback Matt Leinart's favorite target, finishing a remarkable freshman season with eighty-one receptions for

1,265 yards and fourteen touchdowns. He then went out and exceeded all those numbers as a sophomore, catching ninety-five balls for 1,314 yards and sixteen touchdowns, topping it off with a touchdown pass of his own to help win the Rose Bowl Game against Michigan and clinch part of a national championship for the Trojans.

He signed with an agent after his 2003 season, hoping to jump to the NFL before his junior year. But the NFL ruled against him and Ohio State's Maurice Clarett, and when Williams tried to reapply to return to USC, the NCAA ruled him ineligible and his college career was over. Still, he stuffed plenty into those two years, setting an NCAA freshman record for receiving yards, and after just two years, he was ranked fourth on USC's career receptions list with 176. He established new school records for TD catches in a career (thirty), a season (sixteen) and game (three, something he did three times). No one was more effective running after the catch than he was. If there was a stat for breaking tackles as a wide receiver, he would be the easy leader.

He was drafted in the first round as the eleventh overall pick by Detroit in 2005 and continues to play for the Lions.

24. MARVIN POWELL, OT

Another one of the large, overpowering blockers who helped make those USC tailbacks famous, Powell was a two-time All-American and a four-year letterman who, at 6–5 and 265 pounds, was a massive presence upfront for the Trojans. He played on the 1974 national championship team as a freshman, then was a star on the 1975 and 1977 Rose Bowl squads. He also played in the 1975 Liberty Bowl.

A three-time All-Pac-10 selection, he was inducted into the National Football Foundation College Football Hall of Fame in 1994 and is almost a certain pick to be in the USC Athletic Hall of Fame in the near future. After playing in the Hula Bowl and Japan Bowl, he was selected in the first round as the fourth overall pick in the NFL draft by the New York Jets. He played in New York from 1977 through '85 and played for the Tampa Bay Bucs from 1986 through '87. His son, Marvin III, was a fullback-tight end-safety for

USC from 1995 through '98. After his own playing career was over, he became an attorney.

23. JUNIOR SEAU, OLB

Talk about making a major impact in a short time. He was a dynamic player from the moment he stepped on the field, then took it up a notch in 1989 when he enjoyed one of the great defensive seasons in recent USC history, recording seventy-two tackles, twenty-seven of them for losses. A great athlete at 6–3 and 245 pounds, he had the rare combination of strength and speed that made him a devastating pass rusher as well as an unblockable force on the outside. He also played with a passion that was palpable.

Seau was both USC's and the Pac-10's Defensive Player of the Year in 1989 and was voted the Trojans' MVP that season. He played in the 1989 and the '90 Rose Bowls, then was drafted as the fifth overall player in the first round by the San Diego Chargers. In a brilliant thirteen-year career in San Diego, he became a perennial All-Pro and one of the great outside linebackers in modern NFL history. He played in Super Bowl XXIX for the Chargers and then joined the Miami Dolphins as a free-agent in 2003. He owns a popular restaurant in San Diego that bears his name.

22. KEYSHAWN JOHNSON, WR

He is one of the best players and one of the best stories in recent memory at USC. He began as the ballboy who wouldn't go away, a skinny street kid who would show up at USC football practice every afternoon, riding a bus or his bike or whatever it took to get him there. The players at that time, big-time players such as Ronnie Lott, Marcus Allen, and Duane Bickett, fell in love with the kid who would shag balls endlessly with a smile that never left his face. They gave him autographed pictures and wristbands and even let him sleep overnight in their apartments. He became everybody's favorite little brother.

Then Keyshawn grew up. All of a sudden, he was a 6–4, 212-pound JC transfer who was making diving catches all over the place. The flair to his game matched his personality. He was the Trojans' version of Deion Sanders. He loved to play and he loved to talk, and it soon became evident he could do both better than anyone else on the team.

He caught sixty-six passes for 1,362 yards his first season, then broke all the records in USC's books by fielding 102 passes for 1,434 yards as a senior in 1995. He was the Cotton Bowl MVP in 1995 and the Rose Bowl MVP in 1996. He was a unanimous All-American in 1995, the year he was also the Pac-10's Offensive Player of the Year and the winner of the Pop Warner Award as the most valuable senior on the Pacific Coast.

"He was only at USC two years," says coach John Robinson. "If he'd had four years, his numbers would have been super. He dominated his position as much as anybody we had. He was very competitive and a deceptively strong football player."

Keyshawn had seventeen 100-yard games, setting two USC career receiving records, two school season receiving records, and one single-game record. Nobody was ever better at making the tough catches in the middle of the field.

Johnson was the first overall player selected in the 1996 NFL draft by the New York Jets. He played from 1996 throiugh '99 in New York, then moved on to the Tampa Bay Bucs (2000–03), whom he helped get to the Super Bowl, and the Dallas Cowboys, whom he plays for today. He also owns a popular restaurant in Los Angeles, one many of the players who used to take care of him now visit. Like everyone else, they have to admit that he's come a long way from those days as a ballboy.

21. MARLIN McKEEVER, RE-FB
MIKE McKEEVER, G

The most famous brother combination in USC history, these two were legends even before they enrolled in college. They were a pair of the most heavily recruited high school players of their era coming out of Mt. Carmel High in Los Angeles. Both were simply great natural football players. Marlin played fullback and end (it wasn't called wide receiver back then) in college but went on to be a long-time starting linebacker in the NFL. Mike was a two-way guard who was everything but lucky in his career. Both were All-Americans in 1959 and probably would have been again if Mike's senior season hadn't been curtailed when he suffered a major head injury that resulted in surgery for two blood clots on his brain.

Marlin led the Trojans in receptions both in 1959 and '60 and also was the team's punter, but he was noted more for his bruising blocks from both the end and fullback positions. He was named USC's Lineman of the Year in 1960. Mike , who made 199 tackles in two seasons, was the team's Most Inspirational Player in 1959 and was the Football Alumni Club Award winner for being the senior with the highest grade-point average in 1960, the year he was also co-captain. The more dominant of the two brothers in college, Mike was voted into the National Football Foundation's College Hall of Fame in 1987.

Marlin was drafted in the first round by the NFL Los Angeles Rams and in the third round by the AFL San Diego Chargers. He played with the Rams from 1961 through '66 and 1971–72. He also was with the Minnesota Vikings (1967), Washington Redskins (1968–70), and Philadelphia Eagles (1973). After his playing career, he became a stockbroker and insurance executive. Obviously limited after his head injury, Mike was drafted by the Rams and Chargers, as well, but he didn't play in the NFL. He was in the construction business before an automobile accident put him in a coma for twenty-two months. He never recovered, dying in August 1967.

In 1995, the McKeever brothers were inducted into the USC Athletic Hall of Fame the only way they should have been—together.

20. RON MIX, OT

This is another of the great offensive tackles at USC. He played at 6–3 and 215 pounds in a single-platoon era when that made him one of the larger players at the position. There was no question he was one of the great technicians at offensive tackle. A 1959 All-American and a team co-captain that same season, he didn't receive as much recognition as he would have had he played in a more winning period at USC. But there was never any question about his talent.

Drafted by the NFL Baltimore Colts in the first round by the then-Los Angeles Chargers of the AFL, he went on to become a perennial All-Pro both in L.A. and when the franchise moved to San Diego, and he was selected to most of the all-time AFL teams before the merger. Mix played with the Chargers from 1960 through '69, then with the Oakland Raiders in 1971.

He was inducted into the USC Athletic Hall of Fame in 1997 and the Pro Football Hall of Fame in 1979. He also is a member of the Jewish Sports Hall of Fame. After his playing career was over, he became a lawyer working out of the San Diego area.

19. RICKY BELL, TB

Maybe the best of the power-running tailbacks never to win the Heisman Trophy, Bell certainly was the most durable of USC's great runners. You look back at his numbers now, and they are staggering. He ran for 1,957 yards in 385 carries as a junior and 1,433 yards on 280 attempts as a senior. In that final season, against Washington State in a game played on the rock-hard turf of the Seattle King-dome, the player his teammates called "Bulldog" carried a surreal fifty-one times, gaining 347 yards, both still single-game USC records. But not surprisingly, that effort seemed to take something out of him, and he wasn't the same overpowering player the second half of that season.

Even so, he finished third in the Heisman balloting in 1975 and was runner-up in 1976 to Pittsburgh's Tony Dorsett. Bell was Pac-10 Player of the Year in '76 and won the Voit Trophy given to the out-standing player on the Pacific Coast and the Pop Warner Award pre-sented to the most valuable player on the Pacific Coast that same season. He was USC's MVP both his junior and senior seasons and ranks high on the school's career rushing list with 3,689 yards. He played in three Rose Bowls and one Liberty Bowl during his career.

But Bell was another USC star who never had much luck. In the 1977 Rose Bowl against Michigan, he sustained a head injury and had to leave the game early, allowing Charles White, the next tail-back in line, to play the starring role. The first player selected in the '77 NFL draft, by Tampa Bay, he played with the Buccaneers from 1977 through '81, then played the 1982 season for the San Diego Chargers.

After his playing career, he was a restaurant owner until he con-tracted dermatomyositis, a rare inflammation of the skin and mus-cles that led to degenerative heart disease. Bell died on November

28, 1984 at age twenty-nine. "Besides being a great football player, he was one of the nicest human beings I've ever known," says coach John Robinson. "That made his death a double tragedy." Bell was posthumously inducted into the USC Athletic Hall of Fame in 1997 and the College Football Hall of Fame in 2004.

18. SAM CUNNINGHAM, FB

They called him "Sam Bam," a nickname that fit him almost as well as his helmet and shoulder pads. He was pure football player, a tremendously gifted athlete who could have played any number of positions, including tailback and middle linebacker. John McKay put him at fullback because he had so many other great runners and because he blocked better than just about anybody in recent memory. Toss in his legendary dives into the end zone for touchdowns, maybe the single most unstoppable play in USC history, and you get an idea of how valuable this 6–3, 212-pound All-American was.

Bear Bryant certainly knew. After Cunningham had run for 135 yards and two touchdowns in a memorable performance at Alabama in 1970, Bryant realized that he had to integrate his program, and the whole culture of football in the South changed. In the 1973 Rose Bowl, Cunningham scored on four of his famous dives and was named Player of the Game. He was voted onto the 1972 All-America team, the same year he was Trojans captain and was voted the team's Back of the Year award. He was inducted into the Rose Bowl Hall of Fame in 1992 and the USC Athletic Hall of Fame in 2001. He was drafted as the eleventh overall pick in the first round by the New England Patriots, for whom he played from 1973 through '79 and 1981–82. After his playing career was over, he became an owner of a landscaping business.

17. ANTHONY MUNOZ, OT

This is open to argument, we realize, because he only played one full season at USC due to injuries. "But that one year was so dominant, you couldn't believe it," said coach John Robinson. "You'd watch him in practice, and he was so much better than any standard you'd ever set. He's one of the greatest players at any position I ever saw. "

If he'd played even a couple of years, Munoz probably would be in the top ten, if not the top five, on this list. He probably also would rate as perhaps the finest college offensive tackle of all time. He was 6–7, 280 pounds, and all by himself, he could just collapse his side of the line. Bodies would be strewn everywhere when he was finished. He had astonishing feet and agility for someone his size and was a good enough athlete to play basketball and baseball in high school and baseball at USC. After undergoing his third knee injury in the first game of his senior season, he battled back in time to play in the Rose Bowl and helped USC defeat Ohio State, 17–16.

We have been careful not to let success in the NFL affect our rankings, but it is impossible to disregard the fact he went on to become an all-generation player and, many believe, an all-time-great offensive tackle at that level for the Cincinnati Bengals. He was picked in the first round as the third overall player selected in the NFL draft and went on to eleven consecutive years as an All-Pro and Pro Bowl selection. Bengals coach Sam Wyche called him "the greatest offensive tackle I've ever seen." In 1998, he was voted into the Pro Football Hall of Fame in his first year of eligibility.

At first, we were considering placing him lower on this list because of his limited playing time with the Trojans, but when you remember how overpowering he was, even in his short periods on the field, it seemed impossible not to rank him this high.

16. LYNN SWANN, WR

Maybe no one ever had a more fitting name than this gifted athlete who was the most graceful of all USC football players—as graceful as a swan. Put him in this pass-happy era, and there is no telling how many passes he might have caught. As it was, he finished his USC career with ninety-five receptions for 1,562 yards and a 16.2 yard average. He scored eleven touchdowns and added three others as one of more dangerous punt returners of his time.

Swann was a consensus All-American in 1973, the same year he won the Pop Warner Award as the most valuable senior on the Pacific Coast and was USC's MVP. But it wasn't his statistics or his awards that you remember, it is the stylish way he played. He was the Joe DiMaggio of football, so graceful in everything he did, even while

No one was more graceful with a football in his hands or under his arm than Lynn Swann. He was a great receiver who doubled as a dangerous kick runner.

making spectacular, diving catches. His body control was remarkable, and he could run after the catch like a tailback.

He was inducted into the National Football Foundation's College Football Hall of Fame in 1993 and was among the winners of the NCAA Silver Anniversary Award in 1999. He was selected in the first round of the 1974 NFL draft by the Pittsburgh Steelers, played in four Super Bowls, and was MVP in Super Bowl X. He was inducted into the Pro Football Hall of Fame in 2001. After his playing career, he was a successful broadcaster for ABC and this year is running for governor in Pennsylvania.

15. JON ARNETT, HB

Those of us who saw him play can only close our eyes and imagine what he would have been like running in a John McKay or Pete Carroll offense. As it was, operating from a split-back set in a 1950s era that wasn't rich in offensive creativity, he was still the most exciting player in the country. He was a lot like Reggie Bush. Every time he touched the ball, you expected something magical to happen, and it often did.

Arnett had good speed, great moves, and unbelievable balance. He and Hugh McElhenny, who played a few years before him at the University of Washington and then went on to a Hall of Fame career with the San Francisco 49ers, were considered the best broken-field runners of their time. An all-city running back at nearby Manual Arts High, Arnett became an instant star as a sophomore at USC, scoring seven touchdowns in one three-game spurt before an injury slowed him down. As a junior, he blossomed into an All-American, leading the Trojans in both total offense and kick returns and scoring sixteen touchdowns. He also played full time on defense, leading the team in interceptions in 1954. He would have been one of the Heisman Trophy favorites as a senior, but his season was cut short by an NCAA ruling after he was cited as one of several conference seniors who accepted money from boosters. Still, playing only in an abbreviated five-game schedule, Arnett finished tenth in the 1956 Heisman balloting.

He won the Voit Trophy given to the outstanding player on the West Coast in both 1955 and 1956, and the Pop Warner Award given to the most valuable senior on the West Coast in 1956. He was inducted into the College Football Hall of Fame in 2001. A first-round draft pick of the Los Angeles Rams, he stayed home and played with them from 1957 through '63 and finished his career with the Chicago Bears (1964–66). In 1994, he was inducted into the USC Athletic Hall of Fame. He has worked in various areas of sales and marketing, real estate development, and stock brokering after his playing career. He now lives in Oregon.

14. CHARLES YOUNG, TE

If you took a vote, he's be the unanimous winner as the greatest tight end in USC history. At 6–4 and 228 pounds, with the ability to run like a scatback, he was physical mismatch for most teams, even in an era when the Trojans ran the ball a lot more than they threw it. He also blocked as if he were an additional tackle. He gave new meaning to the term "strong side" on offense.

A unanimous All-American in 1972, the year many think USC had its greatest team, he led the squad with twenty-nine receptions that season, averaging 16.2 yards a catch. He was named co-Lineman of the Year with John Grant that season. He played in the 1973 Rose Bowl and was inducted into the College Football Hall of Fame in 2004.

He was drafted as the overall sixth pick in the first round by the Philadelphia Eagles in 1973. He played three seasons with the Eagles, before moving on to the Los Angeles Rams (1977–79), San Francisco 49ers (1980–82), and Seattle Seahawks (1983–85).

He played in Super Bowls XIV and XVI. His daughters, Candace, Cerenity, and Chanel, all went on to compete on the USC track team.

13. MARK CARRIER, S

He is USC's first and only Thorpe Award winner, gaining the honor as the country's finest defensive back in 1989. He was a two-year All-American, gaining unanimous selection in '89, the same year he led the Pac-10 in interceptions with seven. He made 336 tackles in three varsity seasons and is tied for sixth on USC's career interception list with thirteen. He was so good, it was difficult to tell whether he was more effective rushing up to make big hits or dropping back to pick off passes.

He played in three Rose Bowls and a Citrus Bowl at USC, then was selected in the first round as the sixth overall pack of the 1990 NFL draft by the Chicago Bears. He played with the Bears from 1990 through '96, then moved on to the Detroit Lions (1997–99) and Washington Redskins (2000). After his playing career was over, he became a radio sports commentator and college and NFL assistant coach.

12. RICHARD WOOD, MLB

He was USC's lone three-time All-American until he was joined by Matt Leinart just this past season. Wood was honored all three of his seasons (1972–74), a period in which the Trojans finished 31–2–2 and captured two national championships.

They called him "Batman," and he played like a superhero at middle linebacker, where he would range all over the field making tackles and knocking down, or intercepting, passes. He started in three consecutive Rose Bowls and was team captain in 1974. He went on to play in the Senior Bowl, the Hula Bowl and the College All-Star Game. He was inducted into the USC Athletic Hall of Fame in 2003.

Not as big as some middle linebackers, at 6–2 and 213 pounds, he was drafted in the third round by the New York Jets. He played for the Jets in 1975 and the Tampa Bay Buccaneers, under his old coach, John McKay, from 1976 though '84.

He went on to become an assistant coach in the NFL and in Europe, then came home to become a high school football coach in Florida, where he was voted Coach of the Year in 2002.

11. BRAD BUDDE, OG

He is USC's first and only Lombardi Award winner, being recognized as the college lineman who best exemplifies the spirit of Vince Lombardi in 1979. He was also runner-up for the Outland Trophy as the nation's top offensive lineman that season. He was so good, he became a star right from the start, earning the right to be the first freshman to start a USC opener since World War II.

For four years, he was a dominating presence upfront, playing in three Rose Bowls and a Bluebonnet Bowl and earning all-conference honors three of those years. He was USC's Offensive Player of the Year in 1979, the season he was a unanimous All-American and also was honored as the team's Most Inspirational Player. He was inducted into the National Football Foundation's College Hall of Fame in 1998 and was the recipient of an NCAA postgraduate scholarship in 1979.

He was selected as the overall eleventh pick in the first round of the 1980 NFL draft by the Kansas City Chiefs, where he became a perennial All-Pro much like his father, Ed Budde, was. After starring for the Chiefs from 1980 through '86, Brad was inducted into the USC Athletic Hall of Fame in 2001. When his playing career was over, he became a physical therapist.

UNIVERSITY OF SOUTHERN CALIFORNIA

An overpowering blocker at the guard position, Brad Budde is the only USC player to win the prestegious Lombardi Trophy as college football's best lineman.

10. ANTHONY DAVIS, TB

Meet the best USC player not to win the Heisman. Where do you begin with a tailback who was not only a prolific runner but probably the greatest kick-return artist in the history in college football? You don't forget his six touchdown day against Notre Dame in 1972 and that kickoff return in 1974 that ignited the greatest comeback (24–6 to 55–24) in school history, if not the sport's history, or his eleven overall touchdowns against the Irish. This guy is the greatest one-man menace they've ever seen at Notre Dame.

He wasn't too bad against everyone else, either. He had seventeen 100-yard rushing games in his career, and in 1974 he led the nation in kickoff returns with a—are you ready?—42.5 yard average. He holds too many Pac-10 and NCAA records to list. He was the Heisman Trophy runner-up in 1974 and a unanimous All-American that season. He was quick, tough, and amazingly durable for someone who only stood 5–9 and weighed 183 pounds. "A.D.," as he was known, won the 1974 Pop Warner Award given to the most valuable player on the Pacific Coast and the 1974 and the '74 Voit Award as the outstanding player on the Pacific Coast. A good enough athlete to also play baseball on USC's 1973 and '74 national championship teams, he was inducted into the College Football Hall of Fame in 2005 and the USC Athletic Hall of Fame in 1999.

He was drafted in the second round by the New York Jets and played for the Tampa Bay Buccaneers (1977), Houston Oilers (1978), and Los Angeles Rams (1978), as well as in the World Football League and the Canadian Football League. After his playing career was over, he became an actor and a real estate developer.

9. CARSON PALMER, QB

It would have been hard to believe he could have cracked the top ten after his first three years of struggling behind shabby blocking, a major change in head coaches, and a couple of different offensive coordinators. But what he did in his senior season under Pete Carroll and Norm Chow vaulted him past other players faster than one of those bullet spirals he throws.

This is how far Palmer came even in one season: As a junior he threw thirteen TD passes and twelve interceptions. As a senior, those numbers were thirty-three and ten. He went from the disappointing quarterback who might never live up to his potential to USC's fifth Heisman Trophy winner and an All-American in 2002. Before he was finished, he'd set or tied 33 Pac-10 and USC total offense and passing records, winning the Johnny Unitas Golden Arm Award, the Pop Warner Award, and the *Sporting News* National Player of the Year award, all in 2002.

UNIVERSITY OF SOUTHERN CALIFORNIA

USC's only Outland Award winner, Ron Yary was the dominant blocker on those great O.J. Simpson teams in the late 1960s. He went on to become an NFL All-Pro.

When he and the Trojans' offense started really rolling in the second half of 2002, it set the stage for not only a 10–2 record with a BCS bowl victory against Iowa, but for everything that would happen in the next three years with Matt Leinart and the USC offense. He is now first on the Pac-10's career total offense list and passing yardage list. He was inducted into the USC Athletic Hall of Fame in 2003. The first overall pick in the 2003 NFL draft by the Cincinnati Bengals, Palmer is now a Pro Bowl quarterback with an unlimited NFL future who just signed a new $100 million-plus contract extension.

8. RON YARY, OT

USC's first and only Outland Trophy winner. A two-time All-American, he was the 6–5, 245-pound anchor on the offensive line in the Trojans' 1967 national championship season. He was a dominant presence throughout his college career, being selected three times all-conference, the first year as a defensive tackle, and is generally considered the finest offensive lineman in school history. When O. J. Simpson was busting loose for all those yards his first season, in 1967, it was Yary who was opening up many of those holes.

He hit the Hall of Fame trifecta, being selected to the National Football Foundation's College Football Hall of Fame in 1987, the USC Athletic Hall of Fame in 1997, and the Pro Football Hall of Fame in 2001. He was the first USC player to become the first overall pick in the NFL draft when the Minnesota Vikings selected him in 1968. He became a perennial All-Pro for the Vikings from 1968 through '82, finishing his career with the Los Angeles Rams in 1982. He played in two Rose Bowls and in Super Bowls IV, XIII, XI.

After his playing career, he opened a successful photography, printing, and publishing business in the Los Angeles area.

7. CHARLES WHITE, TB

He was USC's third Heisman Trophy winner and the tailback coach John Robinson still describes as "the toughest football player I've ever been around." Unbelievably strong and durable for someone standing a mere 5–10 and weighing 185 pounds, he carried the ball a jaw-dropping 1,147 times for 6,245 yards and forty-nine touchdowns in his four seasons on the job.

There isn't enough room to list all his honors and awards, but he was a two-time unanimous All-American who won the Walter Camp Award and the Maxwell Award, as well as the Heisman in 1979. He set or equaled twenty-two NCAA, Pac-10, USC, and Rose Bowl records, finishing as the NCAA's second-leading career rusher and the Pac-10's top career rusher. He was inducted into the College Hall of Fame in 1996 and into the USC Athletic Hall of Fame in 1995.

In his senior season of 1979, he carried the ball 332 times averaging an extraordinary 6.2 yards per carry on his way to a 2,050-yard season with nineteen touchdowns. He was selected in the first round of the 1980 NFL draft by the Cleveland Browns. He played with the Browns from 1980 through '84, then for the Los Angeles Rams, where he was reunited with his former USC coach Robinson from 1985 through '88. After his playing career, he was an assistant coach at USC, worked in the USC athletic department, and was a computer consultant.

6. MIKE GARRETT, TB

Garrett was USC's first Heisman Trophy winner, in 1965, and one of the finest all-around players in school history. He was not only a dominant runner, he was an excellent receiver, a fine blocker, and an even bigger threat returning kicks. More important, he was the foundation for the stream of great Trojan tailbacks that would follow. He started the legacy as the one who prompted coach John McKay to go to the power I-formation and revolutionize college football in the 1960s.

"Iron Mike," they called him, a 5–9, 185-pounder with surprising strength and marvelous moves in the open field. He set fourteen NCAA, conference, and USC records in his career and racked up just about every major award imaginable. A wonderful athlete, he also played cornerback on defense and outfield for the USC baseball team, earning all-league honors in that sport, as well.

He was inducted into the College Football Hall of Fame in 1985 and received an NCAA Silver Anniversary Award in 1991. He was drafted by both the NFL Los Angeles Rams and the AFL Kansas City Chiefs, choosing to sign with the latter. He played for the Chiefs from 1966 through '70, starting in Super Bowls I and IV, then played for the San Diego Chargers (1970–73).

He was inducted into the USC Athletic Hall of

UNIVERSITY OF SOUTHERN CALIFORNIA

Mike Garrett set the standard for all USC tailbacks in the future when he became the Trojans' first Heisman Trophy winner in 1965. The school's current athletic director, he hired coach Pete Carroll in 2001.

Fame in 1994, one year after he assumed the position of athletic director at the university, where he has enjoyed almost as much success as he once did on the football field. It was Garrett who hired Pete Carroll as head coach in 2001, demonstrating he is just as good at picking coaches as he once was at picking holes to run through.

5. REGGIE BUSH, TB

If it were a vote for the most electric player in USC history, he'd win by a couple of thousand volts. Maybe part of it is because our memory of him is so fresh, but even if it weren't, it would be hard to disregard the Trojans' seventh Heisman Trophy winner. He was a different kind of USC tailback. He didn't carry the ball forty times a game and pound between the tackles. Instead, Pete Carroll utilized him all over the place, creating mismatches for opposing players and nightmares for opposing defensive coordinators.

His Heisman junior season was his best one yet. He rushed 200 times for 1,740 yards, a sweet 8.7 yards per carry, scoring sixteen touchdowns, then caught thirty-seven passes for 478 yards and two more TDs. His 513-yard, all-purpose show against Fresno State ranks as one of the more eye-popping performances, not just in USC history but in college football history. His great fifty-yard clutch cutback run for a touchdown that night looked eerily like O. J. Simpson's legendary move on his sixty-four-yard touchdown run against UCLA in 1967. It even came at exactly the same spots on the Coliseum floor. But was that any better than his sixty-five-yard punt return for a TD in the fog at Oregon State a year earlier? Or his three long touchdown catches vs. Virginia Tech in the 2004 opener in Landover, Maryland? Or the forty-four-yard punt return that avoided an upset at Stanford? Or, for that matter, any number of great shows he put on in his blur of a three-year career with the Trojans?

No one has ever been more fun to watch in a USC uniform, absolutely no one. He was a two-time All-American and finished fifth in the Heisman balloting as a sophomore the year teammate Matt Leinart won the award. For his career—and remember, it was just three years—he finished with 3,169 yards rushing with twenty-five touchdowns, 1,301 yards receiving with thirteen touchdowns, and four more TDs on kick returns. His total of 6,617 all-purpose yards ranks second in USC history. Expected to be the the top pick in the 2006 NFL draft by the Houston Texans, he surprisingly was selected No. 2 overall by the New Orleans Saints.

4. RONNIE LOTT, S

He is the defensive back against which all others are measured. He was then; he is even more so now. Nobody delivered more jarring hits. Nobody was as effective in coverage. Nobody made more of an overall impact than this 6–2, 200-pound battering ram of a safety. He was a unanimous All-American in 1980, but he was USC's defensive leader the moment he stepped on the field full time as a sophomore.

Lott made 250 tackles and intercepted fourteen passes in his college career, tying for the NCAA lead in the latter category as a senior. He played in two Rose Bowls and a Bluebonnet Bowl and was team captain in 1980, when he was also voted the Trojans' Most Inspirational Player and co-Defensive Player of the Year. He was inducted into three different Halls of Fame, including the College Football Hall of Fame in 2002, the USC Athletic Hall of Fame in 1995, and the Pro Football Hall of Fame in 2000.

He was selected in the first round as the eighth overall pick in the NFL draft by the San Francisco 49ers and became one of the cornerstone players during the Joe Montana-Jerry Rice glory years, playing in Super Bowls XVI, XIX, XXIII, and XXIV all won by the Niners. A perennial All-Pro, he is considered by many to be the greatest strong safety in the history of the NFL.

3. MARCUS ALLEN, TB

In the category of best pure football player, he'd win in a landslide. He started as a fullback blocking for Heisman Trophy winner Charles White, then switched to tailback without having any experience at the position and went on to become USC's fourth Heisman Trophy winner and a running back of record-breaking proportions. He could block, he could catch passes, and as a former high school quarterback, he could even throw passes. In another era, he would have been a brilliant single-wing tailback.

He was the first collegian to rush for more than 2,000 yards in a regular season, finishing with a staggering 2,342 yards in 1981, the year he was a unanimous All-American and Heisman winner, as well as the recipient of the Maxwell and Pop Warner awards. He led the NCAA in all-purpose running in 1980 and 1981 and is second on USC's glittering career rushing list with 4,810 yards. He had twenty-one 100-yard rushing games in his career.

Drafted in the first round as the tenth overall pick by the Oakland Raiders in 1982, he played in Oakland from 1982 to '92, earning MVP honors in Super Bowl XVIII and becoming a perennial Pro Bowl selection. He finished his career with the Kansas City Chiefs (1993–97). He was inducted into the USC Athletic Hall of Fame in 1995, the College Football Hall of Fame in 2000, and the Pro Football Hall of Fame in 2003.

2. O. J. SIMPSON, TB

Apart from anything that occurred after his playing career was over, he remains perhaps the greatest running back in college football history. Doc Blanchard and Glenn Davis became famous in the 1940s as "Mr. Inside" and "Mr. Outside." Well, O. J. was a one-man combination of both. At 6–2 and 207 pounds, he could power between the tackles, carrying the ball forty or forty-five times a game, and he could sprint around the edge with his proven world-class speed (he was a member of USC's world-record-setting 440 relay team). Coach John McKay, who knew something about running backs, called him "the best I've ever seen." Lots of people agreed with him.

A junior college transfer who only played two years as a Trojan, he rushed for 1,543 yards and thirteen touchdowns as a junior, finishing as the Heisman runner-up to UCLA's Gary Beban in 1967. A year later, he ran for 1,880 yards and twenty-three touchdowns to race away with the sport's most cherished trophy. Many experts felt he should have won both years. He led the NCAA in all-purpose running both seasons and was USC's scoring leader both years. He even led the Trojans with twenty-six receptions in 1968.

He was inducted into the College Football Hall of Fame in 1983, the USC Athletic Hall of Fame in 1994, and the Pro Football Hall of Fame in 1985. The No. 1 overall selection of the NFL draft by the Buffalo Bills, he played for the Bills from 1969 through '77, then finished his career with the San Francisco 49ers in 1978–79. He set the NFL season rushing record of 2003 yards in 1973 and finished his career as the NFL's all-time second-leading rusher.

1. MATT LEINART, QB

Let's see, he was a three-time All-American, a Heisman Trophy winner, a two-time BCS bowl-game MVP, and the quarterback who led USC to a thirty-four-game winning streak and two consecutive national championships, coming within inches of a third, going 37–2 in his three-year career with the Trojans.

The smooth, left-handed passer with poise to spare finished his collegiate career throwing for 10,693 yards, completing .648 percent of his passes, with ninety-nine touchdowns and only twenty-three interceptions. He even ran for nine touchdowns, including the one-yard sneak at Notre Dame in 2005 that would probably rank as one of the more dramatic plays in USC history. That's if it weren't overshadowed by his fourth-and-nine throw for sixty-one yards to Dwayne Jarrett just a few seconds earlier. Those were the two signature plays of his career, yet there were so many more highlights—enough, in fact, for Leinart to finish his days at USC ranked among the finest quarterbacks ever to play college football.

If only LenDale White had gained a few more inches on that fourth-down play in the Rose Bowl against Texas, Leinart would have had three national titles to his credit and maybe the unanimous vote as the No. 1 college quarterback of them all. As it is, he had a remarkable run, especially for someone who went into his sophomore season not even sure he would be starting.

From that modest beginning, Leinart finished as the finest quarterback in USC history, the most significant leader, and, at least in the humble opinion of the authors of this book, the greatest of all the great players ever to put on a Trojan uniform.

THE FUTURE

I n the rich tapestry of college athletics, some schools have prospered so long and so well, they've all but reserved a position in the top echelon of their sport year after year. In basketball, you know that Duke and North Carolina, Kansas and Connecticut, UCLA and Arizona will be there come NCAA Tournament time just about every season. If the situation is not quite the same in football, it is close. The elite teams have established themselves across the years, from Oklahoma to Notre Dame, from Ohio State to Florida State, from Texas to Alabama. And then, of course, there is USC, with as much, if not more, glittering history and proud tradition than any of them.

Like their No. 1 nemesis and annual intersectional rival located under the Golden Dome in South Bend, Indiana, the Trojans suffered through some difficult times in the 1980s and 1990s, but they have fought their way back and then some, rising to the pinnacle of college football the past four seasons to forge a dazzling 45-2 record since the middle of 2002, producing two national championships and three BCS bowl victories, three Heisman Trophy winners in four years, and at one point, winning an astounding thirty-four games in a row.

Pete Carroll has become the natural successor to the legacy left by Howard Jones and John McKay, and from all indications, he has only just begun to rack up national championship-caliber seasons in downtown Los Angeles. None of the famous coaches who preceded him, not even Jones and McKay, had such a total grasp of the program as this energized former defensive back from the University of the Pacific. It is not just the way Carroll coaches on the practice field, it is the manner in which he goes about the rest of what can be a remarkably complex job. Whether he is dealing with the large L.A. media contingent or schmoozing with influential alumni, whether he is quietly counseling a player in his office or charming the mother of a prospect in a living room 3,000 miles away, this is a man in total control. Which is exactly why he is not apt to leave for somewhere else anytime in the near future.

The NFL rumors will continue to hover over Carroll, but what people don't understand is that this is a coach who already has found his Nirvana. He loves everything about what he is doing now, and best of all, he doesn't have to deal with an egotistical general manager or a curmudgeonly owner. He is in charge, given total command by Athletic Director Mike Garrett, and as someone who has been there before, that is a luxury he knows he won't ever find in the much more sinister world of professional football.

The boundless energy he has brought to the USC program has become Carroll's enduring trademark. According to Garrett, the man who hired him, Carroll is very much like McKay, only a more extroverted, hyper version of the 1960s-'70s USC legend. Carroll isn't a walking quote book, the way McKay was, but that's only because he is too busy flitting in so many different directions.

Some thought the Trojans' early success under Carroll revolved just as much around excellent assistants such as Norm Chow, the revered offensive guru, and Ed Orgeron, the dynamic defensive line coach who also spearheaded recruiting. But when both left before the 2005 season, Chow for the NFL Tennessee Titans and Orgeron to become the new head coach at Mississippi, the USC program never missed a beat, with the offense setting a flood of new records and the recruiting continuing its remarkable run of No. 1 classes nationally. If there had been any lingering doubt as to whom was the real key to what was happening to this program, it should have ended right there.

Carroll and Garrett are the reasons USC football should flourish for years to come. Sure, they absorbed some hits this past off-season, producing a series of ugly headlines. But much of it had to do more with outside influences than anything emanating from the university. Carroll and Garrett understand that college kids make mistakes, and they are working even harder now to create some kind of buffer zone that will offer their athletes more protection from those trying to capitalize on their success.

Overall, what the coach and athletic director have built now not only is a great resumé, but an undeniable standard for those in the future to follow. They have demonstrated they can overcome what many thought were the impossible challenges of smaller rosters and tougher academic standards and greater competition from schools outside California for local recruits.

The critics said USC couldn't dominate in this era the way it had in the Jones and McKay years. The critics were wrong. Carroll has done it by embracing the past, not eschewing it. He has invited the Ronnie Lotts and Marcus Allens and Sam Cunninghams to return, to stand along the sidelines at games and practices, to stroll through the locker room and shake hands and tell stories. Some of his predecessors were intimidated by what had happened at USC before they arrived. Carroll is intoxicated by it, breathing in all that history and tradition and passing it on to the kids he has brought into the program.

The result is that USC football has found a niche it never had before amid the massive sports menu offered in Southern California. Even with the Dodgers and Lakers, the Angels and Clippers, the Kings and Ducks, all competing for the attention of fans, the Trojans have become the only team to sell out home games regularly. Not even McKay's great teams, in their prime, drew crowds of 92,000 week after week the way USC's teams do now.

It is interesting to note that even when fans, alums, and various sports columnists were expressing doubt that USC could achieve the level of success it had enjoyed so many years ago, there were some who weren't buying it, including a group of great players from the past. Jon Arnett and Pat Haden were among those who went public to disagree vehemently. They raged at any thought that the Trojans couldn't return to national prominence. What was needed, they said, wasn't so much a new blueprint as the right people to come in and implement the one that was already there.

It took a while to find those people, but they are in place now. They are Garrett and Carroll, the two caretakers of all that history and tradition, who understood, even amid some early struggles, what USC football was before and what it should be again. The happy result for all those involved seems more apparent than ever now. As we believe the pages of this book have aptly demonstrated, the glory years of USC football definitely are back.

And from every encouraging, cardinal-and-gold indication, they are not about to go away anytime soon.

TEAM AND INDIVIDUAL RECORDS, STATISTICS, AND ACCOLADES

NATIONAL CHAMPIONSHIPS: (11)
1928, 1931, 1932, 1939, 1962, 1967,
1972, 1974, 1978, 2003, 2004

ALL-TIME RECORD: 732-298-54

HEISMAN TROPHY WINNERS: (7)
MIKE GARRETT, 1965; O. J. SIMPSON, 1967;
CHARLES WHITE, 1979; MARCUS ALLEN, 1981;
CARSON PALMER, 2002; MATT LEINART, 2004;
REGGIE BUSH, 2005

ALL-AMERICANS: 140

RHODES SCHOLAR: PAT HADEN, 1975

OUTLAND TROPHY: RON YARY, 1967

LOMBARDI AWARD: BRAD BUDDE, 1979

THORPE AWARD: MARK CARRIER, 1989

BUTKUS AWARD: CHRIS CLAIBORNE, 1998

NATIONAL FOOTBALL FOUNDATION'S COLLEGE FOOTBALL HALL OF FAME: 27, PLUS COACHES HOWARD JONES AND JOHN MCKAY

ACADEMIC ALL-AMERICANS: 22

NATIONAL FOOTBALL FOUNDATION SCHOLAR-ATHLETES: 12

NCAA POSTGRADUATE SCHOLARSHIP WINNERS: 20

ALL-TIME FIRST-ROUND NFL DRAFT CHOICES: 67
(NO. 1 IN NATION)

INDEX

Michigan State Spartans,
71, 118, 125, 154, 179,
227, 247
Michigan Wolverines, 37,
98, 103, 111, 149, 192,
194, 203-205, 211, 226-
227, 263, 267-268, 272,
276, 284, 305, 341, 345
Miller, Billy, 250
Miller, Lennox, 167
Miller, Ron, 88
Minnesota Gophers, 150,
155, 172
Minnesota Vikings, 268,
333-334, 339, 344, 354
Mississippi (Ole Miss)
Rebels, 264 363
Missouri Tigers, 30, 192,
210, 228
Mix, Ron, 11, 344-345
Mix, Tom, 84
Mohler, Orv, 43, 68, 313
Monday Night Football,
101, 339
Monroe, Marilyn, 69, 86
Montana, Joe, 71, 279
Montana Grizzlies, 67
Moore, Kenney, 203
Moore, Lenny, 109
Moore, Manfred, 134
Morgan, Mike, 178
Morris Trophy, 330, 339-
340
Morton, Johnnie, 119
Moscrip, Monk, 44
Mosebar, Don, 218
Mother Machree, 85
Mt. Carmel High, 343
Muncie, Chuck, 210
Munoz, Anthony, 10, 193,
202, 206, 346-347
Musick, Jim, 35, 68, 313
Mutiny on the Bounty, 87

N
Naked Gun, The, 124
National Collegiate Ath-
letic Association

(NCAA), 103-104, 108,
154-155, 162, 167, 171,
196, 207, 221, 224,
235, 261, 284, 338,
341, 348-349, 351-352,
354-355, 357-358, 361,
366
NCAA Silver Anniver-
sary Award, 348, 355
National Football Founda-
tion, 36, 213, 328, 338-
339, 341, 344, 348,
351, 354, 366
National Football League
(NFL), 19, 41, 55, 72-
74, 78, 81, 89, 102-103,
108, 120, 127, 130-132,
136, 141-145, 156, 160,
182, 185, 187-188, 193,
197-198, 206, 208,
210-211, 218, 221, 225,
229, 239, 242, 247-248,
251, 254-255, 257-258,
260-261, 263-264, 268-
271, 276, 285-286,
288-289, 292-293, 321,
324-330, 332-334, 337-
345, 347-348, 350-351,
353-355, 357-359, 362,
366
NFL draft, 41, 81, 132,
182, 198, 208, 211,
221, 254, 264, 269-270,
276, Nave, Doyle, 35,
49-50, 52, 300-302
Navy Blue and God, 86
Navy Midshipmen, 86,
96-97, 130
NBC, 146, 186
Nebraska Cornhuskers,
41, 72
Nelsen, Bill, 120, 130,
327, 332
Neuheisel, Rick, 243
New England Patriots,
178, 219, 239, 242,
257-258, 346
New Mexico Lobos, 332
New Mexico State Aggies,
150

New Orleans Saints, 144,
334, 357
New York Giants, 101,
115, 336, 339
New York Jets, 239, 242,
257, 329, 341, 343,
350, 352
Neyland, Robert "Bob,"
52, 115, 292-293, 325,
328, 330, 334, 338-339,
341, 343, 345, 347-348,
350-351, 353-354, 357-
358, 366
Nickels, Matt, 251
Niemic, Johnny, 63
Nolan, Tom, 55
North Carolina Tar Heels,
361
Northwestern Wildcats,
63, 171, 199-200, 230
Notre Dame Fighting
Irish, 10-11, 13, 17, 34,
36-40, 43-44, 47, 51,
54, 57-79, 83, 89-90,
99-101, 104, 107, 113,
124, 128, 130, 133,
137-138, 141-142, 148-
149, 154, 159, 162,
164-165, 182-183, 186,
200, 204-207, 211,
224-226, 229-230, 232,
234, 248, 252-253, 256,
259, 263-264, 268, 272,
274, 279-280, 289,
300-301, 303, 307-309,
312-318, 325, 331, 338,
352, 359, 361
Notre Dame Stadium, 312
Nugent, Tom, 136
Nutcracker ballet, 56

O
Oakland Raiders, 55, 143,
188, 191-192, 199, 221,
271, 337, 345, 358
Oas, Rick, 55
Oberlin College, 24
Obradovich, Jim, 304
O'Brien, Pat, 89-90, 128